.NET Framework Essentials

SECOND EDITION

.NET Framework Essentials

Thuan Thai and Hoang Q. Lam

O'REILLY®

Beijing · Cambridge · Farnham · Köln · Paris · Sebastopol · Taipei · Tokyo

.NET Framework Essentials, Second Edition
by Thuan Thai and Hoang Q. Lam

Copyright © 2002, 2001 O'Reilly & Associates, Inc. All rights reserved.
Printed in the United States of America.

Published by O'Reilly & Associates, Inc., 1005 Gravenstein Highway North,
Sebastopol, CA 95472.

O'Reilly & Associates books may be purchased for educational, business, or sales pro-
motional use. Online editions are also available for most titles (*safari.oreilly.com*). For
more information, contact our corporate/institutional sales department: (800) 998-9938
or *corporate@oreilly.com*.

Editor:	Nancy Kotary
Production Editor:	Colleen Gorman
Cover Designer:	Ellie Volckhausen
Interior Designer:	David Futato

Printing History:

June 2001:	First Edition.
February 2002:	Second Edition.

Nutshell Handbook, the Nutshell Handbook logo, and the O'Reilly logo are registered
trademarks of O'Reilly & Associates, Inc. Microsoft, MSDN, .NET logo, Visual Basic,
Visual C++, Visual Studio, and Windows are registered trademarks of Microsoft
Corporation. Many of the designations used by manufacturers and sellers to distinguish
their products are claimed as trademarks. Where those designations appear in this book,
and O'Reilly & Associates, Inc. was aware of a trademark claim, the designations have
been printed in caps or initial caps. The association between the image of shrimp and
the topic of the .NET Framework is a trademark of O'Reilly & Associates, Inc.

While every precaution has been taken in the preparation of this book, the publisher and
the authors assume no responsibility for errors or omissions, or for damages resulting
from the use of the information contained herein.

ISBN: 0-596-00302-1
[M]

Table of Contents

Preface

A condensed introduction to the Microsoft .NET Framework, this book aims to help programmers make the transition from traditional Windows programming into the world of .NET programming. The Microsoft .NET Framework includes the Common Language Runtime (CLR) and a set of base classes that radically simplify the development of large-scale applications and services. This book examines the CLR in detail, so that you can put its new features to good use. The book also illustrates how language integration really works and guides you through component and enterprise development using the .NET Framework. In addition, it introduces you to four key .NET technologies: Data (ADO.NET) and XML, Web Services, Web Forms (ASP.NET), and Windows Forms.

We used the latest release of Microsoft Visual Studio .NET and the .NET Framework SDK to prepare this manuscript and to develop all the examples and figures in this book. While we have done our best to ensure that the technical content of this book is up-to-date, it is possible that some items have changed slightly from the time of writing. To stay up-to-date, regularly check *http://msdn.microsoft.com/net*, *http://www.gotdotnet.com*, and this book's O'Reilly page, *http://www.oreilly.com/catalog/dotnet_frmess2/*.

Audience

While this book is for any person interested in learning about the Microsoft .NET Framework, it targets seasoned developers with experience in building Windows applications with Visual Studio 6 and the Visual Basic and Visual C++ languages. Java™ and C/C++ developers will also be well prepared for the material presented here. To gain the most from this book, you should have experience in object-oriented, component, enterprise, and web application development. COM programming experience is a plus.

About This Book

Based on a short course that Thuan has delivered to numerous companies since August 2000, this book is designed so that each chapter builds on knowledge from the previous one for those unfamiliar with each technology. To give you a heads-up, here are brief summaries for the chapters and appendixes covered in this book.

Chapter 1, *.NET Overview*, takes a brief look at Microsoft .NET and the Microsoft .NET Platform. It then describes the .NET Framework design goals and introduces you to the components of the .NET Framework.

Chapter 2, *The Common Language Runtime*, lifts the hood and peers into the CLR. This chapter surveys the rich runtime of the CLR, as well as other features.

Chapter 3, *.NET Programming*, introduces you to .NET programming. You'll examine a simple program that uses object-oriented and component-based concepts in four different languages: Managed C++, VB.NET, C#, and IL. You'll also experience the benefits of language integration.

Chapter 4, *Working with .NET Components*, demonstrates the simplicity of component and enterprise development in .NET. Besides seeing component-deployment features, you'll also examine complete programs that take advantage of transaction, object pooling, role-base security, and message queuing—all in one chapter.

Chapter 5, *Data and XML*, describes the architecture of ADO.NET and its benefits. Besides being disconnected to promote scalability, the ADO.NET dataset is also tightly integrated with XML to enhance interoperability. This chapter introduces you to the .NET data-access objects, as well as the XML namespace.

Chapter 6, *Web Services*, describes the next generation of software components that can be accessed through the Internet. In this chapter, we discuss the protocols that support Web Services, as well as how to publish and discover them. You will see how XML, used in conjunction with HTTP, breaks the proprietary nature of current component-oriented software development and enables greater interoperability.

Chapter 7, *Web Forms*, introduces you to ASP.NET, which now supports object-oriented and event-driven programming, as opposed to conventional ASP development. In this chapter, Web Forms and server controls take the center stage. In addition, we examine how to build custom server controls, perform data binding to various .NET controls, and survey state management features in ASP.NET.

Chapter 8, *Windows Forms*, takes conventional form-based programming a step into the future with the classes in the System.Windows.Forms namespace. Similar to Win32-based applications, Windows Forms are best used for to build so-called rich or "fat" clients; however, with the new zero-effort installation procedure of .NET and the advent of Web Services, Windows Forms are appropriate for a host of applications.

Appendix A, *.NET Languages*, contains a list of links to web sites with information regarding languages that targets the CLR, including some burgeoning open source projects.

Appendix B, *Common Acronyms*, contains a list of commonly used acronyms that are used in .NET literature and presentations.

Appendix C, *Common Data Types*, contains several lists of commonly used datatypes in .NET. This appendix also illustrates the use of several of its collection classes.

Appendix D, *Common Utilities*, surveys the important tools that the .NET SDK provides to ease the tasks of .NET development.

Now that you know what this book is about, we should explain what it is not about. This book does not focus on the marketing aspects of .NET or on other components of the .NET Platforms, including .NET Enterprise Servers, .NET Building Block Services, or .NET Operating Systems. Likewise, we do not cover the recently announced HailStorm service or the work Microsoft is doing to make the .NET Framework available on a host of devices.

Assumptions This Book Makes

This book assumes that you are a Windows and web application developer fluent in object-oriented and component-based programming. It also assumes that you have some basic knowledge of XML. While COM is not a crucial prerequisite, if you have COM programming experience, you will appreciate this book and the .NET Framework all the more.

Conventions Used in This Book

We use the following font conventions in this book.

Italic is used for:

- Pathnames, filenames, and program names
- Internet addresses, such as domain names and URLs
- New terms where they are defined

`Constant width` is used for:

- Command lines and options that should be typed verbatim
- Direct quotes and specific method names from code examples, as well as specific values for attributes and settings within code
- XML element tags

`Constant width bold` is used for:

- User input in code that should be typed verbatim
- Items in code to which we'd like to draw the reader's attention

`Constant width italic` is used for replaceable items in code, which should be replaced with the appropriate terms.

In code syntax examples, we sometimes use [*value*]⁺ to represent one or more instances of a value and [*value*]* to mean zero or more instances of a value.

How to Contact Us

We have tested and verified the information in this book to the best of our ability, but you may find that features have changed (or even that we have made mistakes!). Please let us know about any errors you find, as well as your suggestions for future editions, by writing to:

> O'Reilly & Associates, Inc.
> 1005 Gravenstein Highway North
> Sebastopol, CA 95472
> (800) 998-9938 (in the United States or Canada)
> (707) 829-0515 (international/local)
> (707) 829-0104 (FAX)

You can also send us messages electronically. To be put on the mailing list or request a catalog, send email to:

> *info@oreilly.com*

To ask technical questions or comment on the book, send email to:

> *bookquestions@oreilly.com*

We have a web site for the book, where we'll list examples, errata, and any plans for future editions. You can access this page at:

> *http://www.oreilly.com/catalog/dotnetfrmess2/*

For more information about this book and others, see the O'Reilly web site:

> *http://www.oreilly.com*

For more information on .NET in general, visit the O'Reilly .NET Center at *http://dotnet.oreilly.com* and the .NET DevCenter at *http://www.oreillynet. com/dotnet/*.

Acknowledgments

The folks at O'Reilly never cease to amaze us with the support that they provide. We'd like to thank John Osborn for extending us the contract to write this book and for his continuous support throughout the project. We'd also like to thank Nancy Kotary for the hard work that she went through to get the book out under a rigorous schedule. Nancy did a great job reviewing our materials and coordinating the project. Without John and Nancy, this book would not have been possible. Thanks to the production and design folks at O'Reilly for making this book a reality: Emma Colby, Tatiana Diaz, David Futato, Colleen Gorman, Robert Romano, Mike Sierra, Ellie Volckhausen, and Joe Wizda.

Thanks to Brian Jepson who has contributed significantly to this book since the beginning of this project. Brian did an unquestionably outstanding job reading, testing, and ensuring that the technical content in every chapter lines up with the latest release. He also gave us invaluable guidance and support throughout this project. We'd also like to thank Dennis Angeline and Brad Merrill at Microsoft for answering technical questions on the CLR and languages.

Hoang would like to thank his parents and family for their support and understanding of his being missing-in-action for several months. Mom and Dad, your ongoing efforts to put your children where they are today can never be repaid. Hoang would like to thank his wife, VanDu, the source of his inspiration. Don't underestimate your contribution to this book. And last, but not least, a personal *thank you* to Thuan, who has always pushed me toward the bleeding edge.

CHAPTER 1

.NET Overview

Microsoft announced the .NET intitiative in July 2000. The .NET platform is a new development framework with a new programming interface to Windows services and APIs, integrating a number of technologies that emerged from Microsoft during the late 1990s. Incorporated into .NET are COM+ component services; the ASP web development framework; a commitment to XML and object-oriented design; support for new web services protocols such as SOAP, WSDL, and UDDI; and a focus on the Internet.

The platform consists of four separate product groups:

Development tools
> A set of languages, including C# and VB.NET; a set of development tools, including Visual Studio.NET; a comprehensive class library for building web services and web and Windows applications; as well as the Common Language Runtime to execute objects built within this framework.

Specialized servers
> A set of .NET Enterprise Servers, formerly known as SQL Server 2000, Exchange 2000, BizTalk 2000, and so on, that provide specialized functionality for relational data storage, email, and B2B commerce.

Web services
> An offering of commercial web services, specifically the .NET My Services initiative (formerly called HailStorm); for a fee, developers can use these services in building applications that require knowledge of user identity.

Devices
> New .NET-enabled non-PC devices, from cell phones to game boxes.

Microsoft is devoting considerable resources to the development and success of .NET and related technologies: their bets are on .NET as the next big thing in computing.

Microsoft .NET

Microsoft has spent the last four years creating Microsoft .NET, which was publicly launched at PDC 2000 in Orlando, Florida. While the main strategy of .NET is to enable software as a service, .NET is much more than that. Aside from embracing the Web, Microsoft .NET acknowledges and responds to the following trends within the software industry today:

Distributed computing
> Simplifies the development of robust client/server applications. Current distributed technologies require high vendor-affinity and lack interoperation with the Web. Microsoft .NET provides a remoting architecture that exploits open Internet standards, including the Hypertext Transfer Protocol (HTTP), Extensible Markup Language (XML), and Simple Object Access Protocol (SOAP).

Componentization
> Simplifies the integration of software components developed by different vendors. The Component Object Model (COM) has brought reality to software plug-and-play, but COM component development and deployment are too complex. Microsoft .NET provides a simpler way to build and deploy components.

Enterprise services
> Allow the development of scalable enterprise applications without writing code to manage transactions, security, or pooling. Microsoft .NET continues to support enterprise services, since these services greatly reduce the development time and effort involved in building large-scale applications.

Web paradigm shifts
> Represents changes in web technologies to simplify the development of web applications. Over the last few years, web application development has shifted from connectivity (TCP/IP), to presentation (HTML), to programmability (XML and SOAP). A key goal of Microsoft .NET is to enable software to be sold and distributed as a service.

Maturity factors
> Represents lessons that the software industry has learned from developing large-scale enterprise and web applications. A commercial web application must support interoperability, scalability, availability, and manageability. Microsoft .NET facilitates all these goals.

Although these are the main concepts that Microsoft .NET incorporates, what's more notable is that Microsoft .NET uses open Internet standards (HTTP, XML, and SOAP) at its core to transmit an object from one machine to another across the Internet. In fact, there is bidirectional mapping between XML and objects in .NET. For example, a class can be expressed as an XML Schema Definition (XSD); an object can be converted to and from an XML buffer; a method can be specified using an XML format called Web Services Description Language (WSDL); and an invocation (method call) can be expressed using an XML format called SOAP.

The .NET Platform

The Microsoft .NET Platform consists of five main components, as shown in Figure 1-1. At the lowest layer lies the operating system (OS), which can be one of a variety of Windows platforms, including Windows XP, Windows 2000, Windows Me, and Windows CE. As part of the .NET strategy, Microsoft has promised to deliver more .NET device software to facilitate a new generation of smart devices.

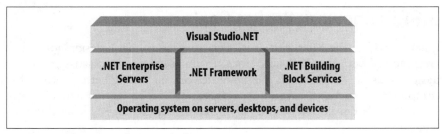

Figure 1-1. The Microsoft .NET platform

On top of the operating system is a series of .NET Enterprise Server products that shortens the time required to develop large-scale business systems. These server products include Application Center 2000, BizTalk Server 2000, Commerce Server 2000, Exchange Server 2000, Host Integration Server 2000, Internet Security and Acceleration Server 2000, and SQL Server 2000.

Since Web Services are highly reusable across the Web, Microsoft plans to provide a number of building-block services that applications developers can use, for a fee. An example of building-block service is Microsoft Passport, which allows you to use a single username and password at all web sites that support Passport authentication. In March 2001, Microsoft announced another set of Web Services with the codename HailStorm, now called .NET My Services. This product encompasses a set of building-block services that support personalization, centered entirely on consistent user experiences.*

---

* For more information on .NET My Services, see the forthcoming .NET My Services Essentials by Culbert and Murphy (O'Reilly).

Microsoft plans to add newer services, such as calendar, directory, and search services. Third-party vendors are also creating new Web Services of their own.

At the top layer of the .NET architecture is a brand new development tool called Visual Studio.NET (VS.NET), which makes possible the rapid development of Web Services and other applications. A successor of Microsoft Visual Studio 6.0, VS.NET is an Integrated Development Environment (IDE) that supports four different languages and features such as cross-language debugging and the XML Schema Editor.

And at the center of .NET is the Microsoft .NET Framework—the main focus of this book. The .NET Framework is a new development and runtime infrastructure that will change the development of business applications on the Windows platform. It includes the Common Language Runtime (CLR) and a common framework of classes that can be used by all .NET languages.

.NET Framework Design Goals

Inherent within the Microsoft .NET Framework are many design goals that are practical yet extremely ambitious. In this section, we discuss the main design goals of the Microsoft .NET Framework, including better support for components, language integration, application interoperation across cyberspace, simple development and deployment, better reliability, and greater security.

Component Infrastructure

Prior to the existence of COM technology, Microsoft developers had no simple way to integrate binary libraries without referring to or altering their source code. With the advent of COM, programmers were able to integrate binary components into their applications, similar to the way we plug-and-play hardware components into our desktop PCs. Although COM was great, the grungy details of COM gave developers and administrators many headaches.

While COM permits you to integrate binary components developed using any language, it does require you to obey the COM identity, lifetime, and binary layout rules. You must also write the plumbing code that is required to create a COM component, such as DllGetClassObject, CoRegister-ClassObject, and others.

Realizing that these requirements result in frequent rewrites of similar code, .NET sets out to remove them. In the .NET world, all classes are ready to be reused at the binary level. You don't have to write extra plumbing code to support componentization in the .NET Framework. You simply write a .NET class, which then becomes a part of an assembly (to be discussed in Chapter 2), and supports plug-and-play.*

In addition to providing a framework to make development easier, .NET removes the pain of developing COM components. Specifically, .NET removes the use of the registry for component registration and eliminates the requirements for extraneous plumbing code found in all COM components, including code to support IUnknown, class factories, component lifetime, registration, dynamic binding, and others.

 "Component" is a nasty word because one person may use it to refer to an object and another may use it to refer to a binary module. To be consistent, this book uses the term "COM component" (or simply "component") to refer to a binary module, such as a DLL or an EXE.

Language Integration

COM supports *language independence*, which means that you can develop a COM component in any language you want. As long as your component meets all the rules spelled out in the COM specification, it can be instantiated and used by your applications. While this supports binary reuse, it doesn't support *language integration*. In other words, you can't reuse the code in the COM components written by someone else; you can't extend a class hosted in the COM component; you can't catch exceptions thrown by code in the COM component; and so forth.

Microsoft .NET supports not only language independence, but also language integration. This means that you can inherit from classes, catch exceptions, and take advantage of polymorphism across different languages. The .NET Framework makes this possible with a specification called the Common Type System (CTS), which all .NET components must support. For example, everything in .NET is an object of a specific class that derives from the root class called System.Object. The CTS supports the general concepts of classes, interfaces, delegates (which support callbacks), reference types, and value types. The .NET base classes provide most of the base system types, such as ones that support integer, string, and file manipulation. Because every language compiler must meet a minimum set of rules

---

*COM still plays a role in the .NET Framework. In fact, if you use *dumpbin.exe* to dump a Portable Executable (PE) file created by the compilers available in the prerelease or Beta 1 version of the .NET SDK, you will see some COM residues, specifically a mention of something called the COM+Header. See ".NET Portable Executable File" in Chapter 2 for more information.

stipulated by the Common Language Specification (CLS) and generate code to conform to the CTS, different .NET languages can intermingle with one another. We will examine the CTS and CLS in Chapter 2.

Internet Interoperation

COM supports distributed computing through its Distributed COM (DCOM) wire protocol. A problem with DCOM is that it embeds the host TCP/IP address inside the Network Data Representation (NDR) buffer, such that it will not work through firewalls and Network Address Translation (NAT) software. In addition, the DCOM dynamic activation, protocol negotiation, and garbage-collection facilities are proprietary, complex, and expensive. The solution is an open, simple, and lightweight protocol for distributed computing. The .NET Framework uses the new industry-supported SOAP protocol, which is based on the widely accepted XML and HTTP standards.

Simple Development

If you have developed software for the Windows platforms since their appearance, you have seen everything from the Windows APIs to the Microsoft Foundation Classes (MFC), the Active Template Library (ATL), the system COM interfaces, and the countless other environments, such as Visual Interdev, Visual Basic, JScript, and other scripting languages. Each time you set out to develop something in a different compiler, you had to learn a new API or a class library, because there is no consistency or commonality among these different libraries or interfaces.

The .NET solution provides a set of framework classes and lets every language use it. Such a framework removes the need for learning a new API each time you switch languages. Put differently, it's certainly easier to go through ten methods of a particular class than to go through a thousand API functions.

Simple Deployment

Imagine this scenario: your Windows application, which uses three shared DLLs, works just fine for months, but stops working one day after you've installed another software package that overwrites the first DLL, does nothing to the second DLL, and adds an additional copy of the third DLL into a different directory. If you have ever encountered such a brutal—yet entirely possible—problem, you have entered *DLL Hell*. And if you ask a group of seasoned developers whether they have experienced DLL Hell, they will grimace at you in disgust, not because of the question you've posed, but because they have indeed experienced the pain and suffering.

To avoid DLL Hell on Windows 2000 (at least for system DLLs), Windows 2000 stores system DLLs in a cache. If you install an application that overwrites system DLLs, Windows 2000 will overwrite the added system DLLs with the original versions from the cache.

Microsoft .NET further diminishes DLL Hell. In the .NET environment, your executable will use the shared DLL with which it was built. This is guaranteed, because a shared DLL must be registered against something similar to the Windows 2000 cache, called the Global Assembly Cache (GAC). In addition to this requirement, a shared DLL must have a unique hash value, public key, locale, and version number. Once you've met these requirements and registered your shared DLL in the GAC, its physical filename is no longer important. In other words, if you have two versions of a DLL that are both called *MyDll.dll*, both of them can live and execute on the same system without causing DLL Hell. Again, this is possible because the executable that uses one of these DLLs is tightly bound to the DLL during compilation.

In addition to eradicating DLL Hell, .NET also removes the need for component-related registry settings. A COM developer will tell you that half the challenge of learning COM is understanding the COM-specific registry entries for which the developer is responsible. Microsoft .NET stores all references and dependencies of .NET assemblies within a special section called a *manifest* (see Chapter 2). In addition, assemblies can be either private or shared. Private assemblies are found using logical paths or XML-based application configuration files, and public assemblies are registered in the GAC; in both cases the system will find your dependencies at runtime. If they are missing, you get an exception telling you exactly what happened.

Finally, .NET brings back the concept of zero-impact installation and removal. This concept is the opposite of what you have to deal with in the world of COM. To set up a COM application, you have to register all your components after you have copied them over to your machine. If you fail to perform this step correctly, nothing will work and you'll end up pulling your hair out. Likewise, to uninstall the application, you should unregister your components (to remove the registry entries) prior to deleting your files. Again, if you fail to perform this step correctly, you will leave remnants in the registry that will be forever extant.

Unlike COM, but like DOS, to set up an application in .NET, you simply xcopy your files from one directory on a CD to another directory on your machine, and the application will run automatically.* Similarly, you can just delete the directory to uninstall the application from your machine.

Reliability

There are many programming languages and platforms in the commercial software industry, but few of them attempt to provide both a reliable language and a robust runtime or infrastructure. The most successful language that we have seen in the commercial software industry is the Java™ language and the Java Virtual Machine™, which have brought the software-development community much satisfaction. Microsoft is positioning .NET as the next big thing.

Microsoft .NET requires type safety. Unlike C++, every class in .NET is derived from the mother of all classes, Object, which supports runtime type-identification features, content-dumping features, and so on. The CLR must recognize and verify types before they can be loaded and executed. This decreases the chances for rudimentary programming errors and prevents buffer overruns, which can be a security weakness.

Traditional programming languages don't provide a common error-handling mechanism. C++ and Java support exception handling, but many others leave you in the dust, forcing to invent your own error-handling facilities. Microsoft .NET supports exceptions in the CLR, providing a consistent error-handling mechanism. Put another way: exceptions work across all .NET-compatible languages.

When you program in C++, you must deallocate all heap-based objects that you have previously allocated. If you fail to do this, the allocated resources on your system will never be reclaimed even though they are no longer needed. And if this is a server application, it won't be robust because the accumulation of unused resources in memory will eventually bring down the system. Similar to Java, the .NET runtime tracks and garbage-collects all allocated objects that are no longer needed.

Security

When developing applications in the old days of DOS, Microsoft developers cared little about security because their applications ran on a single desktop with a single thread of execution. As soon as developers started developing client and server applications, things got a bit complicated: multiple users

---

* This is true for private assemblies, but not for shared assemblies. See Chapter 4 for more details.

might then have accessed the servers, and sensitive data might be exchanged between the client and the server. The problem became even more complex in the web environment, since you could unknowingly download and execute malicious applets on your machine.

To mitigate these problems, .NET provides a number of security features. Windows NT and Windows 2000 protect resources using access-control lists and security identities, but don't provide a security infrastructure to verify access to parts of an executable's code. Unlike traditional security support in which only access to the executable is protected, .NET goes further to protect access to specific parts of the executable code. For example, to take advantage of declarative security checks, you can prefix your method implementations with security attributes without having to write any code. To take advantage of imperative security checks, you write the code in your method to explicitly cause a security check. There are many other security facilities that .NET provides in an attempt to make it harder to penetrate your applications and system.

.NET Framework

Now that you are familiar with the major goals of the .NET Framework, let's briefly examine its architecture. As you can see in Figure 1-2, the .NET Framework sits on top of the operating system, which can be a few different flavors of Windows,* and consists of a number of components. (Each of these components is discussed in greater detail starting with Chapter 4, as described in the Preface.) .NET is essentially a system application that runs on Windows.

The most important component of the Framework is something called the CLR. If you are a Java programmer, think of the CLR as the .NET equivalent of the Java Virtual Machine (JVM). If you don't know Java, think of the CLR as the heart and soul of the .NET architecture. At a high level, the CLR activates objects, performs security checks on them, lays them out in memory, executes them, and garbage-collects them.

Conceptually, the CLR and the JVM are similar in that they are both runtime infrastructures that abstract the underlying platform differences. However, while the JVM currently supports only the Java language, the CLR supports all languages that can be represented in the Common Intermediate Language (CIL). The JVM executes bytecode, so it could technically support

---

* In fact, the operating system can be—potentially—any flavor of Unix or other operating systems. This is possible due to the architecture of the CLR, which is discussed in Chapter 2.

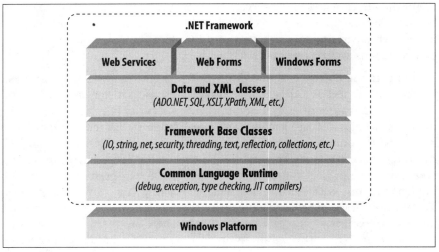

Figure 1-2. The .NET Framework

many different languages, too. Unlike Java's bytecode, though, IL is never interpreted. Another conceptual difference between the two infrastructures is that Java code runs on multiple platforms with a JVM, whereas .NET code runs only on the Windows platforms with the CLR (at the time of this writing). Microsoft has submitted the Common Language Infrastructure (CLI), which is functional a subset of the CLR, to ECMA, so a third-party vendor could theoretically implement a CLR for a platform other than Windows. For more information on third-party vendors, see Appendix A.

In Figure 1-2, the layer on top of the CLR is a set of framework base classes. This set of classes is similar to the set of classes in STL, MFC, ATL, or Java. These classes support rudimentary input and output functionality, string manipulation, security management, network communications, thread management, text management, reflection functionality, and collections functionality, as well as other functions.

On top of the framework base classes is a set of classes that extend the base classes to support data management and XML manipulation. The data classes support persistent data management—data that is stored on backend databases. These classes include the Structured Query Language (SQL) classes to let you manipulate persistent data stores through a standard SQL interface. Similar to the SQL classes, the set of classes called ADO.NET allow you to manipulate persistent data. Alongside of the data classes, the .NET Framework supports a number of classes to let you manipulate XML data, perform XML searching, and perform XML translations.

Classes in three different technologies (including Web Services, Web Forms, and Windows Forms) extend the framework base classes and the data and XML classes. Web Services include a number of classes that support the development of lightweight distributed components, which will work even in the face of firewalls and NAT software. These components support plug-and-play across cyberspace, because Web Services employ standard HTTP and SOAP.

Web Forms include a number of classes that allow you to rapidly develop web Graphical User Interface (GUI) applications. If you're currently developing web applications with Visual Interdev, you can think of Web Forms as a facility that allows you to develop web GUIs using the same drag-and-drop approach as if you were developing the GUIs in Visual Basic. Simply drag and drop controls onto your Web Form, double-click on a control, and write the code to respond to the associated event.

Windows Forms support a set of classes that allow you to develop native-Windows GUI applications. You can think of these classes collectively as a much better version of MFC because they support easier GUI development and provide a common, consistent interface that can be used in all languages.

In the next chapter, we examine the internals of the CLR and how it supports and executes .NET components, formally called *assemblies* in .NET.

CHAPTER 2
The Common Language Runtime

The most important component of the .NET Framework is the Common Language Runtime (CLR). The CLR manages and executes code written in .NET languages and is the basis of the .NET architecture, similar to the Java Virtual Machine. The CLR activates objects, performs security checks on them, lays them out in memory, executes them, and garbage-collects them.

In this chapter, we describe the CLR environment, executables (with examples in several languages), metadata, assemblies, manifests, the CTS, and the CLS.

CLR Environment

The CLR is the underlying .NET infrastructure. Its facilities cover all the goals that we spelled out in Chapter 1. Unlike software libraries such as MFC or ATL, the CLR is built from a clean slate. The CLR manages the execution of code in the .NET Framework.

 An *assembly* is the basic unit of deployment and versioning, consisting of a manifest, a set of one or more modules, and an optional set of resources.

Figure 2-1 shows the two portions of the .NET environment, with the bottom portion representing the CLR and the top portion representing the CLR executables or Portable Executable (PE) files, which are .NET assemblies or units of deployment. The CLR is the runtime engine that loads required classes, performs just-in-time compilation on needed methods, enforces security checks, and accomplishes a bunch of other runtime functionalities. The CLR executables shown in Figure 2-1 are either EXE or DLL files that consist mostly of metadata and code.

Figure 2-1. The CLR environment

CLR Executables

Microsoft .NET executables are different from typical Windows executables in that they carry not only code and data, but also metadata (see "Metadata" and "Intermediate Language" later in this chapter). In this section, we start off with the code for several .NET applications, and discuss the .NET PE format.

Hello, World: Managed C++

Let's start off by examining a simple *Hello, World* application written in Managed C++, a Microsoft .NET extension to the C++ language. Managed C++ includes a number of new .NET-specific keywords that permit C++ programs to take advantage of .NET's new features, including garbage collection. Here's the Managed C++ version of our program:

```
#using <mscorlib.dll>
using namespace System;

void main( )
{
   Console::WriteLine(L"C++ Hello, World!");
}
```

As you can see, this is a simple C++ program with an additional directive, #using (shown in bold). If you have worked with the Microsoft Visual C++ compiler support features for COM, you may be familiar with the #import directive. While #import reverse-engineers type information to generate wrapper classes for COM interfaces, #using makes all types accessible from the specified DLL, similar to a #include directive in C or C++. However, unlike #include, which imports C or C++ types, #using imports types for any .NET assembly, written in any .NET language.

The one and only statement within the main( ) method is self-explanatory— it means that we are invoking a static or class-level method, WriteLine( ), on the Console class. The L that prefixes the literal string tells the C++ compiler to convert the literal into a Unicode string. You may have already guessed that the Console class is a type hosted by *mscorlib.dll*, and it takes one string parameter.

One thing that you should also notice is that this code signals to the compiler that we're using the types in the System namespace, as indicated by the using namespace statement. This allows us to refer to Console instead of having to fully qualify this class as System::Console.

Given this simple program, compile it using the new C++ command-line compiler shipped with the .NET SDK:

```
cl hello.cpp /CLR /link /entry:main
```

The /CLR command-line option is extremely important, because it tells the C++ compiler to generate a .NET PE file instead of a normal Windows PE file.

When this statement is executed, the C++ compiler generates an executable called *hello.exe*. When you run *hello.exe*, the CLR loads, verifies, and executes it.

Hello, World: C#

Because .NET is serious about language integration, we'll illustrate this same program using Microsoft's new C# language specially designed for .NET. Borrowing from Java and C++ syntax, C# is a simple and object-oriented language that Microsoft has used to write the bulk of the .NET base classes and tools. If you are a Java (or C++) programmer, you should have no problem understanding C# code. Here's *Hello, World* in C#:

```
using System;

class MainApp
{
  public static void Main( )
  {
    Console.WriteLine("C# Hello, World!");
  }
}
```

C# is similar to Java in that it doesn't have the concept of a header file: class definitions and implementations are stored in the same *.cs* file. Another similarity to Java is that Main( ) is a public, static function of a particular class, as you can see from the code. This is different from C++, where the main( ) method itself is a global function.

The using keyword here functions similar to using namespace in the previous example, in that it signals to the C# compiler that we want to use types within the System namespace. Here's how to compile this C# program:

```
csc hello.cs
```

In this command, csc is the C# compiler that comes with the .NET SDK. Again, the result of executing this command is an executable called *hello. exe*, which you can execute like a normal EXE but is managed by the CLR.

Hello, World: VB.NET

And since we're on a roll, here is the same program in Visual Basic.NET (VB.NET):

```
Imports System

Public Module modmain
  Sub Main( )
    Console.WriteLine ("VB Hello, World!")
  End Sub
End Module
```

If you are a VB programmer, you may be in for a surprise. The syntax of the language has changed quite a bit, but luckily these changes make the language mirror other object-oriented languages, such as C# and C++. Look carefully at this code snippet, and you will see that you can translate each line of code here into an equivalent in C#. Whereas C# uses the keywords using and class, VB.NET uses the keywords Import and Module, respectively. Here's how to compile this program:

```
vbc /t:exe /out:Hello.exe Hello.vb
```

Microsoft now provides a command-line compiler, *vbc*, for VB.NET. The /t option specifies the type of PE file to be created. In this case, since we have specified an EXE, *hello.exe* will be the output of this command.

 In all three versions of this *Hello, World* program, the Console class and the WriteLine( ) method have remained constant. That is, no matter which language you're using, once you know how to do something in one language, you can do it in all the other languages. This is an extreme change from traditional Windows programming, in which if you know how to write to a file in C++, you may not necessarily know how to do it for VB, Java, or Cobol.

.NET Portable Executable File

A Windows executable, EXE or DLL, must conform to a file format called the *PE* file format, which is a derivative of the Microsoft Common Object File Format (COFF). Both of these formats are fully specified and publicly available. The Windows OS knows how to load and execute DLLs and EXEs because it understands the format of a PE file. As a result, any compiler that wants to generate Windows executables must obey the PE/COFF specification.

Standard Windows PE files are divided into two major sections. The first section includes the PE/COFF headers that reference the contents within the PE file. In addition to the header section, the PE file holds a number of native image sections, including the .data, .rdata, .rsrc, and .text sections. These are the standard sections of a typical Windows executable, but Microsoft's C/C++ compiler allows you to add your own custom sections into the PE file using a compiler pragma statement. For example, you can create your own data section to hold encrypted data that only you can read. Taking advantage of this ability, Microsoft has added a few new sections to the normal PE file specifically to support the CLR's functionality. The CLR understands and manages the new sections. For example, the CLR will read these sections and determine how to load classes and execute your code at runtime.

As shown in Figure 2-2, the sections that Microsoft has added to the normal PE format are the CLR header and the CLR data sections. While the CLR header stores information to indicate that the PE file is a .NET executable, the CLR data section contains metadata and IL code, both of which determine how the program will be executed.

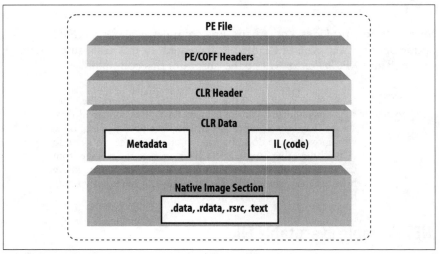

Figure 2-2. The format of a .NET PE file

If you want to prove to yourself that a .NET executable contains both of these sections, use the *dumpbin.exe* utility, which dumps the content of a

Windows executable in readable text. For example, running the following command on the command prompt:

```
dumpbin.exe hello.exe /all
```

generates the following data (for brevity, we have shown only the main elements that we want to illustrate):

```
Microsoft (R) COFF/PE Dumper Version 7.00.9344.1
Copyright (C) Microsoft Corporation.  All rights reserved.

Dump of file hello.exe

PE signature found

File Type: EXECUTABLE IMAGE

FILE HEADER VALUES  [MS-DOS/COFF HEADERS]
  14C machine (x86)
   3 number of sections
   . . .

OPTIONAL HEADER VALUES  [PE HEADER]
  10B magic # (PE32)
  . . .

SECTION HEADER #1  [SECTION DATA]
  . . .
  Code
  Execute Read

RAW DATA #1
  . . .

  clr Header:
    . . .

  Section contains the following imports:
    mscoree.dll
      402000 Import Address Table
      4022B8 Import Name Table
      . . .

      0 _CorExeMain
```

Looking at this text dump of a .NET PE file, you can see that a PE file starts off with the MS-DOS and COFF headers, which all Windows programs must include. Following these headers, you will find the PE header that supports Windows 32-bit programs. Immediately after the PE header, you will find the first data section in the executable file. In a .NET PE file, this is the section (SECTION HEADER #1 as shown here) that stores the CLR header and data.

Notice that it is marked as Code and Execute Read, telling the OS loader and the CLR that this section includes code to be executed at runtime by the CLR.

In the CLR Header, you should note that there is an imported function called _CorExeMain, which is implemented by *mscoree.dll*, the core execution engine of the CLR.* At the time of this writing, Windows 98, 2000, and Me have an OS loader that knows how to load standard PE files. To prevent massive changes to these operating systems and still allow .NET applications to run on them, Microsoft has updated the OS loaders for all these platforms. The updated loaders know how to check for the CLR header, and, if this header exists, it executes _CorExeMain, thus not only jumpstarting the CLR but also surrendering to it. You can then guess that your Main() function will eventually be called by the CLR.

Now that we've looked at the contents of the CLR header, let's examine the contents of the CLR data, including metadata and code, which are arguably the most import elements in .NET.

Metadata

Metadata is machine-readable information about a resource, or "data about data." Such information might include details on content, format, size, or other characteristics of a data source. In .NET, metadata includes type definitions, version information, external assembly references, and other standardized information.

In order for two systems, components, or objects to interoperate with one another, at least one must know something about the other. In COM, this "something" is an interface specification, which is implemented by a component provider and used by its consumers. The interface specification contains method prototypes with full signatures, including the type definitions for all parameters and return types.

Only C/C++ developers were able to readily modify or use Interface Definition Language (IDL) type definitions—not so for VB or other developers, and more importantly, not for tools or middleware. So Microsoft invented something other than IDL that everyone could use, called a *type library*. In COM, type libraries allow a development environment or tool to read, reverse engineer, and create wrapper classes that are most appropriate and

---

* We invite to you run *dumpbin.exe* and view the exports of *mscoree.dll* at your convenience. You will also find _CorDllMain, _CorExeMain, _CorImageUnloading, and other interesting exports. It's interesting to note that this DLL is an in-process COM server, attesting that .NET is created using COM techniques.

convenient for the target developer. Type libraries also allow runtime engines, such as the VB, COM, MTS, or COM+ runtime, to inspect types at runtime and provide the necessary plumbing or intermediary support for applications to use them. For example, type libraries support dynamic invocation and allow the COM runtime to provide universal marshaling* for cross-context invocations.

Type libraries are extremely rich in COM, but many developers criticize them for their lack of standardization. The .NET team invented a new mechanism for capturing type information. Instead of using the term "type library," we call such type information *metadata* in .NET.

Type Libraries on Steroids

Just as type libraries are C++ header files on steroids, metadata is a type library on steroids. In .NET, metadata is a common mechanism or dialect that the .NET runtime, compilers, and tools can all use. Microsoft .NET uses metadata to describe all types that are used and exposed by a particular .NET assembly. In this sense, metadata describes an assembly in detail, including descriptions of its identity (a combination of an assembly name, version, culture, and public key), the types that it references, the types that it exports, and the security requirements for execution. Much richer than a type library, metadata includes descriptions of an assembly and modules, classes, interfaces, methods, properties, fields, events, global methods, and so forth.

Metadata provides enough information for any runtime, tool, or program to find out literally everything that is needed for component integration. Let's take a look at a short list of consumers that make intelligent use of metadata in .NET, just to prove that metadata is indeed like type libraries on steroids:

CLR
> The CLR uses metadata for verification, security enforcement, cross-context marshaling, memory layout, and execution. The CLR relies heavily on metadata to support these runtime features, which we will cover in a moment.

Class loader
> A component of the CLR, the class loader uses metadata to find and load .NET classes. This is because metadata records detailed information for a specific class and where the class is located, whether it is in

---

* In COM, *universal marshaling* is a common way to marshal all datatypes. A universal marshaler can be used to marshal all types, so you don't have to provide your own proxy or stub code.

the same assembly, within or outside of a specific namespace, or in a dependent assembly somewhere on the network.

Just-in-Time (JIT) compilers

JIT compilers use metadata to compile Microsoft Intermediate Language (IL) code. IL is an intermediate representation that contributes significantly to language-integration support, but it is not VB code or bytecode, which must be interpreted. .NET JIT compiles IL into native code prior to execution, and it does this using metadata.

Tools

Tools use metadata to support integration. For example, development tools can use metadata to generate callable wrappers that allow .NET and COM components to intermingle. Tools such as debuggers, profilers, and object browsers can use metadata to provide richer development support. One example of this is the IntelliSense features that Microsoft Visual Studio.NET supports. As soon as you have typed an object and a dot, the tool displays a list of methods and properties from which you can choose. This way, you don't have to search header files or documentation to obtain the exact method or property names and calling syntax.

Like the CLR, any application, tool, or utility that can read metadata from a .NET assembly can make use of that assembly. You can use the reflection classes in the Microsoft .NET Framework to inspect a .NET PE file and know everything about the data types that the assembly uses and exposes. The CLR uses the same set of reflection classes to inspect and provide runtime features, including memory management, security management, type checking, debugging, remoting, and so on.

Metadata ensures language interoperability, an essential element to .NET, since all languages must use the same types in order to generate a valid .NET PE file. The .NET runtime cannot support features such as memory management, security management, memory layout, type checking, debugging, and so on without the richness of metadata. Therefore, metadata is an extremely important part of .NET—so important that we can safely say that there would be no .NET without metadata.

Examining Metadata

At this point, we introduce an important .NET tool, the IL disassembler (*ildasm.exe*), which allows you to view both the metadata and IL code within a given .NET PE file. For example, if you execute *ildasm.exe* and open the *hello.exe* .NET PE file that you built earlier in this chapter, you will see something similar to Figure 2-3.

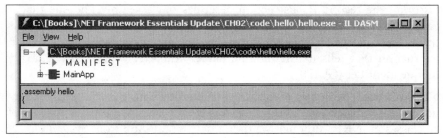

Figure 2-3. -3. The ildasm.exe tool

The *ildasm.exe* tool displays the metadata for your .NET PE file in a tree view, so that you can easily drill down from the assembly, to the classes, to the methods, and so on. To get full details on the contents of a .NET PE file, you can press Ctrl-D to dump the contents out into a text file.* Here's an example of an *ildasm.exe* dump, showing only the contents that are relevant to the current discussion:

```
.assembly extern mscorlib
{
}
.assembly hello
{
}
.module hello.exe
// MVID: {6181DB3C-D7B0-4897-B8F7-013540F29313}
.class private auto ansi beforefieldinit MainApp
       extends [mscorlib]System.Object
{
  .method public hidebysig static
          void Main( ) cil managed
  {
  } // end of method MainApp::Main

  .method public hidebysig specialname rtspecialname
          instance void .ctor( ) cil managed
  {
  } // end of method MainApp::.ctor

} // end of class MainApp
```

As you can see, this dump fully describes the type information and dependencies in a .NET assembly. While the first IL instruction, .assembly extern, tells us that this PE file references (i.e., uses) an external assembly called

---

* The *ildasm.exe* tool also supports a command-line interface. You can execute ildasm.exe /h to view the command-line options. As a side note, if you want to view exactly which types are defined and referenced, press Ctrl-M in the *ildasm.exe* GUI, and it will show you further details.

mscorlib, the second IL instruction describes our assembly, the one that is called hello. We will discuss the contents of the .assembly blocks later, as these are collectively called a *manifest*. Below the manifest, you see an instruction that tells us the module name, *hello.exe*, which has a globally unique identifier (GUID).

Next, you see a definition of a class in IL, starting with the .class IL instruction. Notice this class, MainApp, derives from System.Object, the mother of all classes in .NET. Although we didn't derive MainApp from System.Object when we wrote this class earlier in Managed C++, C#, or VB.NET, the compiler automatically added this specification for us because System.Object is the implicit parent of all classes that omit the specification of a base class.

Within this class, you see two methods. While the first method, Main( ), is a static method that we wrote earlier, the second method, .ctor( ), is automatically generated. Main( ) serves as the main entry point for our application, and .ctor( ) is the constructor that allows anyone to instantiate MainApp.

As this example illustrates, given a .NET PE file, we can examine all the metadata that is embedded within a PE file. The important thing to keep in mind here is that we can do this without the need for source code or header files. If we can do this, imagine the exciting features that the CLR or a third-party tool can offer by simply making intelligent use of metadata. Of course, everyone can now see your code, unless you use different techniques (e.g., encryption) to protect your property rights.

Inspecting and Emitting Metadata

To load and inspect a .NET assembly to determine what types it supports, use a set of classes provided by the .NET Framework. Unlike API functions, these classes encapsulate a number of methods to give you an easy interface for inspecting and manipulating metadata. In .NET, these classes are collectively called the *Reflection API*, which includes classes from the System.Reflection and System.Reflection.Emit namespaces. The classes in the System.Reflection namespace allow you to inspect metadata within a .NET assembly, as shown in the following example:

```
using System;
using System.IO;
using System.Reflection;

public class Meta
{
  public static int Main( )
  {
    // First load the assembly.
```

```
Assembly a = Assembly.LoadFrom("hello.exe");

// Get all the modules that the assembly supports.
Module[] m = a.GetModules();

// Get all the types in the first module.
Type[] types = m[0].GetTypes();

// Inspect the first type.
Type type = types[0];
Console.WriteLine("Type [{0}] has these methods:", type.Name);

// Inspect the methods supported by this type.
MethodInfo[] mInfo = type.GetMethods();
foreach ( MethodInfo mi in mInfo )
{
    Console.WriteLine("  {0}", mi);
}

        return 0;
    }
}
```

Looking at this simple C# program, you'll notice that we first tell the compiler that we want to use the classes in the System.Reflection namespace because we want to inspect metadata. In Main(), we load the assembly by a physical name, *hello.exe*, so be sure that you have this PE file in the same directory when you run this program. Next, we ask the loaded assembly object for an array of modules that it contains. From this array of modules, we pull off the array of types supported by the module, and from this array of types, we then pull off the first type. For *hello.exe*, the first and only type happens to be MainApp. Once we have obtained this type or class, we loop through the list of its exposed methods. If you compile and execute this simple program, you see the following result:

```
Type [MainApp] has these methods:
    Int32 GetHashCode()
    Boolean Equals(System.Object)
    System.String ToString()
    Void Main()
    System.Type GetType()
```

Although we've written only the Main() function, our class actually supports four other methods, as is clearly illustrated by this output. There's no magic here, because MainApp inherits these method implementations from System.Object, which once again is the root of all classes in .NET.

As you can see, the System.Reflection classes allow you to inspect metadata, and they are really easy to use. If you have used type library interfaces in COM before, you know that you can do this in COM, but with much more effort. However, what you can't do with the COM type library interfaces is create a COM component at runtime—a missing feature in COM but an awesome feature in .NET. By using the simple System.Reflection.Emit classes, you can write a simple program to generate a .NET assembly dynamically at runtime. Given the existence of System.Reflection.Emit, anyone can write a custom .NET compiler.

Interoperability Support

Because it provides a common format for specifying types, metadata allows different components, tools, and runtimes to support interoperability. As demonstrated earlier, you can inspect the metadata of any .NET assembly. You can also ask an object at runtime for its type, methods, properties, events, and so on. Tools can do the same. The Microsoft .NET SDK ships four important tools that assist interoperability, including the .NET assembly registration utility (*RegAsm.exe*), the type library exporter (*tlbexp.exe*), the type library importer (*tlbimp.exe*), and the XML schema definition tool (*xsd.exe*).

You can use the .NET assembly registration utility to register a .NET assembly into the registry so COM clients can make use of it. The type library exporter is a tool that generates a type library file (*.tlb*) when you pass it a .NET assembly. Once you have generated a type library from a given .NET assembly, you can import the type library into VC++ or VB and use the .NET assembly in exactly the same way as if you were using a COM component. Simply put, the type library exporter makes a .NET assembly look like a COM component. The following command-line invocation generates a type library, called *hello.tlb*:

```
tlbexp.exe hello.exe
```

Microsoft also ships a counterpart to *tlbexp.exe*, the type library importer; its job is to make a COM component appear as a .NET assembly. So if you are developing a .NET application and want to make use of an older COM component, use the type library importer to convert the type information found in the COM component into .NET equivalents. For example, you can generate a .NET PE using the following command:

```
tlbimp.exe COMServer.tlb
```

Executing this command will generate a .NET assembly in the form of a DLL (e.g., *COMServer.dll*). You can reference this DLL like any other .NET assembly in your .NET code. When your .NET code executes at runtime, all invocations of the methods or properties within this DLL are directed to the original COM component.

Be aware that the type library importer doesn't let you reimport a type library that has been previously exported by the type library exporter. In other words, if you try to use *tlbimp.exe* on *hello.tlb*, which was generated by *tlbexp.exe*, *tlbimp.exe* will barf at you.

Another impressive tool that ships with the .NET SDK is the XML schema definition tool, which allows you to convert an XML schema into a C# class, and vice versa. This XML schema:

```
<schema xmlns="http://www.w3.org/2001/XMLSchema"
  targetNamespace="urn:book:car"
  xmlns:t="urn:book:car">
  <element name="car" type="t:CCar"/>
  <complexType name="CCar">
    <all>
      <element name="vin" type="string"/>
      <element name="make" type="string"/>
      <element name="model" type="string"/>
      <element name="year" type="int"/>
    </all>
  </complexType>
</schema>
```

represents a type called CCar. To convert this XML schema into a C# class definition, execute the following:

```
xsd.exe /c car.xsd
```

The /c option tells the tool to generate a class from the given XSD file. If you execute this command, you get *car.cs* as the output that contains the C# code for this type.

The XML schema definition tool can also take a .NET assembly and generate an XML schema definition (XSD) that represents the types within the .NET assembly. For example, if you execute the following, you get an XSD file as output:

```
xsd.exe somefile.exe
```

Before we leave this topic, we want to remind you to try out these tools for yourself, because they offer many impressive features that we won't cover in this introductory book.

Assemblies and Manifests

As we just saw, types must expose their metadata to allow tools and programs to access them and benefit from their services. Metadata for types alone is not enough. To simplify software plug-and-play and configuration or installation of the component or software, we also need metadata about the component that hosts the types. Now we'll talk about .NET assemblies (deployable units) and manifests (the metadata that describes the assemblies).

Assemblies Versus Components

During the COM era, Microsoft documentation inconsistently used the term *component* to mean a COM class or a COM module (DLLs or EXEs), often forcing readers or developers to consider the context of the term each time they encountered it. In .NET, Microsoft has addressed this confusion by introducing a new concept, *assembly*, which is a software component that supports plug-and-play, much like a hardware component. Theoretically, a .NET assembly is approximately equivalent to a COM module. In practice, an assembly can contain or refer to a number of types and physical files (including bitmap files, .NET PE files, and so forth) that are needed at runtime for successful execution. In addition to hosting IL code, an assembly is a basic unit of versioning, deployment, security management, side-by-side execution, sharing, and reuse, as we discuss next.

To review: an assembly is a logical DLL or EXE, and a manifest is a detailed description (metadata) of an assembly, including its version, what other assemblies it uses, and so on.

Unique Identities

Type uniqueness is important in RPC, COM, and .NET. Given the vast number of GUIDs in COM (application, library, class, and interface identifiers), development and deployment can be tedious because you must use these magic numbers in your code and elsewhere all the time. In .NET, you refer to a specific type by its readable name and its namespace. Since a readable name and its namespace are not enough to be globally unique, .NET guarantees uniqueness by using unique public/private key pairs. All assemblies that are shared (called *shared assemblies*) by multiple applications must be built with a public/private key pair. Public/private key pairs are used in public-key cryptography. Since public-key cryptography uses asymmetric encryption, an assembly creator can sign an assembly with a private key, and anyone can verify that digital signature using the assembly creator's public key.

To sign an assembly digitally, you must use a public/private key pair to build your assembly. At build time, the compiler generates a hash of the assembly files, signs the hash with the private key, and stores the resulting digital signature in a reserved section of the PE file. The public key is also stored in the assembly.

To verify the assembly's digital signature, the CLR uses the assembly's public key to decrypt the assembly's digital signature, resulting in the original, calculated hash. In addition, the CLR uses the information in the assembly's manifest to dynamically generate a hash. This hash value is then compared with the original hash value. These values must match, or we must assume that someone has tampered with the assembly.

Now that we know how to sign and verify an assembly in .NET, let's talk about how the CLR ensures that a given application loads the trusted assembly with which it was built. When you or someone else builds an application that uses a shared assembly, the application's assembly manifest will include an 8-byte hash of the shared assembly's public key. When you run your application, the CLR dynamically derives the 8-byte hash from the shared assembly's public key and compares this value with the hash value stored in your application's assembly manifest. If these values match, the CLR assumes that it has loaded the correct assembly for you.*

IL Code

An assembly contains the IL code—see "Intermediate Language (IL)" later in this chapter—that the CLR executes at runtime. The IL code typically uses types defined within the same assembly, but it also may use or refer to types in other assemblies. While nothing special is required to take advantage of the former, the assembly must define references to other assemblies to do the latter, as we will see in a moment. There is one caveat: each assembly can have at most one entry point, such as DllMain(), WinMain(), or Main(). You must follow this rule because when the CLR loads an assembly, it searches for one of these entry points to start assembly execution.

Versioning

There are four types of assemblies in .NET:

Static assemblies
> These are the .NET PE files that you create at compile time. You can create static assemblies using your favorite compiler: *csc*, *cl*, or *vbc*.

---

* You can use the .NET Strong (a.k.a. Shared) Name (*sn.exe*) utility to generate a new key pair for a shared assembly. Before you can share your assembly, you must register it in the Global Assembly Cache, or GAC (see "Side-by-Side Execution" later in this chapter)—you can do this by using the .NET Global Assembly Cache Utility (*gacutil.exe*). The GAC is simply a directory called *Assembly* located under the Windows system (%windir%) directory, which is typically *WINNT* if you're using Windows 2000.

Dynamic assemblies

These are PE-formatted, in-memory assemblies that you dynamically create at runtime using the classes in the System.Reflection.Emit namespace.

Private assemblies

These are static assemblies used by a specific application.

Public or shared assemblies

These are static assemblies that must have a unique shared name and can be used by any application.

An application uses a private assembly by referring to the assembly using a static path or through an XML-based application configuration file. While the CLR doesn't enforce versioning policies—checking whether the correct version is used—for private assemblies, it ensures that an application uses the correct shared assemblies with which the application was built. Thus, an application uses a specific shared assembly by referring to the specific shared assembly, and the CLR ensures that the correct version is loaded at runtime.

In .NET, an assembly is the smallest unit to which you can associate a version number; it has the following format:

```
<major_version>.<minor_version>.<build_number>.<revision>
```

Deployment

Since a client application's assembly manifest (to be discussed shortly) contains information on external references—including where the external assembly lives and what version of the assembly the application uses—you no longer have to use the registry to store activation and marshaling hints as in COM. Using the version and security information recorded in your application's manifest, the CLR will load the correct shared assembly for you. The CLR does lazy loading of external assemblies and will retrieve them on demand when you use their types. Because of this, you can create downloadable applications that are small, with many small external assemblies. When a particular external assembly is needed, the runtime downloads it automatically without involving registration or computer restarts.

Security

The concept of a user identity is common in all development and operating platforms, but the concept of a *code identity*, in which even a piece of code has an identity, is new to the commercial software industry. In .NET, an assembly itself has a code identity, which includes information such as the assembly's shared name, version number, culture, and public key. Using this concept, the CLR can verify whether an assembly is permitted to access system resources or make calls to other assemblies.

To coincide with the concept of a code identity, the CLR supports the concept of *code access*. In other words, the runtime determines the access to a specific assembly based on a set of permissions. The CLR checks these permissions and determines whether to grant execution requests at the assembly level. When you create an assembly, you can specify a set of permissions that the client application must have in order to use your assembly. At runtime, if the client application has code access to your assembly, it can make calls to your assembly's objects—otherwise, it won't be able to use your assembly.

Side-by-Side Execution

We have said that an assembly is a unit of versioning and deployment, and we've talked briefly about DLL Hell, something that .NET intends to minimize. The CLR allows any versions of the same, shared DLL (shared assembly) to execute at the same time, on the same system, and even in the same process. This concept is known as *side-by-side execution*. Microsoft .NET accomplishes side-by-side execution by using the versioning and deployment features that are innate to all shared assemblies. This concept allows you to install any versions of the same, shared assembly on the same machine, without versioning conflicts or DLL Hell. The only caveat is that your assemblies must be public or shared assemblies, meaning that you must register them against the GAC using a tool such as the .NET Global Assembly Cache Utility (*gacutil.exe*). Once you have registered different versions of the same shared assembly into the GAC, the human-readable name of the assembly no longer matters—what's important is the information provided by .NET's versioning and deployment features.

Recall that when you build an application that uses a particular shared assembly, the shared assembly's version information is attached to your application's manifest. In addition, an 8-byte hash of the shared assembly's public key is also attached to your application's manifest. Using these two pieces of information, the CLR can find the exact shared assembly that your application uses, and it will even verify that your 8-byte hash is indeed equivalent to that of the shared assembly. Given that the CLR can identify and load the exact assembly, .NET should mean that the end of DLL Hell is in sight.

Sharing and Reuse

When you want to share your assembly with the rest of the world, your assembly must have a shared or strong name, and you must register it in the GAC. Likewise, if you want to use or extend a particular class that is hosted by a particular shared assembly, you don't just import that specific class, but you import the whole assembly into your application. Therefore, the whole assembly is a unit of sharing.

Assemblies turn out to be an extremely important feature in .NET because they are an essential part of the runtime. In .NET, an assembly encapsulates all types that are defined within the assembly. For example, while two different assemblies, Personal and Company, can define and expose the same type, Car, Car by itself has no meaning unless you qualify it as [Personal]Car or [Company]Car. Given this, all types are scoped to their containing assembly, and for this reason, the CLR cannot make use of a specific type unless the CLR knows the type's assembly. In fact, if you don't have an assembly manifest, which describes the assembly, the CLR will not execute your program.

Manifests: Assembly Metadata

An assembly *manifest* is metadata that describes everything about the assembly, including its identity, a list of files belonging to the assembly, references to external assemblies, exported types, exported resources, and permission requests. In short, it describes all the details that are required for component plug-and-play. Since an assembly contains all these details, there's no need for storing this type of information in the registry, as in the COM world.

In COM, when you use a particular COM class, you give the COM library a class identifier. The COM library looks up in the registry to find the COM component that exposes that class, loads the component, tells the component to give it an instance of that class, and returns a reference to this instance. In .NET, instead of looking into the registry, the CLR peers right into the assembly manifest, determines which external assembly is needed, loads the exact assembly that's required by your application, and creates an instance of the target class.

Let's examine the manifest for the *hello.exe* application that we built earlier. Recall that we used the *ildasm.exe* tool to pick up this information.

```
.assembly extern mscorlib
{
  .publickeytoken = (B7 7A 5C 56 19 34 E0 89 )
```

```
    .ver 1:0:3200:0
}

.assembly hello
{
  .hash algorithm 0x00008004
  .ver 0:0:0:0
}
.module hello.exe
// MVID: {F828835E-3705-4238-BCD7-637ACDD33B78}
```

You'll notice that this manifest starts off identifying an external or referenced assembly, with mscorlib as the assembly name, which this particular
application references. The keywords .assembly extern tell the CLR that this
application doesn't implement mscorlib, but makes use of it instead. This
external assembly is one that all .NET applications will use, so you will see
this external assembly defined in the manifest of all assemblies. You'll notice
that, inside this assembly definition, the compiler has inserted a special
value called the *publickeytoken*, which is basic information about the publisher of mscorlib. The compiler generates the value for .publickeytoken by
hashing the public key associated with the mscorlib assembly. Another thing
to note in the mscorlib block is the version number of mscorlib.*

Now that we've covered the first .assembly block, let's examine the second,
which describes this particular assembly. You can tell that this is a manifest
block that describes our application's assembly because there's no extern keyword. The identity of this assembly is made up of a readable assembly name,
hello, its version information, 0:0:0:0, and an optional culture, which is missing. Within this block, the first line indicates the hash algorithm that is used to
hash selected contents of this assembly, the result of which will be encrypted
using the private key. However, since we are not sharing this simple assembly, there's no encryption and there's no .publickey value.

The last thing to discuss is .module, which simply identifies the output filename of this assembly, *hello.exe*. You'll notice that a module is associated
with a GUID, which means you get a different GUID each time you build
the module. Given this, a rudimentary test for exact module equivalence is
to compare the GUIDs of two modules.

Because this example is so simple, that's all we get for our manifest. In a
more complicated assembly, you can get all this, including much more in-
depth detail about the make up of your assembly.

---

* The fascinating details are explained in *Partition II Metadata.doc* and *Partition III CIL.doc*, which
  come with the .NET SDK. If you really want to understand metadata IL, read these documents.

Creating Assemblies

An assembly can be a *single-module assembly* or a *multi-module assembly*. In a single-module assembly, everything in a build is clumped into one EXE or DLL, an example of which is the *hello.exe* application that we developed earlier. This is easy to create because a compiler takes care of creating the single-module assembly for you.

If you wanted to create a multi-module assembly, one that contains many modules and resource files, you have a few choices. One option is to use the Assembly Linker (*al.exe*) that is provided by the .NET SDK. This tool takes one or more IL or resource files and spits out a file with an assembly manifest.

Using Assemblies

To use an assembly, first import the assembly into your code, the syntax of which is dependent upon the language that you use. For example, this is how we import an assembly in C#, as we have seen previously in the chapter:

```
using System;
```

When you build your assembly, you must tell the compiler that you are referencing an external assembly. Again, how you do this is different depending on the compiler that you use. If you use the C# compiler, here's how it's done:

```
csc /r:mscorlib.dll hello.cs
```

Earlier, we showed you how to compile *hello.cs* without the /r: option, but both techniques are equivalent. The reference to *mscorlib.dll* is inherently assumed because it contains all the base framework classes.

Intermediate Language (IL)

In software engineering, the concept of *abstraction* is extremely important. We often use abstraction to hide the complexity of system or application services, providing instead a simple interface to the consumer. As long as we can keep the interface the same, we can change the hideous internals, and different consumers can use the same interface.

In language advances, scientists introduced different incarnations of language-abstraction layers, such as *p-code* and *bytecode*. Produced by the Pascal-P compiler, p-code is an intermediate language that supports procedural programming. Generated by Java compilers, bytecode is an intermediate language that supports object-oriented programming. Bytecode is a language abstraction that allows Java code to run on different operating platforms, as long as the platforms have a Java Virtual Machine (JVM) to execute bytecode.

Microsoft calls its own language-abstraction layer the Common Intermediate Language (CIL). Similar to bytecode, IL supports all object-oriented features, including data abstraction, inheritance, polymorphism, and useful concepts such as exceptions and events. In addition to these features, IL supports other concepts, such as properties, fields, and enumeration. Any .NET language may be converted into IL, so .NET supports multiple languages and perhaps multiple platforms in the future (as long as the target platforms have a CLR).

Shipped with the .NET SDK, *Partition III CIL.doc* describes the important IL instructions that language compilers should use. In addition to this specification, the .NET SDK includes another important document, *Partition II Metadata.doc*. Both of these documents are intended for developers who write compilers and tools, but you should read them to further understand how IL fits into .NET. While you can develop a valid .NET assembly using the supported IL instructions and features, you'll find IL to be very tedious because the instructions are a bit cryptic. However, should you decide to write pure IL code, you could use the IL Assembler (*ilasm.exe*) to turn your IL code into a .NET PE file.*

Enough with the theory: let's take a look at some IL. Here's an excerpt of IL code for the *hello.exe* program that we wrote earlier:†

```
.class private auto ansi beforefieldinit MainApp
   extends [mscorlib]System.Object
{
   .method public hidebysig static
           void Main() cil managed
   {
     .entrypoint
     .maxstack  1
     ldstr "C# hello world!"
     call void [mscorlib]System.Console::WriteLine(string)
     ret
   } // end of method MainApp::Main

   .method public hidebysig specialname rtspecialname
      instance void .ctor() cil managed
   {
     .maxstack  1
     ldarg.0
     call instance void [mscorlib]System.Object::.ctor()
```

---

* You can test this utility using the IL disassembler to load a .NET PE file and dump out the IL to a text file. Once you've done this, use the IL Assembler to covert the text file into a .NET PE file.

† Don't compile this IL code: it's incomplete because we've extracted unclear details to make it easier to read. If you want to see the complete IL code, use *ildasm.exe* on *hello.exe*.

```
      ret
    } // end of method MainApp::.ctor

  } // end of class MainApp
```

Ignoring the weird-looking syntactic details, you can see that IL is conceptually the same as any other object-oriented language. Clearly, there is a class
that is called MainApp that derives from System.Object. This class supports
a static method called Main(), which contains the code to dump out a text
string to the console. Although we didn't write a constructor for this class,
our C# compiler has added the default constructor for MainApp to support
object construction.

Since a lengthy discussion of IL is beyond the scope of this book, let's just
concentrate on the Main() method to examine its implementation briefly.
First, you see the following method signature:

```
.method public hidebysig static
        void Main( ) cil managed
```

This signature declares a method that is public (meaning that it can be called
by anyone) and static (meaning it's a class-level method). The name of this
method is Main(). Main() contains IL code that is to be managed or executed by the CLR. The hidebysig attribute says that this method hides the
same methods (with the same signatures) defined earlier in the class hierarchy. This is simply the default behavior of most object-oriented languages,
such as C++. Having gone over the method signature, let's talk about the
method body itself:

```
{
    .entrypoint
    .maxstack 1
    ldstr "C# hello world!"
    call void [mscorlib]System.Console::WriteLine(string)
    ret
} // end of method MainApp::Main
```

This method uses two directives: .entrypoint and .maxstack. The .entrypoint
directive specifies that Main() is the one and only entry point for this assembly. The .maxstack directive specifies the maximum stack slots needed by this
method; in this case, the maximum number of stack slots required by Main()
is one. Stack information is needed for each IL method because IL instructions are stack-based, allowing language compilers to generate IL code easily.

In addition to these directives, this method uses three IL instructions. The
first IL instruction, ldstr, loads our literal string onto the stack so that the
code in the same block can use it. The next IL instruction, call, invokes the
WriteLine() method, which picks up the string from the stack. The call IL
instruction expects the method's arguments to be on the stack, with the first

argument being the first object pushed on the stack, the second argument being the second object pushed onto the stack, and so forth. In addition, when you use the call instruction to invoke a method, you must specify the method's signature. For example, examine the method signature of WriteLine():

```
void [mscorlib]System.Console::WriteLine(string)
```

and you'll see that WriteLine() is a static method of the Console class. The Console class belongs to the System namespace, which happens to be a part of the *mscorlib* assembly. The WriteLine() method takes a string (an alias for System.String) and returns a void. The last thing to note in this IL snippet is that the ret IL instruction simply returns control to the caller.

The CTS and CLS

Having seen the importance of metadata and IL, let's examine the CTS and the CLS. Both the CTS and the CLS ensure language compatibility, interoperability, and integration.

The Common Type System (CTS)

Because .NET treats all languages as equal, a class written in C# should be equivalent to a class written in VB.NET, and an interface defined in Managed C++ should be exactly the same as one that is specified in managed COBOL. Languages must agree on the meanings of these concepts before they can integrate with one another. In order to make language integration a reality, Microsoft has specified a common type system to which every .NET language must abide. In this section, we outline the common types that have the same conceptual semantics in every .NET language. Microsoft .NET supports a rich set of types, but we limit our discussion to the important ones, including value types, reference types, classes, interfaces, and delegates.

Value types

In general, the CLR supports two different types: value types and reference types. *Value types* represent values allocated on the stack. They cannot be null and must always contain some data. When value types are passed into a function, they are passed by value, meaning that a copy of the value is made prior to function execution. This implies that the original value won't change, no matter what happens to the copy during the function call. Since intrinsic types are small in size and don't consume much memory, the resource cost of making a copy is negligible and outweighs the performance drawbacks of object management and garbage collection. Value types include primitives, structures, and enumerations; examples are shown in the following C# code listing:

```
int i;                    // primitive
struct Point { int x, y; } // structure
enum State { Off, On }    // enumeration
```

You can also create a value type by deriving a class from System.ValueType. One thing to note is that a value type is *sealed*, meaning that once you have derived a class from System.ValueType, no one else can derive from your class.

Reference types

If a type consumes significant memory resources, then a reference type provides more benefits over a value type. *Reference types* (including objects, interfaces, and pointers) are so called because they contain references to heap-based objects and can be null. These types are passed by reference, meaning that when you pass such an object into a function, an address of or pointer to the object is passed—not a copy of the object, as in the case of a value type. Since you are passing a reference, the caller will see whatever the called function does to your object. The first benefit here is that a reference type can be used as an output parameter, but the second benefit is that you don't waste extra resources because a copy is not made. If your object is large (consuming lots of memory), then reference types are a better choice. In .NET, one drawback of a reference type is that it must be allocated on the managed heap, which means it requires more CPU cycles because it must be managed and garbage-collected by the CLR. In .NET, the closest concept to destruction is finalization, but unlike destructors in C++, finalization is non-deterministic. In other words, you don't know when finalization will happen because it occurs when the garbage collector executes (by default, when the system runs out of memory). Since finalization is nondeterministic, another drawback of reference types is that if reference-type objects hold on to expensive resources that will be released during finalization, system performance will degrade because the resources won't be released until these objects are garbage-collected. Reference types include classes, interfaces, arrays, and delegates; examples of which are shown in the following C# code listing:

```
class Car {}              // class
interface ISteering {}    // interface
int[] a = new int[5];     // array
delegate void Process();  // delegate
```

Classes, interfaces, and delegates will be discussed shortly.

Boxing and unboxing

Microsoft .NET supports value types for performance reasons, but everything in .NET is ultimately an object. In fact, all primitive types have corresponding classes in the .NET Framework. For example, int is in fact an alias of System.Int32, and System.Int32 happens to derive from System.Value-Type, meaning that it is a value type. Value types are allocated on the stack by default, but they can always be converted into a heap-based reference-type object, called *boxing*. The following code snippet shows that we can create a box and copy the value of i into it:

```
int i = 1;        // i - a value type
object box = i;   // box - a reference object
```

When you box a value, you get an object upon which you can invoke methods, properties, and events. For example, once you have converted the integer into an object, as shown in this code snippet, you can call methods that are defined in System.Object, including ToString(), Equals(), and so forth.

The reverse of boxing is of course *unboxing*, which means that you can convert a heap-based reference-type object into its value-type equivalent, as shown here:

```
int j = (int)box;
```

This example simply uses the cast operator to cast a heap-based object called box into a value-type integer.

Classes, properties, indexers

The CLR provides full support for object-oriented concepts (such as encapsulation, inheritance, and polymorphism) and class features (such as methods, fields, static members, visibility, accessibility, nested types, and so forth). In addition, the CLR supports new features that are nonexistent in many traditional object-oriented programming languages, including properties, indexers, and events.* Events are covered in Chapter 8. For now let's briefly talk about properties and indexers.

A property is similar to a field (a member variable), with the exception that there is a getter and a setter method, as follows:

```
using System;

public class Car
{
  private string make;
```

---

* An event is a callback that is implemented using delegates, which is covered shortly.

```
  public string Make
  {
    get { return make; }
    set { make = value; }
  }

  public static void Main( )
  {
    Car c = new Car( );
    c.Make = "Acura";  // use setter
    String s = c.Make; // use getter
    Console.WriteLine(s);
  }
}
```

Although this is probably the first time you've seen such syntax, this example is straightforward and really needs no explanation, with the exception of the keyword value. This is a special keyword that represents the one and only argument to the setter method.

Syntactically similar to a property, an indexer is analogous to operator[ ] in C++, as it allows array-like access to the contents of an object. In other words, it allows you to access an object like you're accessing an array, as shown in the following example:

```
using System;

public class Car
{
  Car( )
  {
    wheels = new string[4];
  }

  private string[] wheels;
  public string this[int index]
  {
    get { return wheels[index]; }
    set { wheels[index] = value; }
  }


  public static void Main( )
  {
    Car c = new Car( );
    c[0] = "LeftWheel";  // c[0] can be an l-value or an r-value
    Console.WriteLine(c[0]);
  }
}
```

Here's one note before we leave this topic: unlike C++ but similar to Java, classes in .NET support only single-implementation inheritance.

Interfaces

Interfaces support exactly the same concept as a C++ abstract base class (ABC) with only pure virtual functions. An ABC is a class that declares one or more pure virtual functions and thus cannot be instantiated. If you know COM or Java, interfaces in .NET are conceptually equivalent to a COM or Java interface. You specify them, but you don't implement them. A class that derives from your interface must implement your interface. An interface may contain methods, properties, indexers, and events. In .NET, a class can derive from multiple interfaces.

Delegates

One of the most powerful features of C is its support for function pointers. Function pointers allow you to build software with hooks that can be implemented by someone else. In fact, function pointers allow many people to build expandable or customizable software. Microsoft .NET supports a type-safe version of function pointers, called *delegates*. Here's an example that may take a few minutes to sink in, but once you get it, you'll realize that it's really simple:

```
using System;
class TestDelegate
{
    // 1. Define callback prototype
    delegate void MsgHandler(string strMsg);

    // 2. Define callback method
    void OnMsg(string strMsg)
    {
        Console.WriteLine(strMsg);
    }

    public static void Main( )
    {
        TestDelegate t = new TestDelegate( );

        // 3. Wire up our callback method
        MsgHandler f = new MsgHandler(t.OnMsg);

        // 4. Invoke the callback method indirectly
        f("Hello, Delegate.");
    }
}
```

The first thing to do is to define a callback function prototype, and the important keyword here is delegate, which tells the compiler that you want an object-oriented function pointer. Under the hood, the compiler generates a nested class, MsgHandler, which derives from System.MulticastDelegate.* A multicast delegate supports many receivers. Once you've defined your prototype, you must define and implement a method with a signature that matches your prototype. Then, simply wire up the callback method by passing the function to the delegate's constructor, as shown in this code listing. Finally, invoke your callback indirectly. Having gone over delegates, you should note that delegates form the foundation of events, which are discussed in Chapter 8.

The Common Language Specification (CLS)

A goal of .NET is to support language integration in such a way that programs can be written in any language, yet can interoperate with one another, taking full advantage of inheritance, polymorphism, exceptions, and other features. However, languages are not made equal because one language may support a feature that is totally different from another language. For example, Managed C++ is case-sensitive, and VB.NET is not. In order to bring everyone to the same sheet of music, Microsoft has published the Common Language Specification (CLS). The CLS specifies a series of basic rules that are required for language integration. Since Microsoft provides the CLS that spells out the minimum requirements for being a .NET language, compiler vendors can build their compilers to the specification and provide languages that target .NET. Besides compiler writers, application developers should read the CLS and use its rules to guarantee language interoperation.

CLR Execution

Now that you understand the elements of a .NET executable, let's talk about the services that the CLR provides to support management and execution of .NET assemblies. There are many fascinating components in the CLR, but for brevity, we will limit our discussions to just the major components, as shown in Figure 2-4.

The major components of the CLR include the class loader, verifier, JIT compilers, and other execution support, such as code management, security management, garbage collection, exception management, debug management,

---

* If you want to see this, use *ildasm.exe* and view the metadata of the *delegate.exe* sample that we've provided.

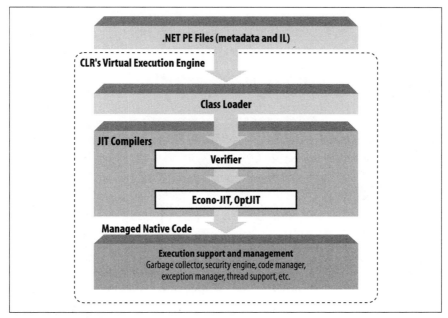

Figure 2-4. Major CLR components: the Virtual Execution System (VES)

marshaling management, thread management, and so on. As you can see from Figure 2-4, your .NET PE files layer on top of the CLR and execute within the CLR's Virtual Execution System (VES), which hosts the major components of the runtime. Your .NET PE files will have to go through the class loader, the type verifier, the JIT compilers, and other execution support components before they will execute.

Class Loader

When you run a standard Windows application, the OS loader loads it before it can execute. At the time of this writing, the default loaders in the existing Windows operating systems, such as Windows 98, Windows Me, Windows 2000, and so forth, recognize only the standard Windows PE files. As a result, Microsoft has provided an updated OS loader for each of these operating systems that support the .NET runtime. The updated OS loaders know the .NET PE file format and can handle the file appropriately.

When you run a .NET application on one of these systems that have an updated OS loader, the OS loader recognizes the .NET application and thus passes control to the CLR. The CLR then finds the entry point, which is typically Main(), and executes it to jump-start the application. But before Main() can execute, the class loader must find the class that exposes Main()

and load the class. In addition, when Main( ) instantiates an object of a specific class, the class loader also kicks in. In short, the class loader performs its magic the first time a type is referenced.

The *class loader* loads .NET classes into memory and prepares them for execution. Before it can successfully do this, it must locate the target class. To find the target class, the class loader looks in several different places, including the application configuration file (*.config*) in the current directory, the GAC, and the metadata that is part of the PE file, specifically the manifest. The information that is provided by one or more of these items is crucial to locating the correct target class. Recall that a class can be scoped to a particular namespace, a namespace can be scoped to a particular assembly, and an assembly can be scoped to a specific version. Given this, two classes, both named Car, are treated as different types even if the version information of their assemblies are the same.

Once the class loader has found and loaded the target class, it caches the type information for the class so that it doesn't have to load the class again for the duration of this process. By caching this information, it will later determine how much memory is needed to allocate for the newly created instance of this class. Once the target class is loaded, the class loader injects a small stub, like a function prolog, into every single method of the loaded class. This stub is used for two purposes: to denote the status of JIT compilation and to transition between managed and unmanaged code. At this point, if the loaded class references other classes, the class loader will also try to load the referenced types. However, if the referenced types have already been loaded, the class loader has to do nothing. Finally, the class loader uses the appropriate metadata to initialize the static variables and instantiate an object of the loaded class for you.

Verifier

Scripting and interpreted languages are very lenient on type usages, allowing you to write code without explicit variable declarations. This flexibility can introduce code that is extremely error-prone and hard to maintain, and that is often a culprit for mysterious program crashes. Unlike scripting and interpreted languages, compiled languages require types to be explicitly defined prior to their use, permitting the compiler to ensure that types are used correctly and the code will execute peacefully at runtime.

The key here is type safety, and it is a fundamental concept for code verification in .NET. Within the VES, the verifier is the component that executes at runtime to verify that the code is type safe. Note that this type verification is done at runtime and that this is a fundamental difference between .NET and other environments. By verifying type safety at runtime, the CLR can prevent the execution of code that is not type safe and ensure that the code is used as intended. In short, type safety means more reliability.

Let's talk about where the verifier fits within the CLR. After the class loader has loaded a class and before a piece of IL code can execute, the verifier kicks in for code that must be verified. The verifier is responsible for verifying that:

- The metadata is well formed, meaning the metadata must be valid.
- The IL code is type safe, meaning type signatures are used correctly.

Both of these criteria must be met before the code can be executed because JIT compilation will take place only when code and metadata have been successfully verified. In addition to checking for type safety, the verifier also performs rudimentary control-flow analysis of the code to ensure that the code is using types correctly. You should note that since the verifier is a part of the JIT compilers, it kicks in only when a method is being invoked, not when a class or assembly is loaded. You should also note that verification is an optional step because trusted code will never be verified but will be immediately directed to the JIT compiler for compilation.

JIT Compilers

JIT compilers play a major role in the .NET platform because all .NET PE files contain IL and metadata, not native code. The JIT compilers convert IL to native code so that it can execute on the target operating system. For each method that has been successfully verified for type safety, a JIT compiler in the CLR will compile the method and convert it into managed native code. Managed native code is required because the execution-support components will manage and execute only managed code on the target operating system.

One advantage of a JIT compiler is that it can dynamically compile code that is optimized for the target machine. If you take the same .NET PE file from a one-CPU machine to a two-CPU machine, the JIT compiler on the two-CPU machine knows about the second CPU and may be able to spit out the native code that takes advantage of the second CPU. Another obvious advantage is that you can take the same .NET PE file and run it on a totally different platform, whether it be Windows, Unix, or whatever, as long as that platform has a CLR.

For optimization reasons, JIT compilation occurs only the first time a method is invoked. Recall that the class loader adds a stub to each method during class loading. At the first method invocation, the VES reads the information in this stub, which tells it that the code for the method has not been JIT-compiled. At this indication, the JIT compiler compiles the method and injects the address of the managed native method into this stub. During subsequent invocations to the same method, no JIT compilation is needed because each time the VES goes to read information in the stub, it sees the address of the native method. Because the JIT compiler only performs its magic the first time a method is invoked, the methods you don't need at runtime will never be JIT-compiled.

The compiled, native code lies in memory until the process shuts down and until the garbage collector clears off all references and memory associated with the process. This means that the next time you execute the process or component, the JIT compiler will again perform its magic.

If you want to avoid the cost of JIT compilation at runtime, you can use a special tool called ngen, which compiles your IL during installation and setup time. Using ngen, you can JIT-compile the code once and cache it on the machine so that you can avoid JIT compilation at runtime (this process is referred to as pre-JITting). In the event that the PE file has been updated, you must PreJIT the PE file again. Otherwise, the CLR can detect the update and dynamically command the appropriate JIT compiler to compile the assembly.

Execution Support and Management

By now, you should see that every component in the CLR that we've covered so far uses metadata and IL in some way to successfully carry out the services that it supports. In addition to the provided metadata and generated managed code, the JIT compiler must generate managed data that the code manager needs to locate and unwind stack frames.* The *code manager* uses managed data to control the execution of code, including performing stack walks that are required for exception handling, security checks, and garbage collection. Besides the code manager, the CLR also provides a number of important execution-support and management services. A detailed discussion of these services is beyond the scope of this book, so we will briefly enumerate a few of them here:

Garbage collection
> Unlike C++, where you must delete all heap-based objects manually, the CLR supports automatic lifetime management for all .NET objects. The

---

* By the way, you can write a custom JIT compiler or a custom code manager for the CLR because the CLR supports the plug-and-play of these components.

---

garbage collector can detect when your objects are no longer being referenced and perform garbage collection to reclaim the unused memory.

Exception handling

Prior to .NET, there was no consistent method for error or exception handling, causing lots of pain in error handling and reporting. In .NET, the CLR supports a standard exception-handling mechanism that works across all languages, allowing every program to use a common error-handling mechanism. The CLR exception-handling mechanism is integrated with Windows Structured Exception Handling (SEH).

Security support

The CLR performs various security checks at runtime to make sure that the code is safe to execute and that the code is not breaching any security requirements. In addition to supporting code-access security, the security engine also supports declarative and imperative security checks. Declarative security requires no special security code, but you have to specify the security requirements through attributes or administrative configuration. Imperative security requires that you write the code in your method to specifically cause security checks.

Debugging support

The CLR provides rich support for debugging and profiling. There is an API that compiler vendors can use to develop a debugger. This API contains support for controlling program execution, breakpoints, exceptions, control flow, and so forth. There is also an API for tools to support the profiling of running programs.

Interoperation support

The CLR supports interoperation between the managed (CLR) and unmanaged (no CLR) worlds. The *COM Interop* facility serves as a bridge between COM and the CLR, allowing a COM object to use a .NET object, and vice versa. The *Platform Invoke (P/Invoke)* facility allows you to call Windows API functions.

This is by no means an exhaustive list. The one thing that we want to reiterate is that like the class loader, verifier, JIT compilers, and just about everything else that deals with .NET, these execution-support and management facilities all use metadata, managed code, and managed data in some way to carry out their services.

Summary

As you can see from this chapter, the .NET architecture strives to support language integration and componentization in every way that makes sense.

Thanks to metadata, programming becomes much easier because you no longer have to worry about the registry for component deployment and other kinks (such as CoCreateInstanceEx, CLSIDs, IIDs, IUnknown, IDL, and so forth) in order to support componentization. Thanks to the CTS, CLS, metadata, and IL, you now have real language integration. Microsoft has shipped a CLR for several flavors of Windows, but is also working on a shared-source version of the CLR that will run on FreeBSD and will no doubt be portable to other Unix-like systems. Non-Microsoft implementations of the CLR have also appeared, including DotGNU Portable.NET (for more information, see *http://www.southern-storm.com.au/portable_net.html*) and Mono (see *http://www.go-mono.com*). .NET is thus a multilanguage and multiplatform architecture.

CHAPTER 3

.NET Programming

Now that you know what .NET is all about, let's talk about programming for the .NET environment. This chapter presents the common programming model that .NET provides, core languages and features that .NET supports, and language integration—how you can take advantage of object-oriented features even across different languages that .NET enables.

Common Programming Model

Without the .NET Framework, programmers must choose from amongst a wealth of APIs or libraries that support system services. For example, if you want to write GUI applications on Windows, you have a slew of options from which to choose, including the Win32 API, MFC, ATL, VB, and so on. Once you've chosen the library, you have to learn how to use the structures, classes, functions, interfaces, and so forth that the library provides. Unfortunately, this knowledge doesn't transfer directly into a different environment. For instance, there's a big difference between the code to manage IO in MFC and the code to manage IO in VB.

One of the goals of the .NET Framework is to bring commonality to application development by providing a framework of common classes to developers who are using compilers that generate IL. This common framework is extremely helpful: if you know how to take advantage of IO functionality in .NET using your favorite language, you can easily port that code to another language. This is possible because the namespaces, classes, methods, and so forth have a consistent representation in all languages. For example, you can output a line of text to the console the same way across all .NET languages by using the WriteLine( ) method of the Console object, as we have seen elsewhere in this book. This consistent framework requires less development training and enables higher programmer productivity.

Since a full discussion of the entire set of classes in the .NET Framework is beyond the scope of this book (see O'Reilly's In a Nutshell .NET series), we talk about the System.Object class and present the major namespaces in the .NET Framework, opening the doors for you to step into this world.

System.Object

Every type in .NET is an object, meaning that it must derive directly or indirectly from the Object class. If you don't specify a base class when you define a class, the compiler will inject this requirement into the IL code. The Object class supports a commonality that all .NET classes inherit and thus automatically provide to their consumers. The Object class exposes the public methods listed in Table 3-1, which you can invoke on any given .NET object at runtime.

Table 3-1. Public methods of the Object class

Methods	Description
Equals( )	Compares two objects and determines whether they are equivalent (having the same content).
ReferenceEquals( )	Compares two object references and determines whether they are referring to the same object.
GetHashCode( )	Gets the object's hash code. In .NET, hash codes are used as an added mechanism for determining object uniqueness at runtime. For instance, if you want your objects to be used as keys in a hash table, you must override this function and provide a unique hash value for each instance of your class.
GetType( )	Obtains the object's type at runtime. Once you have obtained the object's type, you can obtain everything about that type using the Reflection API, as explained in Chapter 2.
ToString( )	Gets a string representation of the object. Normally used for debugging purposes, this method spits out the fully qualified class name by default.

Examine the following program, which illustrates the use of all these methods:

```
using System;
namespace Cpm
{
  class CPModel
  {
    public static void Main( )
    {
      CPModel c = new CPModel( );
      // Test for self equivalence
      Console.WriteLine("Equivalence:\t" +
        c.Equals(c)
      );
```

```
            // Get the hash code from this object
            Console.WriteLine("Object hash:\t" +
              c.GetHashCode( )
            );
            // Use the type to obtain method information
            Console.WriteLine("Object method:\t" +
              c.GetType( ).GetMethods( )[1]
            );
            // Convert the object to a string
            Console.WriteLine("Object dump:\t" +
              c.ToString( )
            );
        }
    }
}
```

If you compile and run this C# program, you get the following output:

```
Equivalence:    True
Object hash:    3
Object method:  Boolean Equals(System.Object)
Object dump:    Cpm.CPModel
```

The boldface line displays the second method of the CPModel class. If you look back at the program's code, you'll see that we use the GetType() method to get the type, and then we use the GetMethods() method to retrieve the array of methods supported by this type. From this array, we pull off the second method, which happens to be Equals(), a method that's implemented by System.Object.

As you can see, the System.Object class provides a mechanism for runtime type identification, equivalence, and inspection for all .NET objects.

Major Namespaces

Table 3-2 is a short list of important namespaces and classes in the .NET Framework that provide support for almost any application that you will develop. These are the namespaces that you'll find yourself using again and again the more you develop .NET applications. For more information, consult MSDN Online or your SDK documentation, as a detailed discussion of these namespaces and classes is beyond the scope of this book.

Table 3-2. Important .NET namespaces and classes

Namespace	Description
System	Includes basic classes almost every program will use. Some simple classes that belong in this namespace are Object, Char, String, Array, and Exception. This namespace also includes more advanced classes such as GC and AppDomain.

Table 3-2. Important .NET namespaces and classes (continued)

Namespace	Description
System.IO	Provides a set of classes to support synchronous and asynchronous IO manipulation for data streams. Also provides classes that allow you to manipulate the filesystem, such as by creating, managing, and deleting files and directories. Some of these classes are FileStream, MemoryStream, Path, and Directory.
System.Collections	Includes a set of classes that allow you to manage collections of objects. Some of these classes are ArrayList, DictionaryBase, Hashtable, Queue, and Stack.
System.Threading	Includes a set of classes that support multithreaded programming. Some of these classes are Thread, ThreadPool, Mutex, and AutoResetEvent.
System.Reflection	Includes a set of classes that support dynamic binding and type inspection. Some of these classes are Assembly, Module, and MethodInfo.
System.Security	Includes a set of classes and child namespaces that provide security support. The interesting child namespaces include Cryptography, Permissions, Policy, and Principal.
System.Net	Includes a set of classes and child namespaces that provide support for network programming. Some of these classes are IPAddress, Dns, and HttpWebRequest.
System.Data	See Chapter 5.
System.Web.Services	See Chapter 6.
System.Web.UI	See Chapter 7.
System.Windows.Forms	See Chapter 8.

Keep in mind that if you know how to use any of the classes in these namespaces, you can write the code to take advantage of them in any language because the class and method names remain consistent across all .NET languages.

Core Features and Languages

Since one of .NET's goals is to support a common paradigm for application programming, it must specify and utilize programming concepts consistently. In this section, we will examine three core Microsoft .NET languages, including Managed C++, VB.NET, and C#, and several core programming concepts that all .NET languages support, including:

Namespace
> Mitigates name collisions.

Interface
> Specifies the methods and properties that must be implemented by objects that expose the interface.

Encapsulation
> In object-oriented languages, allows a class to encapsulate all its data and behavior.

Inheritance

Allows a class to inherit from a parent class so that it can reuse rich functionality that the parent class has implemented, thus reducing development effort and programming errors.

Polymorphism

Permits developers to specify or implement behaviors in a base class that can be overridden by a derived class. This is a very powerful feature because it allows developers to select the correct behavior based on the referenced runtime object.

Exception handling

Allows us to write easier-to-understand code because it allows us to capture all errors in a common, understandable pattern—totally opposite to that of nine levels of nested conditional blocks.

While this is not a complete list of concepts that .NET supports, it includes all the major .NET concepts that we want to cover in this section. We will show you examples of all these features in Managed C++, VB.NET, and C#. These concepts are nothing new: we're merely demonstrating how they're represented in all .NET languages.

Before we start, you should understand first what our examples will accomplish. First, we will create a namespace, called Lang, that encapsulates an interface, ISteering. Then we will create two classes: Vehicle, which is an abstract base class that implements ISteering, and Car, which is a derivative of Vehicle. We will support an entry point that instantiates and uses Car within a try block. We will unveil other details as we work through the examples.

Managed C++ Code

Managed C++ is essentially Microsoft's C++ programming language with some newly added keywords and features to support .NET programming. This allows you to use C++ to develop managed objects, which are objects that run in the CLR. Using Managed C++, you can obtain the performance* that is inherent in C++ programs, and at the same time, you can also take advantage of CLR features.†

Now let's look at an example that includes all the concepts we want to examine. As you can see in the following code listing, we start off creating a

---

* You can easily mix managed and unmanaged code in C++ programs. The unmanaged code will perform better.

† However, if you look carefully at the features and new keywords (__abstract, __box, __delegate, __gc, __nogc, __pin, etc.) that have been added to Microsoft C++, we doubt that you'll want to use Managed C++ to write new code for the CLR, especially when you have C#.

new namespace, Lang, which envelops everything except main(). With the exception of the first two lines and special keywords, the code listing conforms perfectly to the C++ standard:

```
#using <mscorlib.dll>
using namespace System;

namespace Lang
{
```

Next, we specify an interface, called ISteering. If you are a C++ programmer, you will immediately notice that there are two new keywords in the following code listing, __gc and __interface. The new keyword __interface allows you to declare an interface, which is basically equivalent to an abstract base class in C++. In other words, the two method prototypes are specified, but not implemented here. The class that implements this interface provides the implementation for these methods:

```
__gc __interface ISteering
{
  void TurnLeft();
  void TurnRight();
};
```

If you are a COM programmer, you know that in COM you have to manage the lifetimes of your objects and components yourself. Even worse, you also have to rely on your clients to negotiate and interoperate correctly with your COM components, otherwise extant references will never be reclaimed. Managed C++ removes this problem by adding a new keyword, __gc. This new keyword tells the CLR to garbage-collect the references to your interface when they are no longer in use. Aside from these two keywords, the previous code listing requires no other explanation for programmers who have experience with C-like languages.

Now that we have an interface, let's implement it. The following code listing is a Managed C++ class (as indicated by the __gc) that implements our ISteering interface. One thing to notice is that this class is an abstract base class because the ApplyBrakes() method is a pure virtual (meaning that it's polymorphic) function, as indicated by the =0 syntax. Vehicle doesn't provide the implementation for this method, but its derived class must supply the implementation:

```
__gc class Vehicle : public ISteering
{
  public:

  void TurnLeft()
  {
    Console::WriteLine("Vehicle turns left.");
```

```
    }

    void TurnRight( )
    {
      Console::WriteLine("Vehicle turns right.");
    }

    virtual void ApplyBrakes( ) = 0;
  };
```

Since Vehicle is an abstract base class and can't be instantiated, we need to provide a Vehicle derivative, which we will call Car. As you can see in the following listing, everything about the class is C++, with the exception of the keyword __gc. Note that the ApplyBrakes( ) function first dumps a text message to the console and then immediately creates and throws an exception, notifying an exception handler that there has been a brake failure. What is special here is that the Exception class is a part of the .NET Framework, specifically belonging to the System namespace. This is great, because this class works exactly the same way in all languages and there's no longer a need to invent your own exception hierarchy.

```
  __gc class Car : public Vehicle
  {
    public:

    void ApplyBrakes( )
    {
      Console::WriteLine("Car trying to stop.");
      throw new Exception("Brake failure!");
    }
  };

} // This brace ends the Lang namespace.
```

Now that we have a concrete class, we can write the main( ) function to test our Car class. Notice that we have added a try block that encapsulates the bulk of our code so that we can handle any exceptions in the catch block. Looking carefully at the following code listing, you'll see that we've instantiated a new Car on the managed heap, but we've actually referred to this Car instance using a Vehicle pointer. Next, we tell the vehicle to TurnLeft( )—there's no surprise here because we've implemented this method in Vehicle. However, in the following statement, we tell the Vehicle that we're applying the brakes, but ApplyBrakes( ) is not implemented in Vehicle. Since this is a virtual method, the correct vptr and vtbl* will be used, resulting in a call to

---

* Many C++ compilers use vtbls (a vtbl is a table of function pointers) and vptrs (a vptr is a pointer to the vtbl) to support dynamic binding or polymorphism.

Car::ApplyBrakes( ). Of course Car::ApplyBrakes( ) will throw an exception, putting us into the catch block. Inside the catch block, we convert the caught exception into a string and dump it out to the console. We can do this because Exception is a class in the .NET Framework and all classes in the framework must derive from System.Object, which implements a rudimentary ToString( ) function to convert any object into a string:

```
void main( )
{
  try
  {
    Lang::Vehicle *pV = 0;   // namespace qualifier
    pV = new Lang::Car( );   // pV refers to a car
    pV->TurnLeft( );         // interface usage
    pV->ApplyBrakes( );      // polymorphism in action
  }
  catch(Exception *pe)
  {
    Console::WriteLine(pe->ToString( ));
  }
}
```

Notice that you don't have to deallocate your objects on the managed heap when you've finished using them, because the garbage collector will do that for you in .NET.

Although this is a simple example, we have used Managed C++ to illustrate all the major .NET concepts, including namespaces, interfaces, encapsulation, inheritance, polymorphism, and exception handling. Next, we demonstrate that you can translate this code into any other .NET language because they all support these concepts. Specifically, we'll show you this same example in VB.NET, C#, and IL, just to prove that these concepts can be represented the same way in all .NET languages.

VB.NET Code

Microsoft has revamped VB and added full features for object-oriented programming. The new VB language, Visual Basic .NET, or VB.NET, allows you to do all that you can with VB, albeit much more easily. If you are a VB programmer with knowledge of other object-oriented languages, such as C++ or Smalltalk, then you will love the new syntax that comes along with VB.NET. If you are a VB programmer without knowledge of other object-oriented languages, you will be surprised by the new VB.NET syntax at first, but you will realize that the new syntax simplifies your life as a programmer.

In addition to the VB-style Rapid Application Development (RAD) support, VB.NET is a modernized language that gives you full access to the .NET

Framework. The VB.NET compiler generates metadata and IL code, making the language an equal citizen to that of C# or Managed C++. Unlike VB, there will be no interpreter in VB.NET, so there should be no violent arguments about performance drawbacks of VB versus another language.

Perhaps the most potent feature is that now you can write interfaces and classes that look very similar to those written in other .NET languages. The new syntax allows you to inherit from base classes, implement interfaces, override virtual functions, create an abstract base class, and so forth. In addition, it also supports exception handling exactly as does C# and Managed C++, making error handling much easier. Finally, VB.NET ships with a command-line compiler, *vbc.exe*, introduced in Chapter 2.

Let's see how to translate the previous Managed C++ program into VB.NET so that you can see the striking conceptual resemblance. First, we'll start by defining a namespace called Lang, as shown here in bold:

```
Imports System

Namespace Lang
```

Next, we specify the ISteering interface, which is easy to do in VB.NET since the syntax is very straightforward, especially when you compare it with Managed C++. In the following code listing, you'll notice that instead of using opening and closing braces as in Managed C++, you start the interface definition by using the appropriate VB.NET keyword, Interface, and end it by prefixing the associated keyword with the word End. This is just normal VB-style syntax and shouldn't surprise any VB programmer.

```
Interface ISteering
  Sub TurnLeft( )
  Sub TurnRight( )
End Interface
```

With our interface specified, we can now implement it. Since our Vehicle class is an abstract base class, we must add the MustInherit keyword when we define it, explicitly telling the VB.NET compiler that this class cannot be instantiated. In VB.NET, the Class keyword allows you to define a class, and the Implements keyword allows you implement an interface. Another thing that you should be aware of is that ApplyBrakes( ) is not implemented in this class, and we have appropriately signaled this to the VB.NET compiler by using the MustOverride keyword.

```
MustInherit Class Vehicle
  Implements ISteering

  Public Sub TurnLeft( ) Implements ISteering.TurnLeft
    Console.WriteLine("Vehicle turns left.")
  End Sub
```

```
Public Sub TurnRight( ) Implements ISteering.TurnRight
  Console.WriteLine("Vehicle turn right.")
End Sub

Public MustOverride Sub ApplyBrakes( )

End Class
```

As far as language differences go, you must explicitly describe the access (i.e., public, private, and so forth) for each method separately. This is different from C++ because all members take on the previously defined access type.

Now we are ready to translate the concrete Car class. In VB.NET, you can derive from a base class by using the Inherits keyword, as shown in the following code. Since we have said that ApplyBrakes( ) must be overridden, we provide its implementation here. Again, notice that we're throwing an exception.

```
Class Car
  Inherits Vehicle

  Public Overrides Sub ApplyBrakes( )
    Console.WriteLine("Car trying to stop.")
    throw new Exception("Brake failure!")
  End Sub

End Class

End Namespace
```

Now that we have all the pieces in place, let's define a module with an entry point, Main( ), that the CLR will execute. In Main( ), you'll notice that we're handling exceptions exactly as we did in the Managed C++ example. You should also note that this code demonstrates the use of polymorphism because we first create a Vehicle reference that refers to a Car object at run-time. We tell the Vehicle to ApplyBrakes( ), but since the Vehicle happens to be referring to a Car, the object that is stopping is the target Car object.

```
Public Module Driver

  Sub Main( )

    Try

      Dim v As Lang.Vehicle   ' namespace qualifier
      v = New Lang.Car        ' v refers to a car
      v.TurnLeft( )           ' interface usage
      v.ApplyBrakes( )        ' polymorphism in action

    Catch e As Exception
```

```
    Console.WriteLine(e.ToString( ))

  End Try

End Sub

End Module
```

This simple program demonstrates that we can take advantage of .NET object-oriented features using VB.NET. Having seen this example, you should see that VB.NET is very object oriented, with features that map directly to those of Managed C++ and other .NET languages.

C# Code

As you've just seen, VB.NET is a breeze compared to Managed C++, but VB.NET is not the only simple language in .NET—C# is also amazingly simple. Developed from the ground up, C# supports all the object-oriented features in .NET. It maps so closely to the Java and C++ languages that if you have experience with either of these languages, you can pick up C# and be productive with it immediately.

Microsoft has developed many tools using C#; in fact, most of the components in Visual Studio.NET were developed using C#. Microsoft is using C# extensively, and we think that C# will be the language of the next decade.*

Having said that, let's translate our previous program into C# and illustrate all the features we want to see. Again, we start by defining a namespace. As you can see, the syntax for C# maps really closely to that of Managed C++.

```
using System;

namespace Lang
{
```

Following is the IStreering interface specification in C#. Since C# was developed from scratch, we don't need to add any funny keywords like __gc and __interface, as we did in the Managed C++ version of this program.

```
interface ISteering
{
  void TurnLeft( );
  void TurnRight( );
}
```

---

* If you want to learn more about C#, check out O'Reilly's *C# Essentials*, Second Edition (Albahari, Drayton, and Merrill), the forthcoming *C# in a Nutshell* (Drayton, Albahari, and Neward), and *Programming C#*, Second Edition (Liberty).

Having defined our interface, we can now implement it in the abstract Vehicle class. Unlike Managed C++ but similar to VB.NET, C# requires that you explicitly notify the C# compiler that the Vehicle class is an abstract base class by using the abstract keyword. Since ApplyBrakes() is an abstract method—meaning that this class doesn't supply its implementation—you must make the class abstract, otherwise the C# compiler will barf at you. Put another way, you must explicitly signal to the C# compiler the features you want, including abstract, public, private, and so forth, each time you define a class, method, property, and so on.

```
abstract class Vehicle : ISteering
{
  public void TurnLeft( )
  {
    Console.WriteLine("Vehicle turns left.");
  }

  public void TurnRight( )
  {
    Console.WriteLine("Vehicle turn right.");
  }

  public abstract void ApplyBrakes( );
}
```

Here's our Car class that derives from Vehicle and overrides the ApplyBrakes() method declared in Vehicle. Note that we are explicitly telling the C# compiler that we are indeed overriding a method previously specified in the inheritance chain. You must add the override modifier, or ApplyBrakes() will hide the one in the parent class. Otherwise, we are also throwing the same exception as before.

```
class Car : Vehicle
{
  public override void ApplyBrakes( )
  {
    Console.WriteLine("Car trying to stop.");
    throw new Exception("Brake failure!");
  }
}

} // This brace ends the Lang namespace.
```

Finally, here's a class that encapsulates an entry point for the CLR to invoke. If you look at this code carefully, you'll see that it maps directly to the code in both Managed C++ and VB.NET.

```
class Drive
{
  public static void Main( )
  {
```

```
      try
      {
        Lang.Vehicle v = null;   // namespace qualifier
        v = new Lang.Car();      // v refers to a car
        v.TurnLeft();            // interface usage
        v.ApplyBrakes();         // polymorphism in action
      }
      catch(Exception e)
      {
        Console.WriteLine(e.ToString());
      }
    }
  }
```

There are two other interesting things to note about C#. First, unlike C++ but similar to Java, C# doesn't use header files.* Second, the C# compiler generates XML documentation for you if you use XML comments in your code. To take advantage of this feature, start your XML comments with three slashes, as in the following examples:

```
/// <summary>Vehicle Class</summary>
/// <remarks>
///    This class is an abstract class that must be
///    overridden by derived classes.
/// </remarks>
abstract class Vehicle : ISteering
{
  /// <summary>Add juice to the vehicle.</summary>
  /// <param name="gallons">
  ///    Number of gallons added.
  /// </param>
  /// <return>Whether the tank is full.</return>
  public bool FillUp(int gallons)
  {
    return true;
  }
}
```

These are simple examples using the predefined C# tags. You can also use your own XML tags in XML comments, as long as your resulting XML is well formed. Given that you have a source code file with XML comments, you can automatically generate an XML-formatted reference document by using the C# compiler's /doc: option, as follows:

```
csc /doc:doc.xml mylangdoc.cs
```

Although we didn't specify the types of our parameters in the XML comments shown previously, the C# compiler will detect the correct types and

---

* If you've never used C++, a header file is optional and usually contains class and type declarations. The implementation for these classes is usually stored in source files.

add the fully qualified types into the generated XML document. For example, the following generated XML listing corresponds to the XML comments for the FillUp() method. Notice that the C# compiler added System. Int32 into the generated XML document.

```
<member name="M:Lang.Vehicle.FillUp(System.Int32)">
  <summary>Add juice to the vehicle.</summary>
  <param name="gallons">
    Number of gallons added.
  </param>
  <return>Whether the tank is full.</return>
</member>
```

Now that you have the generated XML document, you can write your own XSL document to translate the XML into any visual representation you prefer.

Common Intermediate Language Code

Since all languages compile to IL, let's examine the IL code for the program that we've been studying. As explained in Chapter 2, IL is a set of stack-based instructions that supports an exhaustive list of popular object-oriented features, including the ones that we've already examined in this chapter. It is an intermediary step, gluing .NET applications to the CLR.

Let's start by looking at the namespace declaration. Notice the .namespace IL declaration allows us to create our Lang namespace. Similar to C#, IL uses opening and closing braces:

```
.namespace Lang
{
```

Now for the IStreering interface. In IL, any type that is to be managed by the CLR must be declared using the .class IL declaration. Since the CLR must manage the references to an interface, you must use the .class IL declaration to specify an interface in IL, as shown in the following code listing:

```
.class interface private abstract auto ansi ISteering
{
  .method public hidebysig newslot virtual abstract
          instance void TurnLeft( ) cil managed
  {
  } // end of method ISteering::TurnLeft

  .method public hidebysig newslot virtual abstract
          instance void TurnRight( ) cil managed
  {
  } // end of method ISteering::TurnRight

} // end of class ISteering
```

In addition, you must insert two special IL attributes:

`interface`
> Signals that the current type definition is an interface specification.

`abstract`
> Signals that there will be no method implementations in this definition and that the implementer of this interface must provide the method implementations for all methods defined in this interface.

Other attributes shown in this definition that aren't necessarily needed to specify an interface in IL include the following:

`private`
> Because we haven't provided the visibility of our interface definition in C#, the generated IL code shown here adds the `private` IL attribute to this interface definition. This means that this particular interface is visible only within the current assembly and no other external assembly can see it.

`auto`
> This tells the CLR to perform automatic layout of this type at runtime.

`ansi`
> This tells the CLR to use ANSI string buffers to marshal data across managed and unmanaged boundaries.

Now you know how to specify an interface in IL. Before we proceed further, let's briefly look at the attributes in the `.method` declarations—at least the attributes that we haven't examined, including:

`newslot`
> Tells the JIT compiler to reserve a new slot in the type's vtbl, which will be used by the CLR at runtime to resolve virtual-method invocations.

`instance`
> Tells the CLR that this method is an instance or object-level method, as opposed to a static or class-level method.

Having specified the ISteering interface in IL, let's implement it in our Vehicle class. As you can see in the following code fragment, there's no surprise. We extend the System.Object class (indicated by the extends keyword) and implement Lang.ISteering (as indicated by the implements keyword):

```
.class private abstract auto ansi beforefieldinit Vehicle
       extends [mscorlib]System.Object
       implements Lang.ISteering
{
  .method public hidebysig newslot final virtual
          instance void TurnLeft() cil managed
  {
```

```
    // IL code omitted for clarity.
  } // end of method Vehicle::TurnLeft

  .method public hidebysig newslot final virtual
          instance void TurnRight( ) cil managed
  {
    // IL code omitted for clarity.
  } // end of method Vehicle::TurnRight

  .method public hidebysig newslot virtual abstract
          instance void ApplyBrakes( ) cil managed
  {
  } // end of method Vehicle::ApplyBrakes

  // .ctor omitted for clarity.

} // end of class Vehicle
```

Notice also that this class is an abstract class and that the ApplyBrakes( ) method is an abstract method, similar to what we've seen in the previous examples. Another thing to note is the final IL attribute that you see in the .method declarations for both TurnLeft( ) and TurnRight( ). This IL attribute specifies that these methods can no longer be overridden by subclasses of Vehicle. Having seen all these attributes, you should realize that everything in IL is explicitly declared so that all components of the CLR can take advantage of this information to manage your types at runtime.

Now let's look at the Car class that derives from the Vehicle class. You'll notice that in the ApplyBrakes( ) method implementation, the newobj instance IL instruction creates a new instance of the Exception class. Next, the throw IL instruction immediately raises the exception object just created.

```
.class private auto ansi beforefieldinit Car
        extends Lang.Vehicle
  {
    .method public hidebysig virtual instance void
            ApplyBrakes( ) cil managed
    {
      // IL code omitted for clarity.
      newobj instance void
         [mscorlib]System.Exception::.ctor(class System.String)
      throw
    } // end of method Car::ApplyBrakes

    // .ctor omitted for clarity.

  } // end of class Car

} // end of namespace Lang
```

Finally, let's look at our Main() function, which is part of the Drive class. We've removed most of the IL code—which you've already learned—from this function to make the following code easier to read, but we kept the important elements that must be examined. First, the .locals directive identifies all the local variables for the Main() function. Second, you can see that IL also supports exception handling through the .try instruction. In both the .try and catch block, notice that there is a leave.s instruction that forces execution to jump to the IL instruction on line IL_0024, thus leaving both the .try and catch blocks.

```
.class private auto ansi beforefieldinit Drive
       extends [mscorlib]System.Object
{
  .method public hidebysig static void Main() cil managed
  {
    .entrypoint
    // Code size       37 (0x25)
    .maxstack  1
    .locals (class Lang.Vehicle V_0,
             class [mscorlib]System.Exception V_1)
    .try
    {
      // IL code omitted for clarity.
      leave.s    IL_0024
    }  // end .try
    catch [mscorlib]System.Exception
    {
      // IL code omitted for clarity.
      leave.s    IL_0024
    }  // end handler
    IL_0024:  ret
  } // end of method Drive::Main

  // .ctor omitted for clarity.

} // end of class Drive
```

As you can see, all the major concepts that we've examined apply intrinsically to IL. Since you've seen Managed C++, VB.NET, C#, and IL code that support these features, we won't attempt to further convince you that all these features work in other .NET languages.

Language Integration

In the previous section, we saw that you can take advantage of .NET object-oriented concepts in any .NET language. In this section, we show that you can take advantage of *language integration*—the ability to derive a class from a base that is specified in a totally different language, or to catch exceptions thrown by code written in a different language, or to take advantage of polymorphism across different languages, and so forth.

Before we discuss the examples in this section, let's first understand what we want to accomplish (see Figure 3-1). We will first use Managed C++ to develop a Vehicle class that is an abstract base class. The Vehicle class exposes three polymorphic methods, including TurnLeft(), TurnRight(), and ApplyBrakes(). We will then use VB.NET to develop a Car class that derives from Vehicle and overrides these three virtual methods. In addition, we will use C# to develop the Plane class that derives from Vehicle and overrides these three virtual methods.

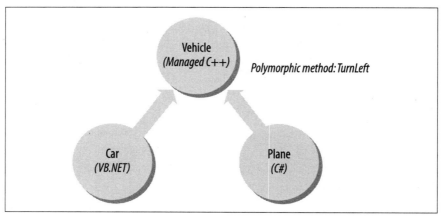

Figure 3-1. Polymorphism across languages

In the upcoming code example, we can tell a Vehicle to TurnLeft() or TurnRight(), but what turns left or right depends upon the target object, whether a Car or a Plane. Unlike the examples in the last section, the examples here illustrate that we can inherit classes and call virtual functions from ones that are defined in another language. In addition, we will demonstrate in our test program that exception handling works across different languages.

Vehicle Class in Managed C++

Let's use Managed C++ to develop the Vehicle class, which is an abstract base class because ApplyBrakes() is a pure virtual function. Vehicle implements the ISteering interface to support turning left and turning right. Since the ApplyBrakes() function is a pure virtual function, any concrete derivative of Vehicle must implement this method:

```
#using <mscorlib.dll>
using namespace System;
```

```
public __gc __interface ISteering
{
  void TurnLeft( );
  void TurnRight( );
};

public __gc class Vehicle : public ISteering
{
  public:

    virtual void TurnLeft( )
    {
      Console::WriteLine("Vehicle turns left.");
    }

    virtual void TurnRight( )
    {
      Console::WriteLine("Vehicle turn right.");
    }

    virtual void ApplyBrakes( ) = 0;
};
```

Given this abstract base class, we can create a DLL that hosts this definition. The first command here shows how we use the Managed C++ compiler to compile (as indicated by the /c option) the *vehicle.cpp* file, which contains the previous code. The second command shows how we use the C++ linker to create a DLL with metadata and IL code:

```
cl /CLR /c vehicle.cpp
link -dll /out:vehicle.dll -noentry vehicle.obj
```

Given just a few lines of Managed C++ code, we can build a DLL that can be used by another component. Note that there is no need to provide code for the functions IUnknown, DllGetClassObject(), DllCanUnloadNow(), DllRegisterServer(), DllUnregisterServer(), and so forth. In the old days, you had to provide code for these functions and interfaces for legacy COM DLLs.

Car Class in VB.NET

Given this abstract Vehicle class, the Car class can derive from it and provide the implementation for the three virtual methods defined by Vehicle. In the following code, note that we've overridden and provided the implementation for TurnLeft(), TurnRight(), and ApplyBrakes(). The ApplyBrakes() method is special in that it throws an exception, which will be caught by code written in C#, as we'll see later.

```
Imports System

Public Class Car
```

```
Inherits Vehicle

Overrides Public Sub TurnLeft()
  Console.WriteLine("Car turns left.")
End Sub

Overrides Public Sub TurnRight()
  Console.WriteLine("Car turns right.")
End Sub

Overrides Public Sub ApplyBrakes()
  Console.WriteLine("Car trying to stop.")
  throw new Exception("Brake failure!")
End Sub

End Class
```

With this code, we can build a DLL using the command-line VB.NET compiler, as follows:

```
vbc /r:vehicle.dll /t:library /out:car.dll car.vb
```

Since we want the VB.NET compiler to generate a DLL, we must signal this by using the /t:library option. Also, since Car derives from Vehicle, the VB.NET compiler must resolve the references to Vehicle. We can tell the VB.NET compiler the location of external references using the /r: option. It is important to note that you don't need to have the source code for the vehicle DLL to reuse its code because all type information can be obtained from any .NET assembly. In addition, you should note that from this example, we have proven that you can derive a VB.NET class from a Managed C++ class.

Plane Class in C#

Now let's use C# to develop the Plane class, which derives from the Vehicle class written in Managed C++. Similar to the Car class, the Plane class implements the three virtual functions from the Vehicle class. Unlike the Car class, though, the ApplyBrakes() method of this class doesn't throw an exception.

```
using System;

public class Plane : Vehicle
{
  override public void TurnLeft()
  {
    Console.WriteLine("Plane turns left.");
  }

  override public void TurnRight()
```

```
  {
    Console.WriteLine("Plane turns right.");
  }

  override public void ApplyBrakes()
  {
    Console.WriteLine("Air brakes being used.");
  }
}
```

You can build a DLL from this code using the following command:

```
csc /r:vehicle.dll /t:library /out:plane.dll plane.cs
```

Notice that we have used the /r: option to tell the C# compiler that Vehicle is defined in *vehicle.dll*.

Test Driver in C#

Having developed *vehicle.dll*, *car.dll*, and *plane.dll*, we are now ready to demonstrate that polymorphism and exception handling work across different languages. Written in C#, the upcoming code listing contains a Main() method with a Vehicle reference and an exception handler.

Inside the try block, we first instantiate a Plane class and refer to this instance using the local Vehicle reference. Instead of telling the Plane to TurnLeft() or ApplyBrakes(), we tell the Vehicle to do so. Similarly, we instantiate a Car and refer to this instance using the local Vehicle reference. Again, instead of telling the Car to TurnLeft() or ApplyBrakes(), we tell the Vehicle to do so. In both cases, we tell the Vehicle either to TurnLeft() or ApplyBrakes(), but the actual vehicle that employs TurnLeft() or ApplyBrakes() is the Plane instance in the first case and the Car instance in the second case; that's polymorphism, and it works across languages.

You should note that the second call to ApplyBrakes() would cause an exception because we threw an exception from Car's ApplyBrakes(). Although Car's ApplyBrakes() was written using VB.NET, we could still catch the exception that it's throwing in C#, proving that exception handling works across languages.

```
using System;

class TestDrive
{
  public static void Main()
  {
    Vehicle v;  // Vehicle reference

    try
    {
```

```
        Plane p = new Plane( );
        v = p;
        v.TurnLeft( );
        v.ApplyBrakes( );

        Car c = new Car( );
        v = c;
        v.TurnLeft( );
        v.ApplyBrakes( );  // Exception
      }
      catch(Exception e)
      {
        Console.WriteLine(e.ToString( ));
      }

    }
  }
```

If you want to test out these features, you can create an EXE using the following command:

```
csc /r:vehicle.dll;car.dll;plane.dll /t:exe /out:drive.exe drive.cs
```

Since we have used the Vehicle, Car, and Plane classes in this code, we must include references to *vehicle.dll*, *car.dll*, and *plane.dll*. And since we are building an EXE, we need to signify this to the C# compiler using the /t:exe option. Once you have built this EXE and executed it, you get the following output:

```
Plane turns left.
Air brakes being used.
Car turns left.
Car trying to stop.
System.Exception: Brake failure!
   at Car.ApplyBrakes( )
   at TestDrive.Main( )
```

As expected, the plane first turns left and then uses its air brakes. Then the car turns left, tries to stop, but can't, so it throws an exception, which is caught in the Main( ) method.

In this simple example, we have shown that you can now take advantage of inheritance, polymorphism, and exception handling across different languages in the .NET Framework.

Summary

We started this chapter by telling you that .NET provides a common programming model, which reduces the learning curve and increases productivity. Once you've learned how to do something using the classes in the .NET

Framework, this knowledge will transfer to any .NET language. We then illustrated that we could write the same type of code, supporting major .NET features, in any given language. Finally, we proved to you that .NET indeed supports language integration, which was never possible using Microsoft platforms and tools, prior to .NET.

CHAPTER 4

Working with .NET Components

Having seen the language-integration examples in the previous chapter, you now know that all .NET assemblies are essentially binary components.* You can treat each .NET assembly as a component that you can plug into another component or application, without the need for source code, since all the metadata for the component is stored inside the .NET assembly. While you have to perform a ton of plumbing to build a component in COM, creating a component in .NET involves no extra work, as all .NET assemblies are components by nature.

In this chapter, we examine the more advanced topics, including component deployment, distributed components, and enterprise services, such as transaction management, object pooling, role-based security, and message queuing.

Deployment Options

For a simple program like *hello.exe* that we built in Chapter 2, deployment is easy: copy the assembly into a directory, and it's ready to run. When you want to uninstall it, remove the file from the directory. However, when you want to share components with other applications, you've got to do some work.

In COM, you must store activation and marshaling† information in the registry for components to interoperate; as a result, any COM developer can

---

* Remember, as we explained in Chapter 1, we're using the term "component" as a binary, deployable unit, not as a COM class.

† Distributed application requires a communication layer to assemble and disassemble application data and network streams. This layer is formally known as a *marshaler* in Microsoft terminology. Assembling and disassembling an application-level protocol network buffer are formally known as *marshaling* and *unmarshaling*, respectively.

discuss at length the pain and suffering inherent in COM and the system registry. In .NET, the system registry is no longer necessary for component integration.

In the .NET environment, components can be *private*, meaning that they are unpublished and used by known clients, or *shared*, meaning that they are published and used by all clients. This section discusses several options for deploying private and shared components.

Private Components

If you have private components that are used only by specific clients, you have two deployment options. You can store the private components and the clients that use these components in the same directory, or you can store the components in a specific directory that the client can access. Since these clients use the exact private components that they referenced at build time, the CLR doesn't support version checking or enforce version policies on private components.

To install your applications in either of these cases, perform a simple xcopy of your application files from the source installation directory to the destination directory. When you want to remove the application, remove these directories. You don't have to write code to store information into the registry, so there's no worrying about whether you've missed inserting a registry setting for correct application execution. In addition, because nothing is stored in the registry, you don't have to worry about registry residues.

One-directory deployment

To specify component location in the same directory as the client application, use the following syntax (as we did in a Chapter 3 example):

```
csc /r:vehicle.dll;car.dll;plane.dll /t:exe /out:drive.exe drive.cs
```

The reference to *plane.dll* does not include a directory path; therefore, the C# compiler stores this reference as is into the client application's assembly manifest so that the CLR can resolve this reference at runtime (i.e., find and load *plane.dll* and activate the Plane class). If you move any of the DLLs to a different directory, you will get an exception when you execute *drive.exe*.

Multiple-directory deployment

Instead of storing all components in the same directory as your client application, you can also use multiple, private paths to segregate your components so that they are easier to find and manage. For example, we will separate the vehicle, car, and plane components into their own private directories, as shown in Figure 4-1. We will leave the *drive.exe* application in the top directory, *MultiDirectories*.

Figure 4-1. Multiple-directory tree of components

When you build the vehicle component, you don't have to do anything special, as it doesn't reference or use any third-party components. However, when you build the car or plane component, you must refer to the correct vehicle component (i.e., the one in the *vehicle* directory). For example, to build the plane component successfully, you must explicitly refer to *vehicle.dll* using a specific or relative path, as shown in the following command (cd to the *plane* directory):

```
csc /r:..\vehicle\vehicle.dll /t:library /out:plane.dll plane.cs
```

You can build the car component the same way you build the plane component. To compile your client application, you must also refer to your dependencies using the correct paths (cd to the main directory, *MultiDirectories*, before you type this command all on one line):

```
csc /r:vehicle\vehicle.dll;car\car.dll;plane\plane.dll
    /t:exe /out:drive.exe drive.cs
```

When you execute this command, the C# compiler records these referenced private paths into your application's assembly manifest. When you execute *drive.exe*, the CLR looks into your application's assembly manifest to find and load the target components.

Shared Components

Unlike application-private assemblies, *shared assemblies*—ones that can be used by any client application—must be published or registered in the system Global Assembly Cache (GAC). When you register your assemblies against the GAC, they act as system components, such as a system DLL that every process in the system can use. A prerequisite for GAC registration is that the component must possess originator and version information. In addition to other metadata, these two items allow multiple versions of the same component to be registered and executed on the same machine. Again, unlike with COM, we don't have to store any information in the system registry for clients to use these shared assemblies.

There are three general steps to registering your shared assemblies against the GAC:

1. Use the shared named (*sn.exe*) utility to obtain a public/private key pair. This utility generates a random key pair for you and saves the key information in an output file—for example, *originator.key*.

2. Build your assembly with an assembly version number and the key information from *originator.key*.

3. Use the .NET Global Assembly Cache Utility (*gacutil.exe*) to register your assembly in the GAC. This assembly is now a shared assembly and can be used by any client.

The commands that we use in this section refer to relative paths, so if you're following along, make sure that you create the directory structure as shown in Figure 4-2. The *vehicle*, *plane*, and *car* directories hold their appropriate assemblies, and the *key* directory holds the public/private key pair that we will generate in a moment. The *car-build* directory holds a car assembly with a modified build number, and the *car-revision* directory holds a car assembly with a modified revision number.

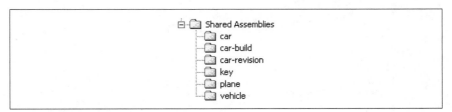

Figure 4-2. Directory structure for examples in this section

Generating a random key pair

We will perform the first step once and reuse the key pair for all shared assemblies that we build in this section. We're doing this for brevity because you can use different key information for each assembly, or even each version, that you build. Here's how to generate a random key pair (be sure to issue this command in the *key* directory):

```
sn -k originator.key
```

The -k option generates a random key pair and saves the key information into the *originator.key* file. We will use this file as input when we build our shared assemblies. Let's now examine steps 2 and 3 of registering your shared assemblies against the GAC.

Making the vehicle component a shared assembly

In order to add version and key information into the vehicle component (developed using Managed C++), we need to make some minor modifications to *vehicle.cpp*, as follows:

```
#using<mscorlib.dll>
using namespace System;

using namespace System::Reflection;
[assembly:AssemblyVersion("1.0.0.0")];
[assembly:AssemblyKeyFile("..\\key\\originator.key")];

public __gc __interface ISteering
{
  void TurnLeft();
  void TurnRight();
};

public __gc class Vehicle : public ISteering
{
  public:

    virtual void TurnLeft()
    {
      Console::WriteLine("Vehicle turns left.");
    }

    virtual void TurnRight()
    {
      Console::WriteLine("Vehicle turn right.");
    }

    virtual void ApplyBrakes() = 0;
};
```

The first boldface line indicates that we're using the Reflection namespace, which defines the attributes that the compiler will intercept to inject the correct information into our assembly manifest. (For a discussion of attributes, see "Attribute-Based Programming" later in this chapter.) We use the AssemblyVersion attribute to indicate the version of this assembly, and we use the AssemblyKeyFile attribute to indicate the file containing the key information that the compiler should use to derive the public-key-token value.

Once you've done this, you can build this assembly using the following commands, which you've seen before:

```
cl /CLR /c vehicle.cpp
link -dll /out:vehicle.dll -noentry vehicle.obj
```

After you've built the assembly, you can use the .NET Global Assembly Cache Utility to register this assembly into the GAC, as follows:

```
gacutil.exe /i vehicle.dll
```

Successful registration against the cache turns this component into a shared assembly. A version of this component is copied into the GAC so that even if you delete this file locally, you will still be able to run your client program.[*]

Making the car component a shared assembly

In order to add version and key information into the car component, we need to make some minor modifications to *car.vb*, as follows:

```vb
Imports System

Imports System.Reflection
<Assembly:AssemblyVersion("1.0.0.0")>
<assembly:AssemblyKeyFile("..\\key\\originator.key")>

Public Class Car
  Inherits Vehicle

  Overrides Public Sub TurnLeft( )
    Console.WriteLine("Car turns left.")
  End Sub

  Overrides Public Sub TurnRight( )
    Console.WriteLine("Car turns right.")
  End Sub

  Overrides Public Sub ApplyBrakes( )
    Console.WriteLine("Car trying to stop.")
    Console.WriteLine("ORIGINAL VERSION - 1.0.0.0.")
    throw new Exception("Brake failure!")
  End Sub

End Class
```

Having done this, you can now build it with the following command:

```
vbc /r:..\vehicle\vehicle.dll /t:library /out:car.dll car.vb
```

Notice he car component uses a specific vehicle component, ..\vehicle\vehicle.dll. At runtime, if the CLR cannot find this specific file here or within the GAC, it will throw an exception. Once you've built this component, you can register it against the GAC:

```
gacutil /i car.dll
```

---

[*] However, don't delete the file now because we need it to build the car and plane assemblies.

At this point, you can delete *car.dll* in the local directory because it has been registered in the GAC.

Making the plane component a shared assembly

In order to add version and key information into the plane component, we need to make some minor modifications to *plane.cs*, as follows:

```
using System;

using System.Reflection;
[assembly:AssemblyVersion("1.0.0.0")]
[assembly:AssemblyKeyFile("..\\key\\originator.key")]

public class Plane : Vehicle
{
  override public void TurnLeft()
  {
    Console.WriteLine("Plane turns left.");
  }

  override public void TurnRight()
  {
    Console.WriteLine("Plane turns right.");
  }

  override public void ApplyBrakes()
  {
    Console.WriteLine("Air brakes being used.");
  }
}
```

Having done this, you can build the assembly with the following commands:

```
csc /r:..\vehicle\vehicle.dll /t:library /out:plane.dll plane.cs
gacutil /i plane.dll
```

Of course, the last line in this snippet simply registers the component into the GAC.

Viewing the GAC

Now that we've registered all our components into the GAC, let's see what the GAC looks like. Microsoft has shipped a shell extension, the Shell Cache Viewer, to make it easier for you to view the GAC. On our machines, the Shell Cache Viewer appears when we navigate to *C:\WINNT\Assembly*, as shown in Figure 4-3.[*]

---

[*] This path is entirely dependent upon the %windir% setting on your machine.

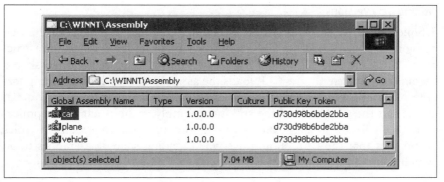

Figure 4-3. Our shared assemblies in the GAC

As you can see, the Shell Cache Viewer shows that all our components have the same version number because we used 1.0.0.0 as the version number when we built our components. Additionally, it shows that all our components have the same public-key-token value, because we used the same key file, *originator.key*.

Building and testing the drive.exe

You should copy the previous *drive.cs* source-code file into the *Shared Assemblies* directory, the root of the directory structure (shown in Figure 4-2) we are working with in this section. Having done this, you can build this component as follows (remember to type everything on one line):

```
csc /r:vehicle\vehicle.dll;car\car.dll;plane\plane.dll
    /t:exe /out:drive.exe drive.cs
```

Once you've done this, you can execute the *drive.exe* component, which will use the *vehicle.dll*, *car.dll*, and *plane.dll* assemblies registered in the GAC. You should see the following as part of your output:

```
ORIGINAL VERSION - 1.0.0.0.
```

To uninstall these shared components, select the appropriate assemblies and press the Delete key (but if you do this now, you must reregister these assemblies because we'll need them in the upcoming examples). When you do this, you've taken all the residues of these components out of the GAC. All that's left is to delete any files that you've copied over from your installation diskette—typically, all you really have to do is recursively remove the application directory.

Adding new versions

Unlike private assemblies, shared assemblies can take advantage of the rich versioning policies that the CLR supports. Unlike earlier OS-level infrastructures, the CLR enforces versioning policies during the loading of all shared assemblies. By default, the CLR loads the assembly with which your application was built, but by providing an application configuration file, you can command the CLR to load the specific assembly version that your application needs. Inside an application configuration file, you can specify the rules or policies that the CLR should use when loading shared assemblies upon which your application depends.

Let's make some code changes to our car component to demonstrate the default versioning support. Remember that Version 1.0.0.0 of our car component's ApplyBrakes() method throws an exception, as follows:

```
Overrides Public Sub ApplyBrakes()
  Console.WriteLine("Car trying to stop.")
  Console.WriteLine("ORIGINAL VERSION - 1.0.0.0.")
  throw new Exception("Brake failure!")
End Sub
```

Let's create a different *build* to remove this exception. To do this, make the following changes to the ApplyBrakes() method (store this source file in the *car-build* directory):

```
Overrides Public Sub ApplyBrakes()
  Console.WriteLine("Car trying to stop.")
  Console.WriteLine("BUILD NUMBER change - 1.0.1.0.")
End Sub
```

In addition, you need to change the build number in your code as follows:

```
<Assembly:AssemblyVersion("1.0.1.0")>
```

Now build this component, and register it using the following commands:

```
vbc /r:..\vehicle\vehicle.dll
    /t:library /out:car.dll car.vb
gacutil /i car.dll
```

Notice that we've specified that this version is 1.0.1.0, meaning that it's compatible with Version 1.0.0.0. After registering this assembly with the GAC, execute your *drive.exe* application, and you will see the following statement as part of the output:

```
ORIGINAL VERSION - 1.0.0.0.
```

This is the default behavior—the CLR will load the version of the assembly with which your application was built. And just to prove this statement further, suppose that you provide Version 1.0.1.1 by making the following code changes (store this version in the *car-revision* directory):

```
Overrides Public Sub ApplyBrakes( )
  Console.WriteLine("Car trying to stop.")
  Console.WriteLine("REVISION NUMBER change - 1.0.1.1.")
End Sub

<Assembly:AssemblyVersion("1.0.1.1")>
```

This time, instead of changing the build number, you're changing the revision number, which should still be compatible to the previous two versions. If you build this assembly, register it against the GAC, and execute *drive.exe* again, you will get the following statement as part of your output:

```
ORIGINAL VERSION - 1.0.0.0.
```

Again, the CLR chooses the version with which your application was built.

As shown in Figure 4-4, you can use the Shell Cache Viewer to verify that all three versions exist on the system simultaneously. This implies that the support exists for side-by-side execution—which terminates DLL Hell in .NET.

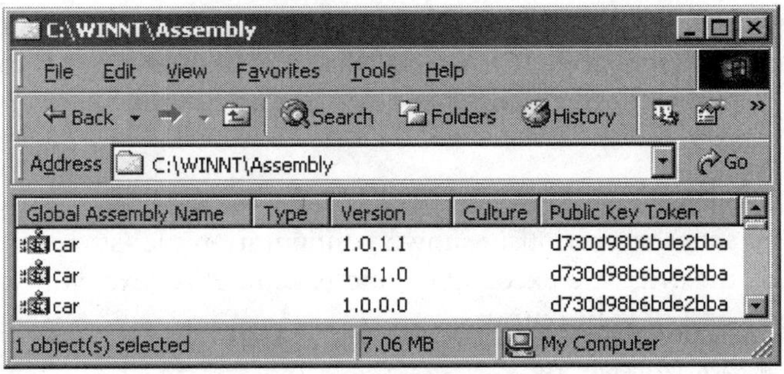

Figure 4-4. Multiple versions of the same shared assembly

If you want your program to use a different compatible version of the car assembly, you have to provide an application configuration file. The name of an application configuration file is composed of the physical executable name and ".config" appended to it. For example, since our client program is named *drive.exe*, its configuration file must be named *drive.exe.config*.

Here's a *drive.exe.config* file that allows you to tell the CLR to load Version 1.0.1.0 of the car assembly for you (instead of loading the default version, 1.0.0.0). The two boldface attributes say that although we built our client with Version 1.0.0.0 (oldVersion) of the car assembly, load 1.0.1.0 (newVersion) for us when we run *drive.exe*.

```
<?xml version ="1.0"?>
<configuration>
  <runtime>
    <assemblyBinding xmlns="urn:schemas-microsoft-com:asm.v1">

      <dependentAssembly>
        <assemblyIdentity name="car"
          publicKeyToken="D730D98B6BDE2BBA"
          culture="" />

        <bindingRedirect oldVersion="1.0.0.0"
                          newVersion="1.0.1.0" />

      </dependentAssembly>
    </assemblyBinding>
  </runtime>
</configuration>
```

In this configuration file, the `name` attribute of the `assemblyIdentity` tag indicates the shared assembly's human-readable name that is stored in the GAC. While the `name` value can be anything, you must replace the `publicKeyToken` value appropriately in order to execute `drive.exe`. The `publicKeyToken` attribute records the public-key-token value, which is an 8-byte hash of the public key used to build this component. There are several ways to get this 8-byte hash: you can copy it from the Shell Cache Viewer, you can copy it from the IL dump of your component, or you can use the Shared Name utility to get it, as follows:

```
sn -T car.dll
```

Once you create the previously shown configuration file (stored in the same directory as the *drive.exe* executable) and execute *drive.exe*, you will see the following as part of your output:

```
BUILD NUMBER change - 1.0.1.0.
```

If you change the configuration file so that `newVersion=1.0.1.1` and if you execute *drive.exe* again, you will see the following as part of your output:

```
REVISION NUMBER change - 1.0.1.1.
```

Having gone over all these examples, you should realize that you have full control over which dependent assembly versions the CLR should load for your applications. It doesn't matter which version was built with your application: you can choose different versions at runtime merely by changing a few attributes in the application configuration file.

Distributed Components

A component technology should support distributed computing, allowing you to activate and invoke remote services, as well as services in another application domain.* Distributed COM, or DCOM, is the wire protocol that provides support for distributed computing using COM. While DCOM is fine for distributed computing, it is inappropriate for global cyberspace because it doesn't work well in the face of firewalls and NAT software. Some other shortcomings of DCOM are expensive lifecycle management, protocol negotiation, and binary formats.

To eliminate or at least mitigate these shortcomings, .NET provides a host of different distributed support. The Remoting API in .NET allows you to use a host of channels, such as TCP and HTTP (which uses SOAP), for distributed computing. It even permits you to plug in your own custom channels, should you require this functionality. Best of all, since the framework is totally object-oriented, distributed computing in .NET couldn't be easier. To show you how simple it is to write a distributed application in .NET, let's look at an example using sockets, otherwise known as the *TCP channel* in .NET.

Distributed Hello Server

In this example, we'll write a distributed Hello application, which outputs a line of text to the console whenever a client invokes its exposed method, SayHello(). Since we're using the TCP channel, we'll tell the compiler that we need the definitions in the System.Runtime.Remoting and System.Runtime.Remoting.Channels.Tcp namespaces.

Note that this class, CoHello, derives from MarshalByRefObject.† This is the key to distributed computing in .NET because it gives this object a distributed identity, allowing the object to be referenced across application domains, or even process and machine boundaries. A marshal-by-reference object requires a proxy to be set up on the client side and a stub to be set up on the server side, but since both of these are automatically provided by the infrastructure, you don't have to do any extra work. Your job is to derive from MarshalByRefObject to get all the support for distributed computing.

---

* Each Windows process requires its own memory address space, making it fairly expensive to run multiple Windows processes. An application domain is a lightweight or virtual process. All application domains of a given Windows process can use the same memory address space.

† If you fail to do this, your object will not have a distributed identity since the default is marshal-by-value, which means that a copy of the remote object is created on the client side.

```csharp
using System;
using System.Runtime.Remoting;
using System.Runtime.Remoting.Channels;
using System.Runtime.Remoting.Channels.Tcp;

public class CoHello : MarshalByRefObject
{
  public static void Main( )
  {
    TcpChannel channel = new TcpChannel(4000);
    ChannelServices.RegisterChannel(channel);

    RemotingConfiguration.RegisterWellKnownServiceType (
      typeof(CoHello),              // Type name
      "HelloDotNet",                // URI
      WellKnownObjectMode.Singleton // SingleCall or Singleton
    );

    System.Console.WriteLine("Hit <enter> to exit...");
    System.Console.ReadLine( );
  }

  public void SayHello( )
  {
    Console.WriteLine("Hello, Universe of .NET");
  }
}
```

The SayHello( ) method is public, meaning that any external client can call
this method. As you can see, this method is very simple, but the interesting
thing is that a remote client application (which we'll develop shortly) can
call it because the Main( ) function uses the TcpChannel class. Look carefully at Main( ), and you'll see that it instantiates a TcpChannel, passing in a
port number from which the server will listen for incoming requests.*

Once we have created a channel object, we then register the channel to the
ChannelServices, which supports channel registration and object resolution.
Having done this, you must then register your object with the Remoting-
Configuration so that it can be activated—you do this by calling the
RegisterWellKnownServiceType( ) method of the RemotingConfiguration
class. When you call this method, you must pass in the class name, a URI,
and an object-activation mode. The URI is important because it's a key element that the client application will use to refer specifically to this registered object. The object-activation mode can be either Singleton, which
means that the same object will service many calls, or SingleCall, which

---

* Believe it or not, all you really have to do is replace TcpChannel with HttpChannel to take advantage of HTTP and SOAP as the underlying communication protocols.

means an object will service at most one call.* Here's how to build this distributed application:

```
csc server.cs
```

Once you've done this, you can start the server program, which will wait endlessly until you hit the Enter key. The server is now ready to service client requests.

Remote Hello Client

Now that we have a server waiting, let's develop a client to invoke the remote SayHello() method. Instead of registering an object with the remoting configuration, we need to activate a remote object. So let's jump into the code now to see how this works. As you examine the following program, note these items:

- We're using types in the System.Runtime.Remoting and System.Runtime.Remoting.Channels.Tcp namespaces, since we want to use the TCP channel.
- Our Client class doesn't need to derive from anything because it's not a server-side object that needs to have a distributed identity.
- Since we're developing a client application, we don't really need to specify a client port when we instantiate the TcpChannel.

Other than these items, the key thing to note is object activation, shown in the second boldface statement in the following code. To invoke remote methods, you must first activate the remote object and obtain an associated proxy on the client side. To activate the object and get a reference to the associated proxy, you call the GetObject() method of the Activator class. When you do this, you must pass along the remote class name and its fully qualified location, including the complete URI. Once you've successfully done this, you can then invoke remote methods.

```
using System;
using System.Runtime.Remoting;
using System.Runtime.Remoting.Channels;
using System.Runtime.Remoting.Channels.Tcp;

public class Client
{
  public static void Main()
```

---

* In this example, we've shown you the code to create a channel, register a channel with the channel services, and register your object with the remoting configuration, but you don't have to write all this code if you provide an application configuration file with all the information.

```
{
  try
  {
    TcpChannel channel = new TcpChannel( );
    ChannelServices.RegisterChannel(channel);

    CoHello h = (CoHello) Activator.GetObject(
      typeof(CoHello),                   // Remote type
      "tcp://127.0.0.1:4000/HelloDotNet" // Location
    );

    h.SayHello( );
  }
  catch(Exception e)
  {
    Console.WriteLine(e.ToString( ));
  }
}
}
```

To build this client application, you must include references to the *server. exe* assembly:

```
csc /r:Server.exe Client.cs
```

If you're familiar with DCOM, you must be relieved to find that it's relatively simple to write distributed applications in .NET.*

Distributed Garbage Collector

Because the new distributed garbage collector is so cool, we must briefly cover this facility. Instead of using DCOM's delta pinging, which requires few network packets when compared to normal pinging (but still too many for a distributed protocol), .NET remoting uses leases to manage object lifetimes. If you've ever renewed the lease to an IP address on your Dynamic Host Configuration Protocol (DHCP) network, you've pretty much figured out this mechanism because it's based on similar concepts.

In .NET, distributed objects give out leases instead of relying on reference counting (as in COM) for lifetime management. An application domain where the remote objects reside has a special object called the *lease manager*, which manages all the leases associated with these remote objects. When a lease expires, the lease manager contacts a sponsor, telling the sponsor that the lease has expired. A *sponsor* is simply a client that has previously registered itself with the lease manager during an activation call,

---

* In fact, if you have a copy of *Learning DCOM* (O'Reilly) handy, compare these programs with
  their DCOM counterparts in Appendix D, and you will see what we mean.

---

indicating to the lease manager that it wants to know when a lease expires. If the lease manager can contact the sponsor, the sponsor may then renew the lease. If the sponsor refuses to renew the lease or if the lease manager can't contact the sponsor after a configurable timeout period, the lease manager will void the lease and remove the object. There are two other ways in which a lease can be renewed: implicitly, via each call to the remote object, or explicitly, by calling the Renew() method of the Lease class.

COM+ Services in .NET

COM programming requires lots of housekeeping and infrastructure-level code to build large-scale, enterprise applications. Making it easier to develop and deploy transactional and scalable COM applications, Microsoft released Microsoft Transaction Server (MTS). MTS allows you to share resources, thereby increasing the scalability of an application. COM+ Services were the natural evolution of MTS. While MTS was just another library on top of COM, COM+ Services were subsumed into the COM library, thus combining both COM and MTS into a single runtime.

COM+ Services have been very valuable to the development shops using the COM model to build applications that take advantage of transactions, object pooling, role-based security, etc. If you develop enterprise .NET applications, the COM+ Services in .NET are a must.

In the following examples, rather than feeding you more principles, we'll show you examples for using major COM+ Services in .NET, including examples on transactional programming, object pooling, and role-based security. But before you see these examples, let's talk about the key element—attributes—that enable the use of these services in .NET.

Attribute-Based Programming

Attributes are the key elements that help you write less code and allow an infrastructure to automatically inject the necessary code for you at runtime. If you've used IDL (Interface Definition Language) before, you have seen the in or out attributes, as in the following example:

```
HRESULT SetAge([in] short age);
HRESULT GetAge([out] short *age);
```

IDL allows you to add these attributes so that the marshaler will know how to optimize the use of the network. Here, the in attribute tells the marshaler to send the contents from the client to the server, and the out attribute tells the marshaler to send the contents from the server to the client. In the SetAge() method, passing age from the server to the client will just waste bandwidth. Similarly, there's no need to pass age from the client to the server in the GetAge() method.

Developing custom attributes

While in and out are built-in attributes the MIDL compiler supports, .NET allows you to create your own custom attributes by deriving from the System.Attribute class. Here's an example of a custom attribute:

```
using System;

public enum Skill {  Guru, Senior, Junior }

[AttributeUsage(AttributeTargets.Class         |
                AttributeTargets.Field         |
                AttributeTargets.Method        |
                AttributeTargets.Property      |
                AttributeTargets.Constructor|
                AttributeTargets.Event)]
public class AuthorAttribute : System.Attribute
{
   public AuthorAttribute(Skill s)
   {
      level = s;
   }
   public Skill level;
}
```

The AttributeUsage attribute that we've applied to our AuthorAttribute class specifies the rules for using AuthorAttribute.* Specifically, it says that AuthorAttribute can prefix or describe a class or any class member.

Using custom attributes

Given that we have this attribute, we can write a simple class to make use of it. To apply our attribute to a class or a member, we simply make use of the attribute's available constructors. In our case, we have only one and it's AuthorAttribute(), which takes an author's skill level. While you can use AuthorAttribute() to instantiate this attribute, .NET allows you to drop the Attribute suffix for convenience, as shown in the following code listing:

```
[Author(Skill.Guru)]
public class Customer
{
   [Author(Skill.Senior)]
   public void Add(string strName)
```

---

* You don't have to postfix your attribute class name with the word Attribute, but this is a standard naming convention that Microsoft uses. C# lets you name your attribute class any way you like; for example, Author is a valid class name for your attribute.

```
    {
    }
    [Author(Skill.Junior)]
    public void Delete(string strName)
    {
    }
}
```

You'll notice that we've applied the Author attribute to the Customer class, telling the world that a guru wrote this class definition. This code also shows that a senior programmer wrote the Add() method and that a junior programmer wrote the Delete() method.

Inspecting attributes

You won't see the full benefits of attributes until you write a simple interceptor-like program, which looks for special attributes and provides additional services appropriate for these attributes. Real interceptors include marshaling, transaction, security, pooling, and other services in MTS and COM+.

Here's a simple interceptor-like program that uses the Reflection API to look for AuthorAttribute and provide additional services. You'll notice that we can ask a type, Customer in this case, for all of its custom attributes. In our code, we ensure that the Customer class has attributes and that the first attribute is AuthorAttribute before we output the appropriate messages to the console. In addition, we look for all members that belong to the Customer class and check whether they have custom attributes. If they do, we ensure that the first attribute is an AuthorAttribute before we output the appropriate messages to the console.

```
using System;
using System.Reflection;

public class interceptor
{
  public static void Main( )
  {
    Object[] attrs = typeof(Customer).GetCustomAttributes(false);
    if ((attrs.Length > 0) && (attrs[0] is AuthorAttribute))
    {
      Console.WriteLine("Class [{0}], written by a {1} programmer.",
          typeof(Customer).Name, ((AuthorAttribute)attrs[0]).level);
    }

    MethodInfo[] mInfo = typeof(Customer).GetMethods( );
    for ( int i=0; i < mInfo.Length; i++ )
    {
      attrs = mInfo[i].GetCustomAttributes(false);
      if ((attrs.Length > 0) && (attrs[0] is AuthorAttribute))
      {
```

```
AuthorAttribute a = (AuthorAttribute)attrs[0];
Console.WriteLine("Method [{0}], written by a {1} programmer.",
    mInfo[i].Name, (a.level));
if (a.level == Skill.Junior)
{
  Console.WriteLine("***Performing automatic " +
    "review of {0}'s code***", a.level);
}
      }
    }
  }
}
```

It is crucial to note that when this program sees a piece of code written by a junior programmer, it automatically performs a rigorous review of the code. If you compile and run this program, it will output the following to the console:

```
Class [Customer], written by a Guru programmer.
Method [Add], written by a Senior programmer.
Method [Delete], written by a Junior programmer.
***Performing automatic review of Junior's code***
```

While our interceptor-like program doesn't intercept any object-creation and method invocations, it does show how a real interceptor can examine attributes at runtime and provide necessary services stipulated by the attributes. Again, the key here is the last boldface line, which represents a special service that the interceptor provides as a result of attribute inspection.

Transactions

It is elementary to write a .NET class to take advantage of the transaction support that COM+ Services provide. All you need to supply at development time are a few attributes, and your .NET components are automatically registered against the COM+ catalog the first time they are used. Put differently, not only do you get easier programming, but you also get just-in-time and automatic registration of your COM+ application.* To develop a .NET class that supports transactions, here's what must happen:

1. Your class must derive from the ServicedComponent class to exploit COM+ Services.

2. You must describe your class with the correct Transaction attribute, such as Transaction(TransactionOption.Required), meaning that instances of your class must run within a transaction.

---

* Automatic registration is nice during development, but don't use this feature in a production environment, because not all clients will have the administrative privilege to set up COM+ applications.

Besides these two requirements, you can use the ContextUtil class (which is a part of the System.EnterpriseServices namespace) to obtain information about the COM+ object context. This class exposes the major functionality found in COM+, including methods such as SetComplete(), SetAbort(), and IsCallerInRole(), and properties such as IsInTransaction and MyTransactionVote.

In addition, while it's not necessary to specify any COM+ application installation options, you should do so because you get to specify what you want, including the name of your COM+ application, its activation setting, its versions, and so on. For example, in the following code listing, if you don't specify the ApplicationName attribute, .NET will use the module name as the COM+ application name, displayed in the Component Services Explorer (or COM+ Explorer). For example, if the name of module is *crm.dll*, the name of your COM+ application will be *crm*. Other than this attribute, we also use the ApplicationActivation attribute to specify that this component will be installed as a library application, meaning that the component will be activated in the creator's process.

```
using System;
using System.Reflection;
using System.EnterpriseServices;

[assembly: ApplicationName(".NET Essentials CRM")]
[assembly: ApplicationActivation(ActivationOption.Library)]
[assembly: AssemblyKeyFile("originator.key")]
[assembly: AssemblyVersion("1.0.0.0")]
```

The rest should look extremely familiar. In the Add() method, we simply call SetComplete() when we've successfully added the new customer into our databases. If something has gone wrong during the process, we will vote to abort this transaction by calling SetAbort().

```
[Transaction(TransactionOption.Required)]
public class Customer : ServicedComponent
{
  public void Add(string strName)
  {
    try
    {
      Console.WriteLine("New customer: {0}", strName);

      // Add the new customer into the system,
      // and make appropriate updates to
      // several databases.

      ContextUtil.SetComplete();
    }
    catch(Exception e)
```

```
    {
      Console.WriteLine(e.ToString());
      ContextUtil.SetAbort();
    }
  }
}
```

Instead of calling SetComplete() and SetAbort() yourself, you can also use the AutoComplete attribute, as in the following code, which is conceptually equivalent to the previously shown Add() method:

```
[AutoComplete]
public void Add(string strName)
{
  Console.WriteLine("New customer: {0}", strName);

  // Add the new customer into the system,
  // and make appropriate updates to
  // several databases.
}
```

Here's how you build this assembly:

```
csc /t:library /out:crm.dll crm.cs
```

Since this is a shared assembly, remember to register it against the GAC by using the GAC utility:

```
gacutil /i crm.dll
```

At this point, the assembly has not been registered as a COM+ application, but we don't need to register it manually. Instead, .NET automatically registers and hosts this component for us in a COM+ application the first time we use this component. So, let's write a simple client program that uses this component at this point. As you can see in the following code, we instantiate a Customer object and add a new customer:

```
using System;

public class Client
{
  public static void Main()
  {
    try
    {
      Customer c = new Customer();
      c.Add("John Osborn");
    }
    catch(Exception e)
    {
      Console.WriteLine(e.ToString());
    }
  }
}
```

We can build this program as follows:

```
csc /r:crm.dll /t:exe /out:client.exe client.cs
```

When we run this application, COM+ Services automatically create a COM+ application called .NET Essentials CRM to host our *crm.dll* .NET assembly, as shown in Figure 4-5. In addition to adding our component to the created COM+ application, .NET also inspects our metadata for provided attributes and configures the associated services in the COM+ catalog.

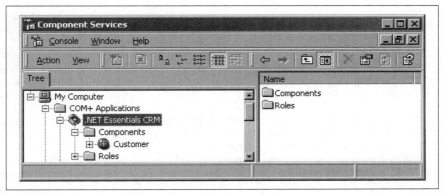

Figure 4-5. The Component Services Explorer

Object Pooling

A *pool* is technical term that refers to a group of resources, such as connections, threads, and objects. Putting a few objects into a pool allows hundreds of clients to share these few objects (you can make the same assertion for threads, connections, and other objects). Pooling is therefore a technique that minimizes the use of system resources, improves performance, and helps system scalability.

Missing in MTS, *object pooling* is a nice feature in COM+ that allows you to pool objects that support transactions but are expensive to create. Similar to providing support for transactions, if you want to support object pooling in a .NET class, you need to derive from ServicedComponent, override any of the Activate(), Deactivate(), and CanBePooled() methods, and specify the object-pooling requirements in an ObjectPooling attribute, as shown in the following example:*

```
using System;
using System.Reflection;
```

---

* Mixing transactions and object pooling should be done with care. See Juval Lowy's *COM and .NET Component Services* (O'Reilly).

```
using System.EnterpriseServices;

[assembly: ApplicationName(".NET Essentials CRM")]
[assembly: ApplicationActivation(ActivationOption.Library)]
[assembly: AssemblyKeyFile("originator.key")]
[assembly: AssemblyVersion("1.0.0.0")]

[Transaction(TransactionOption.Required)]
[ObjectPooling(MinPoolSize=1, MaxPoolSize=5)]
public class Customer : ServicedComponent
{
  public Customer( )
  {
    Console.WriteLine("Some expensive object construction.");
  }

  [AutoComplete]
  public void Add(string strName)
  {
    Console.WriteLine("Add customer: {0}", strName);
    // Add the new customer into the system,
    // and make appropriate updates to
    // several databases.
  }

  override protected void Activate( )
  {
    Console.WriteLine("Activate");
    // Pooled object is being activated.
    // Perform the appropriate initialization.
  }

  override protected void Deactivate( )
  {
    Console.WriteLine("Deactivate");
    // Object is about to be returned to the pool.
    // Perform the appropriate clean up.
  }

  override protected bool CanBePooled( )
  {
    Console.WriteLine("CanBePooled");
    return true; // Return the object to the pool.
  }
}
```

Take advantage of the Activate() and Deactivate() methods to perform appropriate initialization and cleanup. The CanBePooled() method lets you tell COM+ whether your object can be pooled when this method is called. You need to provide the expensive object-creation functionality in the constructor, as shown in the constructor of this class.

Given this Customer class that supports both transaction and object pooling, you can write the following client-side code to test object pooling. For brevity, we will create only two objects, but you can change this number to anything you like so that you can see the effects of object pooling. Just to ensure that you have the correct configuration, delete the current .NET Essentials CRM COM+ application from the Component Services Explorer before running the following code:

```
for (int i=0; i<2; i++)
{
    Customer c = new Customer( );
    c.Add(i.ToString( ));
}
```

Running this code produces the following results:

```
Some expensive object construction.
Activate
Add customer: 0
Deactivate
CanBePooled
Activate
Add customer: 1
Deactivate
CanBePooled
```

We've created two objects, but since we've used object pooling, only one object is really needed to support our calls, and that's why you see only one output statement that says Some expensive object construction. In this case, COM+ creates only one Customer object, but activates and deactivates it twice to support our two calls. After each call, it puts the object back into the object pool. When a new call arrives, it picks the same object from the pool to service the request.

Role-Based Security

Role-based security in MTS and COM+ has drastically simplified the development and configuration of security for business applications. This is because it abstracts away the complicated details for dealing with access control lists (ACL) and security identifiers (SID). All .NET components that are hosted in a COM+ application can take advantage of role-based security. You can fully configure role-based security using the Component Services Explorer, but you can also manage role-based security in your code to provide fine-grain security support that's missing from the Component Services Explorer.

Configuring role-based security

In order to demonstrate role-based security, let's add two roles to our COM+ application, .NET Essentials CRM. The first role represents Agents who can use the Customer class in every way but can't delete customers. You should create this role and add to it the local Users group, as shown in Figure 4-6. The second role represents Managers who can use the Customer class in every way, including deleting customers. Create this role, and add to it the local Administrators group.

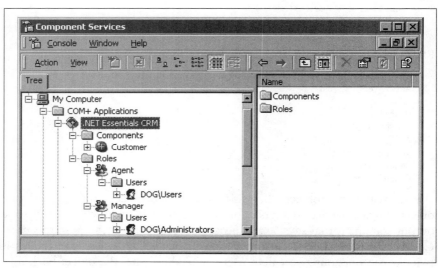

Figure 4-6. Creating roles and adding users to roles

Once you create these roles, you need to enable access checks for the .NET Essentials CRM COM+ application. Launch the COM+ application's Properties sheet (by selecting .NET Essentials CRM and pressing Alt-Enter), and select the Security tab. Enable access checks to your COM+ application by providing the options as shown in Figure 4-7.

Once you have enabled access checks at the application level, you need to enforce access checks at the class level too. To do this, launch Customer's Properties sheet, and select the Security tab. Enable access checks to this .NET class by providing the options shown in Figure 4-8. Here, we're saying that no one can access the Customer class except for those that belong to the Manager or Agent role.

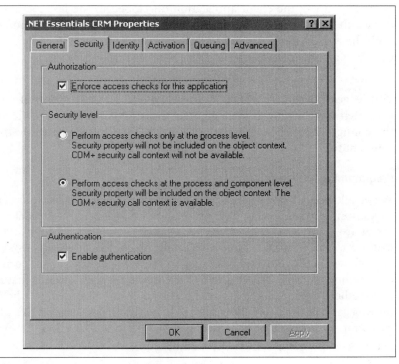

Figure 4-7. Enable authorization for this COM+ application

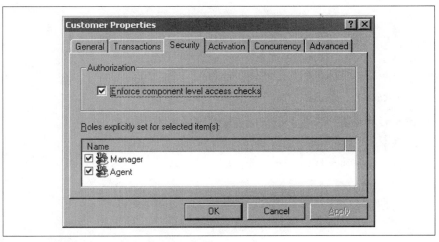

Figure 4-8. Enforce class-level access checks

Now, if you run the client application developed in the last section, every-thing will work because you are a user on your machine. But if you uncheck both the Manager* and Agent roles in Figure 4-8 and rerun the client applica-tion, you get the following message as part of your output:

```
System.UnauthorizedAccessException: Access is denied.
```

You're getting this exception because you've removed yourself from the roles that have access to the Customer class. Once you've verified this, put the configuration back to what is shown in Figure 4-8 to prepare the envi-ronment for the next test that we're about to illustrate.

Programming role-based security

We've allowed anyone in the Agent and Manager roles to access our class, but let's invent a rule allowing only users under the Manager role to delete a cus-tomer from the system (for lack of a better example). So let's add a new method to the Customer class—we'll call this method Delete(), as shown in the following code. Anyone belonging to the Agent or Manager role can invoke this method, so we'll first output to the console the user account that invokes this method. After doing this, we'll check to ensure that this user belongs to the Manager role. If so, we allow the call to go through; otherwise, we throw an exception indicating that only managers can perform a deletion. Believe it our not, this is the basic premise for programming role-based security.

```
[AutoComplete]
public void Delete(string strName)
{
  try
  {
    SecurityCallContext sec;
    sec = SecurityCallContext.CurrentCall;
    string strCaller = sec.DirectCaller.AccountName;

    Console.WriteLine("Caller: {0}", strCaller);

    bool bInRole = sec.IsCallerInRole("Manager");
    if (!bInRole)
    {
      throw new Exception ("Only managers can delete customers.");
    }

    Console.WriteLine("Delete customer: {0}", strName);
```

---

* Since you're a developer, you're probably an administrator on your machine, so you need to uncheck the Manager role, too, in order to see an access violation in the test that we're about to illustrate.

```
   // Delete the new customer from the system,
   // and make appropriate updates to
   // several databases.
 }
 catch(Exception e)
 {
   Console.WriteLine(e.ToString());
 }
}
```

Here's the client code that includes a call to the Delete() method:

```
using System;

public class Client
{
  public static void Main()
  {
    try
    {
      Customer c = new Customer();
      c.Add("John Osborn");
      // Success depends on the role
      // under which this this method
      // is invoked.
      c.Delete("Jane Smith");
    }
    catch(Exception e)
    {
      Console.WriteLine(e.ToString());
    }
  }
}
```

Once you've built this program, you can test it using an account that belongs to the local Users group, since we added this group to the Agent role earlier. On Windows 2000, you can use the following command to launch a command window using a specific account:

```
runas /user:dog\thuant cmd
```

Of course, you should replace dog and thuant with your own machine name and user account, respectively. After running this command, you will need to type in the correct password, and a new command window will appear. Execute the client under this user account, and you'll see the following output:

```
Add customer: John Osborn
Caller: DOG\thuant
System.Exception: Only managers can delete customers.
    at Customer.Delete(String strName)
```

You'll notice that the Add( ) operation went through successfully, but the Delete( ) operation failed because we executed the client application under an account that's missing from the Manager role.

To remedy this, we need to use a user account that belongs to the Manager role—any account that belongs to the Administrators group will do. So, start another command window using the following command:

```
runas /user:dog\administrator cmd
```

Execute the client application again, and you'll get the following output:

```
Add customer: John Osborn
Caller: DOG\Administrator
Delete customer: Jane Smith
```

As you can see, since we've executed the client application using an account that belongs to the Manager role, the Delete( ) operation went through without problems.

Message Queuing

In addition to providing support for COM+ Services, .NET also supports message queuing. If you've used Microsoft Message Queuing (MSMQ) services before, you'll note that the basic programming model is the same but the classes in the System.Messaging namespace make it extremely easy to develop message-queuing applications. The System.Messaging namespace provides support for basic functionality, such as connecting to a queue, opening a queue, sending messages to a queue, receiving messages from a queue, and peeking for messages on the queue. To demonstrate how easy it is to use the classes in System.Messaging, let's build two simple applications: one to enqueue messages onto a private queue on the local computer and another to dequeue these messages from the same queue.*

Enqueue

Here's a simple program that enqueues a Customer object onto a private queue on the local computer. Notice first that we need to include the System.Messaging namespace because it contains the classes that we want to use:

```
using System;
using System.Messaging;
```

---

* To execute these programs, you must have MessageQueuing installed on your system. You can verify this by launching the ComputerManagement console, as shown in Figure 4-9.

While the following Customer structure is very simple, it can be as complex as you want because it will be serialized into an XML-formatted buffer by default before it's placed into the queue.

```
public struct Customer
{
    public string Last;
    public string First;
}
```

Our program first checks whether a private queue on the local computer exists. If this queue is missing, the program will create it. Next, we instantiate a MessageQueue class, passing in the target queue name. Once we have this MessageQueue object, we invoke its Send() method, passing in the Customer object, as shown in the following code. This will put our customer object into our private queue.

```
public class Enqueue
{
    public static void Main( )
    {
        try
        {
            string path = ".\\PRIVATE$\\NE_queue";
            if(!MessageQueue.Exists(path))
            {
                // Create our private queue.
                MessageQueue.Create(path);
            }

            // Initialize the queue.
            MessageQueue q = new MessageQueue(path);

            // Create our object.
            Customer c = new Customer( );
            c.Last = "Osborn";
            c.First = "John";

            // Send it to the queue.
            q.Send(c);
        }
        catch(Exception e)
        {
            Console.WriteLine(e.ToString( ));
        }
    }
}
```

Use the following command to build this program:

```
csc /t:exe /out:enqueue.exe enqueue.cs
```

Execute this program, examine the Computer Management console, and you will see your message in the private queue called ne_queue, as shown in Figure 4-9.

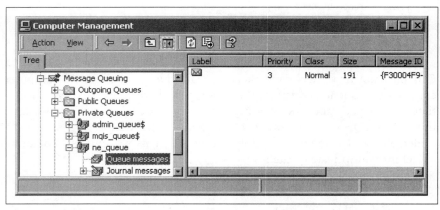

Figure 4-9. Our private queue, ne_queue, with a message

Dequeue

Now that there's a message in our private message queue, let's write a program to dequeue and examine the message. After ensuring that the private queue we want exists, we initialize it by instantiating a MessageQueue class, passing in the path to our private queue. Next, we tell the MessageQueue object that the type of object we want to dequeue is Customer. To actually dequeue the object, we need to invoke the Receive() method, passing in a timeout in terms of a TimeSpan object, whose parameters stand for hours, minutes, and seconds, respectively. Finally, we cast the body of the received Message object into a Customer object and output its contents.

```
using System;
using System.Messaging;
using System.Runtime.Serialization;

public struct Customer
{
  public string Last;
  public string First;
}

public class Dequeue
{
  public static void Main()
  {
    try
    {
```

```
    string strQueuePath = ".\\PRIVATE$\\NE_queue";

    // Ensure that the queue exists
    if (!MessageQueue.Exists(strQueuePath))
    {
        throw new Exception(strQueuePath + " doesn't exist!");
    }

    // Initialize the queue
    MessageQueue q = new MessageQueue(strQueuePath);

    // Specify the types we want to get back
    string[] types = {"Customer, dequeue"};
    ((XmlMessageFormatter)q.Formatter).TargetTypeNames = types;

    // Receive the message (5 sec timeout)
    Message m = q.Receive(new TimeSpan(0,0,5));

    // Convert the body into the type we want
    Customer c = (Customer) m.Body;
    Console.WriteLine("Customer: {0}, {1}", c.Last, c.First);
  }
  catch(Exception e)
  {
    Console.WriteLine(e.ToString());
  }
 }
}
```

Compile and execute this program, look at the Computer Management console, press F5 to refresh the screen, and you will realize that the previous message is no longer there.

Summary

In this chapter, we've touched on many aspects of componentization, including deployment strategies, distributed computing, and enterprise services such as transaction management, object pooling, role-based security, and message queuing. We have to give due credit to Microsoft for making componentization easier in the .NET Framework. Case in point: without .NET, it would be impossible for us to illustrate the complete code for all of these programs in a single chapter of a book.

CHAPTER 5
Data and XML

Almost everything we do in the software industry relates to data in some way. At some point, all software developers must deal with data, perhaps using a database, text file, spreadsheet, or some other method of data storage. There are many different methods and technologies for using, manipulating, and managing data, and newer methods are continually introduced to enhance existing ones. These methods range from function-based APIs to object-based frameworks and proprietary libraries.

Several years ago, it was common for a simple VB desktop application to access a private Microsoft Access database stored on the local hard disk, but this is no longer a typical scenario. Today's applications take advantage of distributed-component technologies to exploit scalability and interoperability, thus widening the reach of the application to the enterprise. While ActiveX Data Objects (ADO) served a typical VB application well a few years ago, it might soon fail to meet the increasing demands for better scalability, performance, and interoperability across multiple platforms.

Here's where ADO.NET comes in. ADO.NET provides huge benefits that allow us to build even better enterprise applications. In this chapter, you will learn the benefits of ADO.NET, the ADO.NET architecture, the main classes in ADO.NET and how they work, and the integration of ADO.NET and XML.

ADO.NET Architecture

Microsoft ADO.NET's object model encompasses two distinct groups of classes: *content components* and *managed-provider components*. The content components include the DataSet class and other supporting classes such as DataTable, DataRow, DataColumn, and DataRelation. These classes contain the actual content of a data exchange. The managed-provider components assist in data retrievals and updates. Developers can use the connection, command, and data reader objects to directly manipulate data. In more typical scenarios, developers use the DataAdapter class as the conduit to move data between the data store and the content components. The data can be actual rows from a database or any other form of data, such as an XML file or an Excel spreadsheet.

Figure 5-1 shows the high-level architecture of ADO.NET. ADO developers should have no problems understanding connection and command objects. We offer a brief overview then go into more detail in the rest of this chapter.

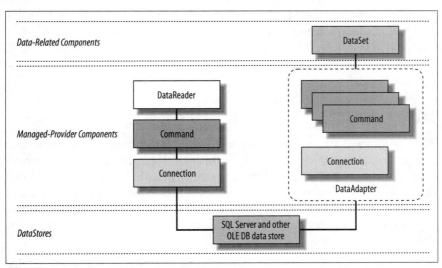

Figure 5-1. High-level architecture of ADO.NET

A data reader is a new object providing fast, forward-only, and read-only access to data. This structure is similar to an ADO Recordset, which has server-side, forward-only, and read-only cursor types.

The DataSet class is analogous to a lightweight cache of a particular database from the data store. It allows reading and writing of data and schema in XML, and it is tightly integrated with XmlDataDocument, as you will see later.

The DataAdapter class serves as a higher-level abstraction of the connection and command classes. It enables you to load content from a data store into a DataSet and reconcile DataSet changes back to the data store.

ADO.NET Benefits

ADO.NET brings with it a number of benefits, which fall into the following categories:

Interoperability
> The ability to communicate across heterogeneous environments.

Scalability
> The ability to serve a growing number of clients without degrading system performance.

Productivity
> The ability to quickly develop robust data access applications using ADO.NET's rich and extensible component object model.

Performance
> An improvement over previous ADO versions due to the disconnected data model.

Interoperability

All communication involves data exchange, whether the communication between distributed components is through a request/response methodology or a message-based facility. Current distributed systems assume that the components involved in the communication are using the same protocol and data format. This assumption is too restrictive for a client base to expand across an enterprise or for multiple companies. Data-access layers should impose no such restrictions.

In current Microsoft Windows Distributed interNet Applications (DNA) Architecture, application components pass data back and forth as ADO disconnected recordsets. The data-providing components, as well as the data-consuming components, are required to use the Component Object Model (COM). The *payload*, the actual content we are passing around, is packaged in a data format called Network Data Representation (NDR). These NDR packages are streamed between components.

There are two issues with current Windows DNA systems. The first is the requirement that both ends of the communication pipe have the COM library. The second issue is that it is difficult to set up and manage these communications across firewalls. If your middle-tier components are COM/DCOM-based and you are using them within your intranet, you are in good shape. To put it another way: if all your components use Microsoft technology, you're fine. With the advent of electronic commerce (e-commerce), however, enterprise applications must interoperate with more than just

Microsoft-development shops. ADO must improve for cross-platform components to seamlessly share data, breaking away from the limitations of COM/DCOM.

ADO.NET addresses the common data-exchange limitation by using XML as its payload data format. Since XML is text-based and simple to parse, it's a good choice for a common, platform-independent, and transportable data format. Furthermore, because XML is nothing more than structured text, employing XML as the data format on top of the HTTP network protocol minimizes firewall-related problems. With ADO and its XML format, the clients do not have to know COM to de-serialize the packaged data. All they need is an XML parser, which is readily available in many flavors on many different platforms. The data producers and consumers need only adhere to the XML schema to exchange data among themselves.

Scalability

In a client/server model, it is typical for a client to acquire and hold onto a connection to the server until all requests are fulfilled. While this solution works fine in small- to medium-scale applications, it is not scalable across a large enterprise. As soon as the number of clients reaches a certain threshold, the server becomes the bottleneck, as database connections eat up network and CPU resources. ADO.NET moves away from the client/server model by promoting the use of disconnected datasets. When a client requests some data, the data is retrieved, it's transferred to the client, and—as soon as possible—the connection is torn down. Since the connection between the client and the data source is short-lived, this technique allows more clients to request information from the server, thus solving the problem of limited connections.

You might think that setting up and tearing down connections is not a good idea since the cost of establishing a connection is usually high. This is a concern only in the absence of connection pooling. ADO.NET automatically keeps connections to a data source in a pool, so when an application thinks it is tearing down a connection, it's actually returning it to the resource pool. This allows connections to be reused, avoiding the cost of reconstructing new connections from scratch.

Working with data in this disconnected fashion is not new to ADO programmers. The disconnected recordset was introduced in early versions of ADO. However, in ADO, it is up to the developer to implement this feature, whereas in ADO.NET, data is disconnected by nature.

ADO.NET has enhanced its predecessor by growing out of the client/server model and into the distributed components model. By using disconnected datasets as the paradigm for data exchange, ADO.NET is much more scalable than its predecessors.

Productivity

ADO.NET's rich framework classes allow developers to boost their productivity. Current ADO developers should have no problems getting up to speed with the object model, because ADO.NET is a natural evolution of ADO. The core functionality remains the same. We still have the connection object, representing the pipeline through which commands are executed.* With ADO.NET, the functionality is factored and distributed to each object in the model—much better than in previous versions of ADO. For example, the connection object is responsible only for connecting to and disconnecting from the data source. In ADO.NET, we can no longer execute a query directly through the connection object. While some developers might miss this ability, it is a step in the right direction for cohesion of component development.

ADO.NET also boosts developers' productivity through extensibility. Because ADO.NET framework classes are managed code, developers can inherit and extend these classes to their custom needs. If you prefer not to do this low-level legwork, you can use the Visual Studio. NET data-design environment to generate these classes for you.

Visual Studio .NET is a great Rapid Application Development (RAD) tool for developing applications with ADO.NET. You can have the Component Designer generate ADO.NET typed DataSets. These typed DataSets are extended types, modeled for your data. The generated code is much more readable, when compared to previous Microsoft code generators. In addition, these generated classes are type-safe, thus reducing the chances for errors and allowing compilers and the CLR to verify type usage.

In short, ADO.NET improves developers' productivity through its rich and extensible framework classes. These features are complemented by the rich toolsets for ADO.NET in Visual Studio .NET, which enable rapid application development.

---

* Along with the familiar connection and command objects, ADO.NET introduces a number of new objects, such as DataSet and DataAdapter. All of these objects are discussed in "ADO.NET Architecture" earlier in this chapter.

Performance

Because ADO.NET is mainly about disconnected datasets, the system benefits from improved performance and scalability. The database server is no longer a bottleneck when the number of connection requests goes up. Managed Providers in ADO.NET also enable implicit connection pooling, which reduces the time required to open a connection.

Previous marshaling of recordsets required type conversion to make sure that the data types were all COM-based. Since the disconnected dataset is in XML format, there is no need for this type conversion during transport, as opposed to dealing with data in Network Data Representation format.

Content Components

Content components encapsulate data. In previous ADO versions, the Recordset object represented such a component. The data contained by the recordset component is in the form of a table, consisting of columns and rows. In ADO.NET, the data encapsulated by the DataSet component is in the form of a relational database, consisting of tables and relationships. This is a major improvement in data-access technology. In this section, we provide a high-level survey of the core classes that make up the content components, including DataSet, DataTable, DataColumn, DataRow, DataView, and DataRelation.*

DataSet

If you are familiar with ADO, you know that data is typically transferred between components in *recordsets*. The recordset contains data in a tabular form. Whether the recordset includes information from one or many tables in the database, the data is still returned in the form of rows and columns as if they were from a single table. ADO.NET allows for more than just a recordset to be shared between application components. This is one of the most important features of ADO.NET: we will be transferring a DataSet instead of a recordset.

The DataSet can be viewed as an in-memory view of the database. It can contain multiple DataTable and DataRelation objects. With previous versions of ADO, the closest you could get to this functionality was to exchange data with a chain of Recordset objects. When the client application receives this

---

* The complete list of all classes can be found in the Microsoft .NET SDK.

chained recordset, it can get to each of the recordsets through NextRecordset(); however, there is no way to describe the relationship between each of the recordsets in the chain. With ADO.NET, developers can navigate and manipulate the collection of tables and their relationships.

As mentioned earlier, ADO.NET involves disconnected datasets because it is geared toward a distributed architecture. Since a DataSet is disconnected, it must provide a way to track changes to itself. The DataSet object provides a number of methods so that all data manipulation done to the DataSet can be easily reconciled with the actual database (or other data source) at a later time. They include: HasChanges(), HasErrors, GetChanges(), AcceptChanges(), and RejectChanges(). You can employ these methods to check for changes that have happened to the DataSet, obtain the modifications in the form of a changed DataSet, inspect the changes for errors, and then accept or reject the changes. If you want to communicate the changes to the data store back end (which is usually the case), just ask the DataSet for an update.

The DataSet is intended to benefit enterprise web applications, which are disconnected by nature. You don't know that the data at the back end has changed until you have updated records you were editing or performed any other tasks that required data reconciliation with the database.

As depicted in Figure 5-2, a DataSet contains two important collections. The first is the Tables (of type DataTableCollection), which holds a collection for all the tables belonging to a given DataSet. The second collection contains all the relationships between the tables, and it is appropriately named the Relations (of type DataRelationCollection).

Creating a DataSet: An example in C#

All the tables and relations inside the DataSet are exposed through the DataSet's Tables and Relations properties, respectively. Normally, you obtain tables from some data sources such as SQL Server or other databases; however, we would like to show the nuts and bolts of the DataSet here first. The following block of C# code demonstrates how to create a DataSet dynamically that consists of two tables, Orders and OrderDetails, and a relationship between the two tables:

```
using System;
using System.Data;

// Class and method declarations omitted for brevity...

// Construct the DataSet object
DataSet m_ds = new DataSet("DynamicDS");

// Add a new table named "Order" to m_ds's collection tables
```

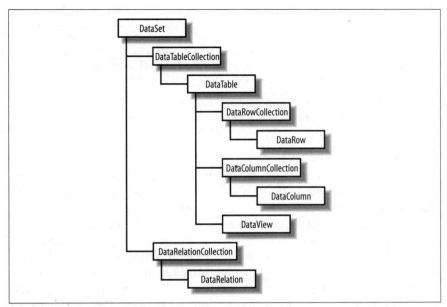

Figure 5-2. Important ADO.NET data objects, including DataSet

```
m_ds.Tables.Add ("Order");

// Add new columns to table "Order"
m_ds.Tables["Order"].Columns.Add("OrderID",
                                    Type.GetType("System.Int32"));
m_ds.Tables["Order"].Columns.Add("CustomerFirstName",
                                    Type.GetType("System.String"));
m_ds.Tables["Order"].Columns.Add("CustomerLastName",
                                    Type.GetType("System.String"));
m_ds.Tables["Order"].Columns.Add("Date",
                                    Type.GetType("System.DateTime"));

// Register the column "OrderID" as the primary key of table "Order"
DataColumn[] keys = new DataColumn[1];
keys[0] = m_ds.Tables["Order"].Columns["OrderID"];
m_ds.Tables["Order"].PrimaryKey = keys;

// Add a new table named "OrderDetail" to m_ds's collection of tables
m_ds.Tables.Add ("OrderDetail");

// Add new columns to table "OrderDetail"
m_ds.Tables["OrderDetail"].Columns.Add("fk_OrderID",
                                    Type.GetType("System.Int32"));
m_ds.Tables["OrderDetail"].Columns.Add("ProductCode",
                                    Type.GetType("System.String"));
m_ds.Tables["OrderDetail"].Columns.Add("Quantity",
                                    Type.GetType("System.Int32"));
```

```
m_ds.Tables["OrderDetail"].Columns.Add("Price",
                                        Type.GetType("System.Currency")));

// Get the DataColumn objects from two DataTable objects in a DataSet.
DataColumn parentCol = m_ds.Tables["Order"].Columns["OrderID"];
DataColumn childCol = m_ds.Tables["OrderDetail"].Columns["fk_OrderID"];

// Create and add the relation to the DataSet.
m_ds.Relations.Add(new DataRelation("Order_OrderDetail",
                                     parentCol,
                                     childCol));
m_ds.Relations["Order_OrderDetail"].Nested = true;
```

Let's highlight some important points in this block of code. After instantiating the DataSet object with the new operator, we add some tables with the Add method of the Tables object. We go through a similar process to add columns to each Table's Columns collection. Each of the added tables or columns can later be referenced by name. In order to assign the primary key for the Order table, we have to create the DataColumn array to hold one or more fields representing a key or a composite key. In this case, we have only a single key field, OrderID. We set the PrimaryKey property of the table to this array of key columns. For the relationship between the two tables, we first create the DataRelation called Order_OrderDetail with the two linking columns from the two tables, and then we add this DataRelation to the collection of relations of the DataSet. The last statement indicates that we want to represent the relationship between the Order and OrderDetail table as a nested structure. This makes dealing with these entities easier in XML.

The following block of C# code shows how to insert data into each of the two tables:

```
DataRow newRow;
newRow = m_ds.Tables["Order"].NewRow( );
newRow["OrderID"] = 101;
newRow["CustomerFirstName"] = "John";
newRow["CustomerLastName"] = "Doe";
newRow["Date"] = new DateTime(2001, 5, 1);;
m_ds.Tables["Order"].Rows.Add(newRow);
newRow = m_ds.Tables["Order"].NewRow( );
newRow["OrderID"] = 102;
newRow["CustomerFirstName"] = "Jane";
newRow["CustomerLastName"] = "Doe";
newRow["Date"] = new DateTime(2001, 4, 29);
m_ds.Tables["Order"].Rows.Add(newRow);

newRow = m_ds.Tables["OrderDetail"].NewRow( );
newRow["fk_OrderID"] = 101;
newRow["ProductCode"] = "Item-100";
newRow["Quantity"] = 7;
```

```
newRow["Price"] = "59.95";
m_ds.Tables["OrderDetail"].Rows.Add(newRow);

newRow = m_ds.Tables["OrderDetail"].NewRow( );
newRow["fk_OrderID"] = 101;
newRow["ProductCode"] = "Item-200";
newRow["Quantity"] = 1;
newRow["Price"] = "9.25";
m_ds.Tables["OrderDetail"].Rows.Add(newRow);

newRow = m_ds.Tables["OrderDetail"].NewRow( );
newRow["fk_OrderID"] = 102;
newRow["ProductCode"] = "Item-200";
newRow["Quantity"] = 3;
newRow["Price"] = "9.25";
m_ds.Tables["OrderDetail"].Rows.Add(newRow);
```

Tables and Relations are important properties of DataSet. Not only do they describe the structure of the in-memory database, but the DataTables inside the collection also hold the content of the DataSet.

XML and tables sets

Now that you have a DataSet filled with tables and relationships, let's see how this DataSet helps in interoperability. XML is the answer. The DataSet has a number of methods that integrate DataSet tightly with XML, thus making it universally interoperable. These methods are WriteXml(), WriteXmlSchema(), ReadXml(), and ReadXmlSchema().

WriteXmlSchema() dumps only the schema of the tables, including all tables and relationships between tables. WriteXml() can dump both the schema and table data as an XML encoded string. Both WriteXmlSchema() and WriteXml() accept a Stream, TextWriter, XmlWriter, or String representing a filename. WriteXml() accepts an XmlWriteMode as the second argument so you can optionally write the schema in addition to the data.

By default, WriteXml() writes only the data. To also write the schema, you will have to pass XmlWriteMode.WriteSchema as the second parameter to the call. You can also retrieve only the data portion of the XML by using the XmlWriteMode.IgnoreSchema property explicitly. Another mode that you can set is XmlWriteMode.DiffGram. In this DiffGram mode, the DataSet will be dumped out as both the original data and changed data. More on this topic when we get to the GetChanges() method of the DataSet.

The DataSet object also provides methods to reconstruct itself from an XML document. Use ReadXmlData() for reading XML data documents, and ReadXmlSchema() for reading XML schema documents.

The following code creates an XML document from the previously created dataset:

```
// Dump the previously shown DataSet to
// the console (and also to an XML file)
m_ds.WriteXml(Console.Out, XmlWriteMode.WriteSchema);
m_ds.WriteXml("DS_Orders.xml", XmlWriteMode.WriteSchema);

// Constructing a new DataSet object
DataSet ds2 = new DataSet("RestoredDS");
ds2.ReadXml("DS_Orders.xml");
```

Let's examine the resulting XML file and its representation of the dataset:

```
<?xml version="1.0" standalone="yes"?>
<DynamicDS>
  <xs:schema id="DynamicDS"
             xmlns=""
             xmlns:xs="http://www.w3.org/2001/XMLSchema"
             xmlns:msdata="urn:schemas-microsoft-com:xml-msdata">
    <xs:element name="DynamicDS" msdata:IsDataSet="true">

      <xs:complexType>
        <xs:choice maxOccurs="unbounded">

          <xs:element name="Order">
            <xs:complexType>
              <xs:sequence>
                <xs:element name="OrderID"
                            type="xs:int" />
                <xs:element name="CustomerFirstName"
                            type="xs:string" minOccurs="0" />
                <xs:element name="CustomerLastName"
                            type="xs:string" minOccurs="0" />
                <xs:element name="Date"
                            type="xs:dateTime" minOccurs="0" />

                <xs:element name="OrderDetail"
                            minOccurs="0" maxOccurs="unbounded">

                  <xs:complexType>
                    <xs:sequence>
                      <xs:element name="fk_OrderID"
                                  type="xs:int" minOccurs="0" />
                      <xs:element name="ProductCode"
                                  type="xs:string" minOccurs="0" />
                      <xs:element name="Quantity"
                                  type="xs:int" minOccurs="0" />
                      <xs:element name="Price"
                                  msdata:DataType="System.Currency,
                                  mscorlib, Version=1.0.3300.0,
                                  Culture=neutral,
```

```
                    PublicKeyToken=b77a5c561934e089"
                    type="xs:string" minOccurs="0" />
            </xs:sequence>
          </xs:complexType>

        </xs:element>

          </xs:sequence>
        </xs:complexType>
      </xs:element>

    </xs:choice>
    </xs:complexType>

    <xs:unique name="Constraint1"
              msdata:PrimaryKey="true">
      <xs:selector xpath=".//Order" />
      <xs:field xpath="OrderID" />
    </xs:unique>

    <xs:keyref name="Order_OrderDetail"
              refer="Constraint1"
              msdata:IsNested="true">
      <xs:selector xpath=".//OrderDetail" />
      <xs:field xpath="fk_OrderID" />
    </xs:keyref>

  </xs:element>
</xs:schema>

<... Data Portion ...>

</DynamicDS>
```

The root element is named DynamicDS because that is the name of the dataset
we created earlier. The xsd:schema tag contains all table and relationship definitions in this DynamicDS dataset. Because we've indicated that the relationship should be nested, the schema shows the xsd:element OrderDetail
nested within the xsd:element Order. All columns are also represented as
xsd:elements.

After the table definitions, the document holds definitions for various key
types. The xsd:unique element is used with msdata:PrimaryKey for keys, as
shown in the xsd:unique named Constraint1. The msdata:PrimaryKey
attribute makes this a primary key, which has the added effect of enforcing
uniqueness (every OrderID in the Order table must be unique).

The xsd:keyref element is used for foreign keys, as shown in the Order_
OrderDetail key that refers to the Constraint1 key. This links the OrderDetail and Order tables where OrderDetail.fk_OrderID = Order.OrderID.

Let's now look at the data portion of the XML file:

```
<Order>
    <OrderID>101</OrderID>
    <CustomerFirstName>John</CustomerFirstName>
    <CustomerLastName>Doe</CustomerLastName>
    <Date>2001-05-01T00:00:00.0000000-04:00</Date>
    <OrderDetail>
        <fk_OrderID>101</fk_OrderID>
        <ProductCode>Item-100</ProductCode>
        <Quantity>7</Quantity>
        <Price>59.95</Price>
    </OrderDetail>
    <OrderDetail>
        <fk_OrderID>101</fk_OrderID>
        <ProductCode>Item-200</ProductCode>
        <Quantity>1</Quantity>
        <Price>9.25</Price>
    </OrderDetail>
</Order>
<Order>
    <OrderID>102</OrderID>
    <CustomerFirstName>Jane</CustomerFirstName>
    <CustomerLastName>Doe</CustomerLastName>
    <Date>2001-04-29T00:00:00.0000000-04:00</Date>
    <OrderDetail>
        <fk_OrderID>102</fk_OrderID>
        <ProductCode>Item-200</ProductCode>
        <Quantity>3</Quantity>
        <Price>9.25</Price>
    </OrderDetail>
</Order>
```

This part of the XML document is fairly self-explanatory. For each row of data in the Order table, we end up with one record of type Order. This is the same for the OrderDetail table. The OrderDetail that relates to a particular Order is nested inside the Order element.

Because the dataset is inherently disconnected from its source, changes to the data inside the dataset have to be tracked by the dataset itself. This is done through the following methods: HasChanges(), GetChanges(), and Merge(). The application can check the changes to the dataset and then ask the DataAdapter object to reconcile the changes with the data source through the DataAdapter Update method.

The following block of code demonstrates how to the track and manage changes to a DataSet:

```
m_ds.AcceptChanges();
/* Make a change to the data set. */
m_ds.Tables["OrderDetail"].Rows[0]["Quantity"] = 12;
```

```
if(m_ds.HasChanges()){

    /* Get a copy of the data set containing the changes. */
    DataSet changeDS = m_ds.GetChanges();

    /* Dump the changed rows. */
    changeDS.WriteXml("ChangedDS.xml" , XmlWriteMode.DiffGram);

    /* Commit all changes. */
    m_ds.AcceptChanges();

}
```

Because we create this DataSet dynamically, we want to tell the DataSet to accept all changes made up to this point by first issuing an AcceptChange() call. Knowing that the DataSet should start tracking the changes again, we then change the quantity of one of the OrderDetail rows. Next we ask the dataset for all the changes and dump it into a new dataset called changeDS. This dataset results in the following XML dump when using DiffGram mode. Notice that because OrderDetail is a child of Order, the change also includes the parent row.

```
<?xml version="1.0" standalone="yes"?>
<diffgr:diffgram xmlns:msdata="urn:schemas-microsoft-com:xml-msdata"
                 xmlns:diffgr="urn:schemas-microsoft-com:xml-diffgram-v1">
  <DynamicDS>
    <Order diffgr:id="Order1" msdata:rowOrder="0">
      <OrderID>101</OrderID>
      <CustomerFirstName>John</CustomerFirstName>
      <CustomerLastName>Doe</CustomerLastName>
      <Date>2001-05-01T00:00:00.0000000-04:00</Date>
      <OrderDetail diffgr:id="OrderDetail1"
                   msdata:rowOrder="0" diffgr:hasChanges="modified">
        <fk_OrderID>101</fk_OrderID>
        <ProductCode>Item-100</ProductCode>
        <Quantity>12</Quantity>
        <Price>59.95</Price>
      </OrderDetail>
    </Order>
  </DynamicDS>

  <diffgr:before>
    <OrderDetail diffgr:id="OrderDetail1" msdata:rowOrder="0">
      <fk_OrderID>101</fk_OrderID>
      <ProductCode>Item-100</ProductCode>
      <Quantity>7</Quantity>
      <Price>59.95</Price>
    </OrderDetail>
  </diffgr:before>

</diffgr:diffgram>
```

We would like to emphasize that the DataSet object is the most important construct in ADO.NET. Because DataSet does not tie to an underlying representation such as SQL Server or Microsoft Access, it is extremely portable. Its data format is self-described in its schema, and its data is in pure XML. A DataSet is self-contained regardless of how it was created, whether by reading data from a SQL Server, from Microsoft Access, from an external XML file, or even by being dynamically generated as we have seen in an earlier example. This portable XML-based entity—without a doubt—should be the new standard for data exchange.

Enough said about DataSet. Let's drill down from DataSet to DataTable.

DataTable

DataTable represents a table of data and thus contains a collection of DataColumns as a Columns property and a collection of DataRows as a Rows property. The Columns property provides the structure of the table, while the Rows property provides access to actual row data. Fields in the table are represented as DataColumn objects, and table records are represented as DataRow objects. Here is some sample code that dumps the name of each column as a row of headers, followed by each row of data:

```
/* Walk the DataTable and display all column headers
 * along with all data rows.
 */
DataTable myTable = m_ds.Tables["OrderDetail"];

/* Display all column names. */
foreach(DataColumn c in myTable.Columns) {
  Console.Write(c.ColumnName + "\t");
}
Console.WriteLine(""); // newline

/* Process each row. */
foreach(DataRow r in myTable.Rows) {

  /* Display each column. */
  foreach(DataColumn c in myTable.Columns) {
    Console.Write(r[c] + "\t");
  }
  Console.WriteLine(""); // newline

}
```

Here is the output of that code:

fk_OrderID	ProductCode	Quantity	Price
101	Item-100	12	59.95
101	Item-200	1	9.25
102	Item-200	3	9.25

Typically, a DataTable has one or more fields serving as a primary key. This functionality is exposed as the PrimaryKey property. Because the primary key might contain more than one field, this property is an array of DataColumn objects. We revisit this excerpt of code here to put things in context. Note that in this example, the primary key consists of only one field, hence the array of size one.

```
// Register the column "OrderID" as the primary key of table "Order"
DataColumn[] keys = new DataColumn[1];
keys[0] = m_ds.Tables["Order"].Columns["OrderID"];
m_ds.Tables["Order"].PrimaryKey = keys;
```

Relations and constraints

Relations define how tables in a database relate to each other. The DataSet globally stores the collection of relations between tables in the Relations property; however, each of the tables participating in the relation also has to know about the relationship. ChildRelations and ParentRelations, two properties of the DataTable object, take care of this. ChildRelations enumerates all relations that this table participates in as a master table. ParentRelations, on the other hand, lists the relations in which this table acts as a slave table. We provide more information on the topic of relations when we explain the DataRelation object in an upcoming section of this chapter.

While we are on the topic of tables and relationships, it is important to understand how to set up constraint enforcements. There are two types of constraints that we can set up and enforce, UniqueConstraint and ForeignKeyConstraint. UniqueConstraint enforces the uniqueness of a field value for a table. ForeignKeyConstraint enforces rules on table relationships. For ForeignKeyConstraint, we can set up UpdateRule and DeleteRule to dictate how the application should behave upon performing update or delete on a row of data in the parent table.

Table 5-1 shows the constraint settings and behavior of ForeignKeyConstraint rules.

Table 5-1. Constraint types and behaviors

Setting	Behavior
None	Nothing.
Cascade	Dependent rows (identified by foreign key) are deleted/ updated when parent row is deleted/updated.
SetDefault	Foreign keys in dependent rows are set to the default value when parent row is deleted.
SetNull	Foreign keys in dependent rows are set to null value when parent row is deleted.

Constraints are activated only when the EnforceConstraint property of the DataSet object is set to true.

The following block of code shows how we have altered the foreign key constraint between the Order and OrderDetail tables to allow cascading deletion:

```
m_ds.Relations["Order_OrderDetail"].ChildKeyConstraint.DeleteRule =
    Rule.Cascade;

m_ds.WriteXml("DS_BeforeCascadeDelete.xml");
m_ds.Tables["Order"].Rows[0].Delete();
m_ds.WriteXml("DS_AfterCascadeDelete.xml");
```

As the result of running this code, the DataSet is left with only one order (order 102), which contains one line item.

DataView

The DataView object is similar to a *view* in conventional database programming. We can create different customized views of a DataTable, each with different sorting and filtering criteria. Through these different views, we can traverse, search, and edit individual records. This ADO.NET concept is the closest to the old ADO recordset. In ADO.NET, DataView serves another important role—data binding to Windows Forms and Web Forms. We show the usage of DataView when we discuss data binding on Windows Forms and Web Forms in Chapters 7 and 8.

DataRelation

A DataSet object as a collection of DataTable objects alone is not useful enough. A collection of DataTable objects returned by a server component provides little improvement upon the chained recordset in previous versions of ADO. In order for your client application to make the most of the returned tables, you also need to return the relations between these DataTables. This is where the DataRelation object comes into play.

With DataRelation, you can define relationships between the DataTable objects. Client components can inspect an individual table or navigate the hierarchy of tables through these relationships. For example, you can find a particular row in a parent table and then traverse all dependent rows in a child table.

The DataRelation contains the parent table name, the child table name, the parent table column (primary key), and the child table column (foreign key).

Because it has multiple DataTables and DataRelations within the DataSet, ADO.NET allows for a much more flexible environment where consumers of the data can choose to use the data in whichever way they wish.

One example might be the need to display all information about a particular parent table and all of its dependent rows in a child table. You have ten rows in the parent table. Each of the rows in the parent table has ten dependent rows in the child table. Let's consider two approaches to getting this data to the data consumer. First, we will just use a join in the query string:

```
Select
    Order.CustomerFirstName, Order.CustomerLastName, Order.OrderDate,
    OrderDetail.ProductCode, OrderDetail.Quantity, OrderDetail.Price
from
    Order, OrderDetail
        where Order.OrderID = OrderDetail.fk_OrderID
```

The result set contains 100 rows, in which each group of ten rows contains duplicate information about the parent row.

A second approach is to retrieve the list of rows from the parent table first, which would be ten rows:

```
Select
    Order.OrderID,
    Order.CustomerFirstName, Order.CustomerLastName, Order.OrderDate
from
    Order
```

Then for each of the ten rows in the parent table, you would retrieve the dependent rows from the child table:

```
Select
    OrderDetail.ProductCode, OrderDetail.Quantity, OrderDetail.Price
from
    OrderDetail where fk_OrderID = thisOrderID
```

This second approach is less of a resource hog since there is no redundant data; however, you end up making 11 round-trips (one time for the parent table, and 10 times for each parent of the child table).

It's better to get the parent table, the child table, and the relation between them using one round-trip, without all the redundant data. This is one of the biggest benefits that DataSet brings. The following block of code demonstrates the power of having tables and relationships:

```
/*
 * Given an order id, display a single order.
 */
public static void DisplaySingleOrder(DataSet m_ds, int iOrderID) {

    Decimal runningTotal = 0;
```

```
Decimal lineTotal = 0;
Decimal dPrice = 0;
int iQty = 0;

DataTable oTable = m_ds.Tables["Order"];

// Find an order from the Order table.
DataRow oRow = oTable.Rows.Find(iOrderID);

/* Navigate to the OrderDetail table
 * through the Order_Details relationship.
 */
DataRow[] arrRows = oRow.GetChildRows("Order_OrderDetail");

/* Display the order information. */
Console.WriteLine ("Order: {0}", iOrderID);
Console.WriteLine ("Name: {0} {1}",
                   oRow["CustomerFirstName"].ToString( ),
                   oRow["CustomerLastName"].ToString( ));
Console.WriteLine ("Date: {0}", oRow["Date"].ToString( ));
Console.WriteLine("--------------------------");


/*
 * Display and calculate line total for each item.
 */
for(int i = 0; i < arrRows.Length; i++)  {

   foreach(DataColumn myColumn in m_ds.Tables["OrderDetail"].Columns)
   {
     Console.Write(arrRows[i][myColumn] + " ");
   }

   iQty = System.Int32.Parse(arrRows[i]["Quantity"].ToString( ));
   dPrice = System.Decimal.Parse(arrRows[i]["Price"].ToString( ));

   lineTotal = iQty * dPrice;
   Console.WriteLine("{0}", lineTotal);

   /* Keep a running total. */
   runningTotal += lineTotal;
}

/* Display the total of the order. */
Console.WriteLine("Total: {0}", runningTotal);
}
```

DisplaySingleOrder finds a single row in the Order table with a given order ID. Once this row is found, we ask the row for an array of dependent rows from the OrderDetail table according to the Order_OrderDetail relationship. With the returned array of DataRows, we then proceed to display all fields in the row. We also calculate the lineTotal value based on the quantity ordered and the price of the item, as well as keeping a runningTotal for the whole order. The following shows the output from the DisplaySingleOrder function:

```
Order: 101
Name: John Doe
Date: 5/1/2001 12:00:00 AM
--------------------------
101 Item-100 12 59.95 719.4
101 Item-200 1 9.25 9.25
Total: 728.65
```

Managed Providers

Managed provider is a term used for a group of .NET components that implement a fixed set of functionality set forth by the ADO.NET architecture. This enforces a common interface for accessing data. In order to build our own managed provider, we must provide our own implementation of System.Data.Common.DbDataAdapter objects and implement interfaces such as IDbCommand, IDbConnection, and IDataReader. We are not building our own managed provider here; however, we do dive into each of these classes and interfaces in this section.

Most of the time, developers don't have to know how to implement managed providers, even though this might increase their productivity with regard to ADO.NET. Understanding how to use the stock managed providers alone is sufficient to develop your enterprise application. Microsoft provides two managed providers in its current release of ADO.NET: OLE DB and SQL. The OLE DB managed provider comes with OleDbConnection, OleDbCommand, OleDbParameter, and OleDbDataReader. The SQL Server managed provider comes with a similar set of objects, whose names start with SqlClient instead of OleDb, as illustrated in Figure 5-3. The implementation of this core function set for managed providers is packaged in the System.Data namespace. The implementation for the OLE DB managed provider is in System.Data.OleDb, and the SQL managed provider is in System.Data.SqlClient.

Both of the included managed providers implement a set of interfaces that access the appropriate data store. The OLE DB provider relies on OLE DB as an access layer to a broad variety of data sources, including Microsoft SQL Server. For performance reasons, the SQL provider uses a proprietary protocol to communicate directly with SQL Server. Regardless of how the data is obtained, the resulting dataset remains the same. This clean separation of managed providers and the XML-based dataset helps ADO.NET achieve portable data.

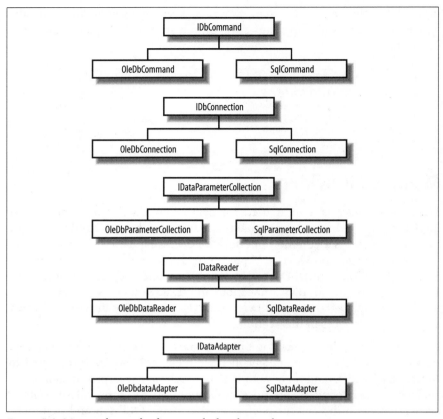

Figure 5-3. Managed provider framework class hierarchy

Figure 5-3 shows the base classes and the two implementations of managed provider: OLE DB and SQL. Because all managed providers, including OLE DB and SQL, adhere to a fixed, common set of interfaces (IDbCommand, IDBConnection, IDataParameterCollection, IDataReader, and IData-Adapter), you can easily adapt your application to switch managed providers as the need arises.

Connection

Both OleDbConnection and SqlConnection implement System.Data.IDb-Connection and thus inherit properties such as the connection string and the state of the connection. They implement the core set of methods specified by IDbConnection, including Open and Close.

Unlike the ADO Connection object, transaction support for the ADO.NET connection object has been moved to a Transaction object (such as

OleDbTransaction and SqlTransaction). The reason is that we cannot assume that the transaction scope is the same as the connection scope. For example, we can have transactions that overlap multiple connections. To create a new transaction, execute the BeginTransaction() method of the OleDbConnection or SqlConnection object. This returns an IDbTransaction implementation that supports transaction-oriented functionality such as Commit and Rollback. The SqlTransaction also supports saving checkpoints so that we can rollback to a specific checkpoint instead of rolling back the whole transaction. Table 5-2 lists the supported providers for OLE DB managed providers.

Table 5-2. ADO managed providers

Driver	Provider
SQLOLEDB	Microsoft OLE DB Provider for SQL Server
MSDAORA	Microsoft OLE DB Provider for Oracle
Microsoft.Jet.OLEDB.4.0	OLE DB Provider for Jet

Again, if you examine the list of methods that both OleDbConnection and SqlConnection support, you will find that the functionality is very much the same as the old ADO Connection object's. However, neither OleDb-Connection nor SqlConnection allows SQL statements or provider-specific text statements to be executed directly any more. In other words, Execute() is no longer supported by the Connection object. This is a better way for distributing functionality between classes. All execution is done through the Command object, which is discussed in the next section along with how to initiate a connection.

The Command and Data Reader Objects

Fortunately for ADO developers, ADO.NET's SqlCommand and OleDb-Command objects behave like ADO's Command object; however, the Command objects are the only way we can make execution requests to insert, update, and delete data in ADO.NET. This makes it easier to learn the object model. Developers are not faced with as many ways of doing the same things, as in the case (with ADO) of whether to execute the query through a Connection, Command, or even a Recordset object.

Command execution

All commands are associated with a connection object through the SqlCommand's or the OleDbCommand's Connection property. Think of the connection object as the pipeline between the data-reading component and the database back end. In order to execute a command, the active connection has to be opened. The command object also accepts parameters to execute a stored procedure at the back end. The top left of Figure 5-5 shows the relationships between command, connection, and parameters objects.

There are two types of execution. The first type is a query command, which returns an IDataReader implementation. It is implemented by the ExecuteReader( ) method. The second type of command typically performs an update, insert, or deletion of rows in a database table. This type of execution is implemented by the ExecuteNonQuery( ) method.

One of the main differences between ADO.NET's Command objects and ADO's Command object is the return data. In ADO, the result of executing a query command is a recordset, which contains the return data in tabular form. In ADO.NET, however, recordsets are no longer supported. The result of executing a query command is now a data reader object (see the following section). This data reader object can be an OleDbDataReader for OLE DB, SqlDataReader for SQL Server, or any class implementing the IDataReader for custom reading needs. Once you've obtained a valid data reader object, you can perform a Read operation on it to get to your data.

Employing the command, connection, and data reader objects is a low-level, direct way to work with the managed provider. As you will find out a little later, the data adapter encapsulates all this low-level plumbing as a more direct way to get the data from the data source to your disconnected dataset.

The data reader object

The data reader is a brand new concept to ADO developers, but it is straightforward. A data reader is similar to a stream object in object-oriented programming (OOP). If you need to access records in a forward-only, sequential order, use a data reader because it is very efficient. Since this is a server-side cursor, the connection to the server is open throughout the reading of data. Because of this continually open connection, we recommend that you exercise this option with care and not have the data reader linger around longer than it should. Otherwise, it might affect the scalability of your application.

The following code demonstrates basic use of OleDbConnection, OleDb-Command, and OleDbDataReader. Though we're using the OLE DB managed provider here, the connection string is very similar to the one we used earlier for ADO.*

```
using System;
using System.Data;
```

---

* In addition, you can create a Command object from the current connection by using this instead: oCmd = oConn.CreateCommand( );.

```
using System.Data.OleDb;

public class pubsdemo {

  public static void Main( ) {

    /* An OLE DB connection string. */
    String sConn =
      "provider=sqloledb;server=(local);database=pubs; Integrated
Security=SSPI";

    /* An SQL statement. */
    String sSQL = "select au_fname, au_lname, phone from authors";

    /* Create and open a new connection. */
    OleDbConnection oConn = new OleDbConnection(sConn);
    oConn.Open( );

    /* Create a new command and execute the SQL statement. */
    OleDbCommand oCmd = new OleDbCommand(sSQL, oConn);
    OleDbDataReader oReader = oCmd.ExecuteReader( );

    /* Find the index of the columns we're interested in. */
    int idxFirstName = oReader.GetOrdinal("au_fname");
    int idxLastName = oReader.GetOrdinal("au_lname");
    int idxPhone = oReader.GetOrdinal("phone");

    /* Retrieve and display each column using their column index. */
    while(oReader.Read( )) {
      Console.WriteLine("{0} {1} {2}",
                        oReader.GetValue(idxFirstName),
                        oReader.GetValue(idxLastName),
                        oReader.GetValue(idxPhone));
    }

  }
}
```

The code opens a connection to the local SQL Server (using integrated security*) and issues a query for first name, last name, and phone number from
the authors table in the pubs database. If you don't have the pubs database
installed on your system, you can load and run *instpubs.sql* in Query Analyzer (*instpubs.sql* can be found under the *MSSQL\Install* directory on your
machine). For those that install the VS.NET Quickstart examples, change

---

* Please be aware that database connection pooling relies on the uniqueness of the connection
  strings. When using the integrated security model of SQL Server, if you make the data access code
  run under the security context of each of the logged-in users, database connection pooling will
  suffer. You must create a small set of Windows accounts to overcome this problem; we don't discuss security in great depth in this book, due to its compact size.

the server parameter of the connection string to server=(local)\\NetSDK because the Quickstart examples installation lays down the NetSDK SQL Server instance that also include the infamous Pubs database. The following example uses SqlClient to get the same information:

```
using System;
using System.Data;
using System.Data.SqlClient;

public class pubsdemo {

  public static void Main( ) {

    /* A SQL Server connection string. */
    String sConn = "server=(local);database=pubs;Integrated Security=SSPI";

    /* An SQL statement. */
    String sSQL = "select au_fname, au_lname, phone from authors";

    /* Create and open a new connection. */
    SqlConnection oConn = new SqlConnection(sConn);
    oConn.Open( );

    /* Create a new command and execute the SQL statement. */
    SqlCommand oCmd = new SqlCommand(sSQL, oConn);
    SqlDataReader oReader = oCmd.ExecuteReader( );

    /* Find the index of the columns we're interested in. */
    int idxFirstName = oReader.GetOrdinal("au_fname");
    int idxLastName = oReader.GetOrdinal("au_lname");
    int idxPhone = oReader.GetOrdinal("phone");

    /* Retrieve and display each column using their column index. */
    while(oReader.Read( )) {
      Console.WriteLine("{0} {1} {2}",
                        oReader.GetValue(idxFirstName),
                        oReader.GetValue(idxLastName),
                        oReader.GetValue(idxPhone));
    }

  }
}
```

The DataAdapter Object

Along with the introduction of data reader, ADO.NET also brings the Data-Adapter object, which acts as the bridge between the data source and the disconnected DataSet. It contains a connection and a number of commands for retrieving the data from the data store into one DataTable in the DataSet and updating the data in the data store with the changes currently cached in the DataSet. Even though each DataAdapter maps only one DataTable in the DataSet, you can have multiple adapters to fill the DataSet object with multiple DataTables. The class hierarchy of DataAdapter is shown in Figure 5-4. Both OleDbDataAdapter and SqlDataAdapter are derived from DbDataAdapter, which in is in turn derived from DataAdapter abstract class. This DataAdapter abstract class implements the IDataAdapter interface, which specifies that it support Fill and Update. IDataAdapter is specified in the System.Data namespace, as is the DataSet itself.

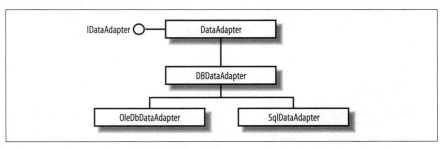

Figure 5-4. DataSetCommand class hierarchy

OleDbDataAdapter and SqlDataAdapter can fill a DataSet with rows and update the data source when you make changes to the dataset. For example, you can use OleDbAdapter to move data from an OLE DB provider into a DataSet using the OleDbDataAdapter.Fill() method. Then you can modify the DataSet and commit the changes you made to the underlying database using the OleDbDataAdapter.Update() method. SqlDataAdapter supports the same methods. These adapters act as the middleman bridging the data between the database back end and the disconnected DataSet.

For data retrieval, a data adapter uses the SQL SELECT command (exposed as the SelectCommand property). This SELECT command is used in the implementation of the IDataAdapter interface's Fill method. For updating data, a data adapter uses the SQL UPDATE, INSERT, and DELETE commands (exposed as the UpdateCommand, InsertCommand, and DeleteCommand properties).

Along with the Fill and Update methods from DbDataAdapter class, both OleDbDataAdapter and SqlDataAdapter also inherit the TableMappings property, a collection of TableMapping objects that enable the mapping of actual database column names to user-friendly column names. This further isolates the DataSet from the source where the actual data comes from. Even table names and column names can be mapped to more readable names, making it easier to use the DataSet. The application developer can be more productive at what he does best, which is to implement business logic and not to decipher cryptic database column names. Figure 5-5 shows the relationship between managed provider components.

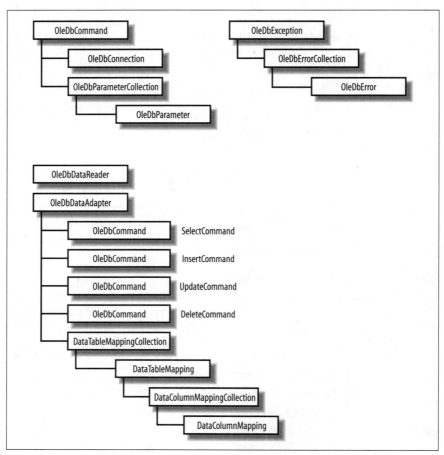

Figure 5-5. OleDbDataAdapter and supporting classes

Out of the four commands in the IDbDataAdapter object, only the SELECT command is required. The rest of the commands are optional since they can be generated automatically by the system. However, the auto-generation of these commands only works when certain conditions are met. For example, if your data adapter fills the data set from some database view that includes more than one table, you will have to explicitly define all four commands. Another example is when your adapter does not return key fields from the table, the system won't be able to generate the insert, update, or delete command. A typical usage of the data adapter involves the following steps:

- Create a data-adapter object (OleDbDataAdapter or SqlDataAdapter)
- Set up the query string for the internal SelectCommand object
- Set up the connection string for the SelectCommand's Connection object
- Set up the InsertCommand, UpdateCommand, or DeleteCommand query strings and connections (Recommended)
- Call Fill() to fill the given dataset with the results from the query string
- Make changes and call the adapter's Update() method with the changed DataSet (Optional)

The following block of code demonstrates these steps:

```
static DataSet GenerateDS() {

    /* Create the DataSet object. */
    DataSet ds = new DataSet("DBDataSet");
    String sConn =
        "provider=SQLOLEDB;server=(local);database=pubs; Integrated
Security=SSPI ";

    /* Create the DataSet adapters. */
    OleDbDataAdapter dsAdapter1 =
        new OleDbDataAdapter("select * from authors", sConn);

    OleDbDataAdapter dsAdapter2 =
        new OleDbDataAdapter("select * from titles", sConn);

    OleDbDataAdapter dsAdapter3 =
        new OleDbDataAdapter("select * from titleauthor", sConn);

    /* Fill the data set with three tables. */
    dsAdapter1.Fill(ds, "authors");
    dsAdapter2.Fill(ds, "titles");
    dsAdapter3.Fill(ds, "titleauthor");

    // Add the two relations between the three tables. */
    ds.Relations.Add("authors2titleauthor",
                    ds.Tables["authors"].Columns["au_id"],
                    ds.Tables["titleauthor"].Columns["au_id"]);

    ds.Relations.Add("titles2titleauthor",
                    ds.Tables["titles"].Columns["title_id"],
                    ds.Tables["titleauthor"].Columns["title_id"]);

    // Return the DataSet
    return ds;

}
```

This is a demonstration of constructing a dataset with three tables from the sample *pubs* database. The DataSet also contains two relationships that tie the three tables together. Let's take a look at the dataset in XML by trying out the next couple lines of code:

```
DataSet ds = GenerateDS( );
ds.WriteXml("DBDataSet.xml", XmlWriteMode.WriteSchema);
```

The content of *DBDataSet.xml* (with some omission for brevity) is shown next:

```
<?xml version="1.0" standalone="yes"?>
<DBDataSet>
  <xsd:schema id="DBDataSet" targetNamespace="" xmlns=""
              xmlns:xsd="http://www.w3.org/2001/XMLSchema"
              xmlns:msdata="urn:schemas-microsoft-com:xml-msdata">
    <xsd:element name="DBDataSet" msdata:IsDataSet="true">
      <xsd:complexType>
        <xsd:choice maxOccurs="unbounded">

          <xsd:element name="authors">
            <xsd:complexType>
              <xsd:sequence>
                <!-- columns simplified for brevity -->
                <xsd:element name="au_id" type="xsd:string" />
                <xsd:element name="au_lname" type="xsd:string" />
                <xsd:element name="au_fname" type="xsd:string" />
                <xsd:element name="phone" type="xsd:string" />
                <xsd:element name="address" type="xsd:string" />
                <xsd:element name="city" type="xsd:string" />
                <xsd:element name="state" type="xsd:string" />
                <xsd:element name="zip" type="xsd:string" />
                <xsd:element name="contract" type="xsd:boolean" />
              </xsd:sequence>
            </xsd:complexType>
          </xsd:element>

          <!-- titles and titleauthor omitted for brevity -->

        </xsd:choice>
      </xsd:complexType>

      <xsd:unique name="Constraint1">
        <xsd:selector xpath=".//authors" />
        <xsd:field xpath="au_id" />
      </xsd:unique>

      <xsd:unique name="titles_Constraint1"
                  msdata:ConstraintName="Constraint1">
        <xsd:selector xpath=".//titles" />
        <xsd:field xpath="title_id" />
      </xsd:unique>

      <xsd:keyref name="titles2titleauthor"
                  refer="titles_Constraint1">
```

```
      <xsd:selector xpath=".//titleauthor" />
      <xsd:field xpath="title_id" />
    </xsd:keyref>

    <xsd:keyref name="authors2titleauthor"
                refer="Constraint1">
      <xsd:selector xpath=".//titleauthor" />
      <xsd:field xpath="au_id" />
    </xsd:keyref>

  </xsd:element>
</xsd:schema>

<!-- Most rows removed for brevity -->

<authors>
  <au_id>899-46-2035</au_id>
  <au_lname>Ringer</au_lname>
  <au_fname>Anne</au_fname>
  <phone>801 826-0752</phone>
  <address>67 Seventh Av.</address>
  <city>Salt Lake City</city>
  <state>UT</state>
  <zip>84152</zip>
  <contract>true</contract>
</authors>

<titles>
  <title_id>PS2091</title_id>
  <title>Is Anger the Enemy?</title>
  <type>psychology  </type>
  <pub_id>0736</pub_id>
  <price>10.95</price>
  <advance>2275</advance>
  <royalty>12</royalty>
  <ytd_sales>2045</ytd_sales>
  <notes>Carefully researched study of the effects of strong
  emotions on the body. Metabolic charts included.</notes>
  <pubdate>1991-06-15T00:00:00.0000</pubdate>
</titles>
  <title_id>MC3021</title_id>
  <title>The Gourmet Microwave</title>
  <type>mod_cook</type>
  <pub_id>0877</pub_id>
  <price>2.99</price>
  <advance>15000</advance>
  <royalty>24</royalty>
  <ytd_sales>22246</ytd_sales>
  <notes>Traditional French gourmet recipes adapted for modern
  microwave cooking.</notes>
  <pubdate>1991-06-18T00:00:00.0000</pubdate>
</titles>
```

```
<titleauthor>
  <au_id>899-46-2035</au_id>
  <title_id>MC3021</title_id>
  <au_ord>2</au_ord>
  <royaltyper>25</royaltyper>
</titleauthor>
<titleauthor>
  <au_id>899-46-2035</au_id>
  <title_id>PS2091</title_id>
  <au_ord>2</au_ord>
  <royaltyper>50</royaltyper>
</titleauthor>

</DBDataSet>
```

The tables are represented as `<xsd:element name="table name">...</xsd:element>` tag pairs that contain column definitions. In addition to one xsd:element for each table, we have one xsd:unique for each key and one xsd:keyref for each relationship. The xsd:unique specifies the key of the parent table in a relationship. The tag xsd:keyref is used for child tables in a relationship. This xsd:keyref serves as the foreign key and refers to the key in the parent table.

For brevity, we've stripped down the data portion of the XML to contain just one author, `Anne Ringer`, and two books she authored.

We can have many different DataAdapters populating the DataSet. Each of these DataAdapters can be going against a completely different data source or data server. In other words, you can construct a DataSet object filled with data that is distributed across multiple servers. In the previous example, we have three different DataAdapters; however, all of them are going to the same server.

DataSets and XML

XML has rapidly gained popularity. Enterprise applications are using XML as the main data format for data exchanges.

ADO.NET breaks away from the COM-based recordset and employs XML as its transport data format. Because XML is platform independent, ADO.NET extends the reach to include anyone who is able to encode/decode XML. This is a big advantage over ADO because a COM-based recordset is not platform independent.

XML parsers

Even though XML is text-based and readable by humans, you still should have some way of programmatically reading, inspecting, and changing XML.

This is the job of XML parsers. There are two kinds of XML parsers: tree-based and stream-based. Depending on your needs, these two types of parsers should complement each other and serve you well.

Tree-based XML parsers read the XML file (or stream) in its entirety to construct a tree of XML nodes. Think of these XML nodes as your XML tag:

```
<car>
  <vin>VI00000383148374</vin>
  <make>Acura</make>
  <model>Integra</model>
  <year>1995</year>
</car>
```

When parsed into a tree, this information would have one root node: car; under car, there are four nodes: vin, make, model, and year. As you might have suspected, if the XML stream is very large in nature, then a tree-based XML parser might not be a good idea. The tree would be too large and consume a lot of memory.

A Stream-based XML parser reads the XML stream as it goes. SAX (Simple API for XML) is a specification for this kind of parsing. The parser raises events as it reads the data, notifying the application of the tag or text the parser just read. It does not attempt to create the complete tree of all XML nodes as does the tree-based parser. Therefore, memory consumption is minimal. This kind of XML parser is ideal for going through large XML files to look for small pieces of data. The .NET framework introduces another stream-based XML parser: the XmlReader. While SAX pushes events at the application as it reads the data, the XmlReader allows the application to pull data from the stream.

Microsoft implements both types of parsers in its XML parser. Because XML is so powerful, Microsoft, among other industry leaders, incorporates XML usage in almost all the things they do. That includes, but is not limited to, the following areas:

- XML+HTTP in SOAP
- XML+SQL in SQL2000
- XML in BizTalk
- XML+DataSet in ADO.NET
- XML in Web Services and Web Services Discovery (DISCO) (see Chapter 6)

In this chapter, we will discuss XML+Dataset in ADO.NET, and XML in Web Services will be examined in the next chapter. Because XML is used everywhere in the .NET architecture, we also provide a high-level survey of the XML classes.

XML Classes

To understand the tree-based Microsoft XML parser, which supports the Document Object Model (DOM Level 2 Core standard), there are only a handful of objects you should know:

- XmlNode and its derivatives
- XmlNodeList, as collection XmlNode
- XmlNamedNodeMap, as a collection of XmlAttribute

We will walk through a simple XML example to see how XML nodes are mapped into these objects in the XML DOM.

XmlNode and its derivatives

XmlNode is a base class that represents a single node in the XML document. In the object model, almost everything derives from XmlNode. This includes: XmlAttribute, XmlDocument, XmlElement, and XmlText, among other XML node types.

The following XML excerpt demonstrates mapping of XML tags to the node types in the DOM tree:

```
<books>
    <book category="How To">
        <title>How to drive in DC metropolitan</title>
        <author>Jack Daniel</author>
        <price>19.95</price>
    </book>
    <book category="Fiction">
        <title>Bring down the fence</title>
        <author>Jack Smith</author>
        <price>9.95</price>
    </book>
</books>
```

After parsing this XML stream, you end up with the tree depicted in Figure 5-6. It contains one root node, which is just a derivative of XmlNode. This root node is of type XmlDocument. Under this books root node, you have two children, also derivatives of XmlNode. This time, they are of type XmlElement. Under each book element node, there are four children. The first child is category. This category node is of type XmlAttribute, a derivative of XmlNode. The next three children are of type XmlElement: title, author, and price. Each of these elements has one child of type XmlText.

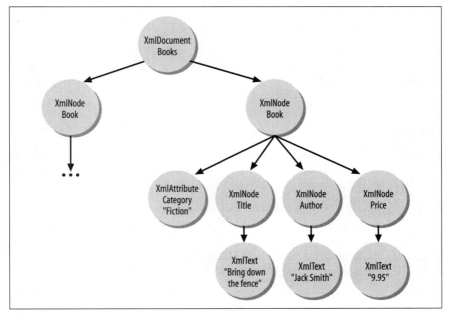

Figure 5-6. Tree representation of the XML document

As a base class, XmlNode supports a number of methods that aid in the constructing of the XML document tree. These methods include: AppendChild(), PrependChild(), InsertBefore(), InsertAfter(), and Clone().

XmlNode also supports a group of properties that aid in navigation within the XML document tree. These properties include: FirstChild, NextSibling, PreviousSibling, LastChild, ChildNodes, and ParentNode. You can use the ChildNodes property to navigate down from the root of the tree. For traversing backward, use the ParentNode property from any node on the tree.

XmlNodeList

Just as an XmlNode represents a single XML element, XmlNodeList represents a collection of zero or more XmlNodes. The ChildNodes property of the XmlNode is of type XmlNodeList. Looking at the root node books, we see that its ChildNodes property would be a collection of two XmlNodes. XmlNodeList supports enumeration, so we can iterate over the collection to get to each of the XmlNode objects. We can also index into the collection through a zero-based index.

Each of the book XmlElement objects would have a ChildNodes collection that iterates over title, author, and price XmlElements.

XmlNamedNodeMap

Similar to XmlNodeList, XmlNamedNodeMap is also a collection object. XmlNamedNodeMap is a collection of XmlAttribute objects that enable both enumeration and indexing of attributes by name. Each XmlNode has a property named Attributes. In the case of the book elements, these collections contain only one attribute, which is category.

XmlDocument

In addition to all methods and properties supported by XmlNode, this derivative of XmlNode adds or restricts methods and properties. Here, we inspect only XmlDocument as an example of a derivative of XmlNode.

XmlDocument extends XmlNode and adds a number of helper functions. These helper functions are used to create other types of XmlNodes such as XmlAttribute, XmlComment, XmlElement, and XmlText. In addition to allowing for the creation of other XML node types, XmlDocument also provides the mechanism to load and save XML contents.

The following code demonstrates how an XmlDocument is programmatically generated with DOM:

```
using System;
using System.Xml;

public class XmlDemo {

  public static void Main( ) {

    // Code to demonstrate creating of XmlDocument programmatically
    XmlDocument xmlDom = new XmlDocument( );
    xmlDom.AppendChild(xmlDom.CreateElement("", "books", ""));
    XmlElement xmlRoot = xmlDom.DocumentElement;
    XmlElement xmlBook;
    XmlElement xmlTitle, xmlAuthor, xmlPrice;
    XmlText xmlText;

    xmlBook= xmlDom.CreateElement("", "book", "");
    xmlBook.SetAttribute("category", "", "How To");

    xmlTitle = xmlDom.CreateElement("", "title", "");
    xmlText = xmlDom.CreateTextNode("How to drive in DC metropolitan");
    xmlTitle.AppendChild(xmlText);
    xmlBook.AppendChild(xmlTitle);

    xmlAuthor = xmlDom.CreateElement("", "author", "");
    xmlText = xmlDom.CreateTextNode("Jack Daniel");
    xmlAuthor.AppendChild(xmlText);
    xmlBook.AppendChild(xmlAuthor);
```

```
xmlPrice = xmlDom.CreateElement("", "price", "");
xmlText = xmlDom.CreateTextNode("19.95");
xmlPrice.AppendChild(xmlText);
xmlBook.AppendChild(xmlPrice);

xmlRoot.AppendChild(xmlBook);

xmlBook= xmlDom.CreateElement("", "book", "");
xmlBook.SetAttribute("category", "", "Fiction");

xmlTitle = xmlDom.CreateElement("", "title", "");
xmlText = xmlDom.CreateTextNode("Bring down the fence");
xmlTitle.AppendChild(xmlText);
xmlBook.AppendChild(xmlTitle);

xmlAuthor = xmlDom.CreateElement("", "author", "");
xmlText = xmlDom.CreateTextNode("Jack Smith");
xmlAuthor.AppendChild(xmlText);
xmlBook.AppendChild(xmlAuthor);

xmlPrice = xmlDom.CreateElement("", "price", "");
xmlText = xmlDom.CreateTextNode("9.95");
xmlPrice.AppendChild(xmlText);
xmlBook.AppendChild(xmlPrice);

xmlRoot.AppendChild(xmlBook);

Console.WriteLine(xmlDom.InnerXml);

    }

}
```

The XmlDocument also supports LoadXml and Load methods, which build
the whole XML tree from the input parameter. LoadXml takes a string in
XML format, whereas Load can take a filename, a TextReader, or an Xml-
Reader. The following example continues where the previous one left off.
The XML tree is saved to a file named *books.xml*. Then this file is loaded
back into a different XML tree. This new tree outputs the same XML stream
as the previous one:

```
...
xmlDom.Save("books.xml");
XmlDocument xmlDom2 = new XmlDocument();
xmlDom2.Load("books.xml");
Console.WriteLine(xmlDom2.InnerXml);
```

XmlReader

The XmlReader object is a fast, noncached, forward-only way of accessing
streamed XML data. There are two derivatives of XmlReader: XmlTextReader

and XmlNodeReader. Both of these readers read XML one tag at a time. The only difference between the two is the input to each reader. As the name implies, XmlTextReader reads a stream of pure XML text. XmlNodeReader reads a stream of nodes from an XmlDocument. The stream can start at the beginning of the XML file for the whole XmlDocument or only at a specific node of the XmlDocument for partial reading.

Consider the following XML excerpt for order processing. If this file is large, it is not reasonable to load it into an XmlDocument and perform parsing on it. Instead, we should read only nodes or attributes we are interesting in and ignore the rest. We can use XmlReader derived classes to do so.

```
<Orders>
<Order id="ABC001" ...>
<Item code="101" qty="3" price="299.00" ...>17in Monitor</Item>
<Item code="102" qty="1" price="15.99" ...>Keyboard</Item>
<Item code="103" qty="2" price="395.95" ...>CPU</Item>
</Order>
<Order id="ABC002" ...>
<Item code="101b" qty="1" price="499.00" ...>21in Monitor</Item>
<Item code="102" qty="1" price="15.99" ...>Keyboard</Item>
</Order>
<...>
</Orders>
```

The following block of code traverses and processes each order from the large Orders.xml input file:

```csharp
using System;
using System.IO;
using System.Xml;

class TestXMLReader
{

static void Main(string[] args)
{
    TestXMLReader tstObj = new TestXMLReader( );
    StreamReader myStream = new StreamReader("Orders.xml");
    XmlTextReader xmlTxtRdr = new XmlTextReader(myStream);
    while(xmlTxtRdr.Read( ))
    {
        if(xmlTxtRdr.NodeType == XmlNodeType.Element
            && xmlTxtRdr.Name == "Order")
        {
            tstObj.ProcessOrder(xmlTxtRdr);
        }
    }
}

public void ProcessOrder(XmlTextReader reader)
{
```

```
Console.WriteLine("Start processing order: " +
                reader.GetAttribute("id"));
while(!(reader.NodeType == XmlNodeType.EndElement
    && reader.Name == "Order")
    && reader.Read())
{
    // Process Content of Order
    if(reader.NodeType == XmlNodeType.Element
        && reader.Name == "Item")
    {
        Console.WriteLine("itemcode:" + reader.GetAttribute("code") +
                        ". Qty: " + reader.GetAttribute("qty"));
    }
}
}

}
```

Let's take a closer look at what is going on. Once we have established the XmlTextReader object with the stream of data from the string, all we have to do is loop through and perform a Read() operation until there is nothing else to read. While we are reading, we start to process the order only when we come across a node of type XmlElement and a node named Order. Inside the ProcessOrder function, we read and process all items inside an order until we encounter the end tag of Order. In this case, we return from the function and go back to looking for the next Order tag to process the next order.

XmlNodeReader is similar to XmlTextReader because they both allow processing of XML sequentially. However, XmlNodeReader reads XML nodes from a complete or fragment of an XML tree. This means XmlNodeReader is not helpful when processing large XML files.

XmlWriter

The XmlWriter object is a fast, noncached way of writing streamed XML data. It also supports namespaces. The only derivative of XmlWriter is XmlTextWriter.

XmlWriter supports namespaces by providing a number of overloaded functions that take a namespace to associate with the element. If this namespace is already defined and there is an existing prefix, XmlWriter automatically writes the element name with the defined prefix. Almost all element-writing methods are overloaded to support namespaces.

The following code shows how to use an XmlTextWriter object to write a valid XML file:

```
XmlTextWriter writer =
    new XmlTextWriter("test.xml", new System.Text.ASCIIEncoding());
writer.Formatting = Formatting.Indented;
```

```
writer.Indentation = 4;
writer.WriteStartDocument( );
writer.WriteComment("Comment");
writer.WriteStartElement("ElementName", "myns");
writer.WriteStartAttribute("prefix", "attrName", "myns");
writer.WriteEndAttribute( );
writer.WriteElementString("ElementName", "myns", "value");
writer.WriteEndElement( );
writer.WriteEndDocument( );
writer.Flush( );
writer.Close( );
```

This produces the following XML document in *test.xml*:

```
<?xml version="1.0" encoding="us-ascii"?>
<!--Comment-->
<ElementName prefix:attrName="" xmlns:prefix="myns" xmlns="myns">
    <prefix:ElementName>value</prefix:ElementName>
</ElementName>
```

XslTransform

XslTransform converts XML from one format to another. It is typically used in data-conversion programs or to convert XML to HTML for the purpose of presenting XML data in a browser. The following code demonstrates how such a conversion takes place:

```
using System;
using System.Xml;          // XmlTextWriter
using System.Xml.Xsl;      // XslTransform
using System.Xml.XPath;    // XPathDocument
using System.IO;           // StreamReader

public class XSLDemo {
  public static void Main( ) {
    XslTransform xslt = new XslTransform( );
    xslt.Load("XSLTemplate.xsl");
    XPathDocument xDoc = new XPathDocument("Books.xml");
    XmlTextWriter writer = new XmlTextWriter("Books.html", null);
    xslt.Transform(xDoc, null, writer);
    writer.Close( );
    StreamReader stream = new StreamReader("Books.html");
    Console.Write(stream.ReadToEnd( ));
  }
}
```

The code basically transforms the XML in the *Books.xml* file, which we've seen earlier, into HTML to be displayed in a browser. Even though you can replace the XPathDocument with XmlDocument in the previous code, XPathDocument is the preferred class in this case because it is optimized for

XSLT processing.* Figure 5-7 and Figure 5-8 show the source XML and the output HTML when viewed in a browser.

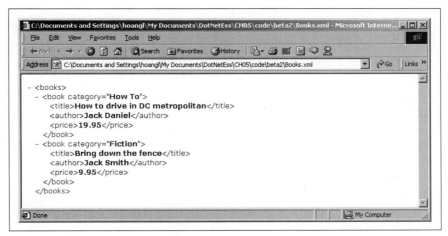

Figure 5-7. Books.xml shown in IE

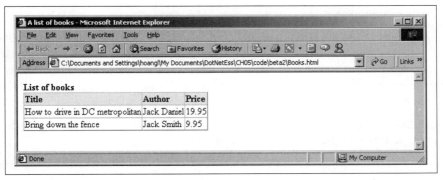

Figure 5-8. Books.html shown in IE

The template XSL file that was used to transform the XML is as follows:

```
<xsl:stylesheet version="1.0"
  xmlns:xsl="http://www.w3.org/1999/XSL/Transform">
<xsl:template match = "/" >

<html>
<head><title>A list of books</title></head>
<style>
.hdr { background-color=#ffeedd; font-weight=bold; }
```

---

* XPathDocument loads data faster than XmlDocument because it does not maintain node identity and it does not perform rule checking. One catch to this advantage is that the content is read-only.

```
  </style>
  <body>
  <B>List of books</B>
  <table style="border-collapse:collapse" border="1">
  <tr>
    <td class="hdr">Title</td>
    <td class="hdr">Author</td>
    <td class="hdr">Price</td>
  </tr>
  <xsl:for-each select="//books/book">
  <tr>
    <td><xsl:value-of select="title"/></td>
    <td><xsl:value-of select="author"/></td>
    <td><xsl:value-of select="price"/></td>
  </tr>
  </xsl:for-each>
  </table>
  </body>
  </html>

  </xsl:template>
  </xsl:stylesheet>
```

XmlDataDocument

One of the most important points in ADO.NET is the tight integration of
DataSet with XML. DataSet can easily be streamed into XML and vice versa,
making it easy to exchange data with any other components in the enterprise system. The schema of the DataSet can be loaded and saved as XML
Schema Definition (XSD), as described earlier.

XmlDataDocument can be associated with DataSet. The following code
excerpt illustrates how such an association takes place:

```
using System;
using System.Data;
using System.Data.OleDb;
using System.Xml;

class TestXMLDataDocument
{

static void Main(string[] args)
{
    TestXMLDataDocument tstObj = new TestXMLDataDocument();

    // construct the XmlDataDocument with the DataSet
    XmlDataDocument doc = tstObj.GenerateXmlDataDocument();

    XmlNodeReader myXMLReader = new XmlNodeReader(doc);
    while (myXMLReader.Read())
    {
```

```
        if(myXMLReader.NodeType == XmlNodeType.Element
            && myXMLReader.Name == "Orders")
        {
            tstObj.ProcessOrder(myXMLReader);
        }
    }
}

public void ProcessOrder(XmlNodeReader reader)
{
    Console.Write("Start processing order: ");
    while(!(reader.NodeType == XmlNodeType.EndElement
        && reader.Name == "Orders")
        && reader.Read())
    {
        if(reader.NodeType == XmlNodeType.Element
            && reader.Name == "OrderID")
        {
            reader.Read();
            Console.WriteLine(reader.Value);
        }
        if(reader.NodeType == XmlNodeType.Element
            && reader.Name == "OrderDetails")
        {
            ProcessLine(reader);
        }
    }
}

public void ProcessLine(XmlNodeReader reader)
{
    while(!(reader.NodeType == XmlNodeType.EndElement
        && reader.Name == "OrderDetails")
        && reader.Read())
    {
        if(reader.NodeType == XmlNodeType.Element && reader.Name ==
"ProductID")
        {
            reader.Read();
            Console.Write(".  ItemCode: " + reader.Value);
        }
        if(reader.NodeType == XmlNodeType.Element && reader.Name ==
"Quantity")
        {
            reader.Read();
            Console.WriteLine(".  Quantity: " + reader.Value);
        }
    }
}
public XmlDataDocument GenerateXmlDataDocument()
{
    /* Create the DataSet object. */
    DataSet ds = new DataSet("DBDataSet");
```

```
String sConn =
    "provider=SQLOLEDB;server=(local);database=NorthWind;Integrated
Security=SSPI";

/* Create the DataSet adapters. */
OleDbDataAdapter dsAdapter1 =
    new OleDbDataAdapter("select * from Orders", sConn);

OleDbDataAdapter dsAdapter2 =
    new OleDbDataAdapter("select * from [Order Details]", sConn);

/* Fill the data set with three tables. */
dsAdapter1.Fill(ds, "Orders");
dsAdapter2.Fill(ds, "OrderDetails");

DataColumn[] keys = new DataColumn[1];
keys[0] = ds.Tables["Orders"].Columns["OrderID"];
ds.Tables["Orders"].PrimaryKey = keys;


// Add the two relations between the three tables. */
ds.Relations.Add("Orders_OrderDetails",
    ds.Tables["Orders"].Columns["OrderID"],
    ds.Tables["OrderDetails"].Columns["OrderID"]);

ds.Relations["Orders_OrderDetails"].Nested = true;
//ds.WriteXml("NorthWindOrders.xml");

return new XmlDataDocument(ds);

    }

}
```

The previous section describing DataSet has already shown you that once we have a DataSet, we can persist the data inside the DataSet into an XML string or file. This time, we demonstrated how to convert the DataSet into an XmlDataDocument that we can manipulate in memory.

Summary

This chapter describes the core of ADO.NET. Having focused on the disconnected dataset, ADO.NET enables us not only to build high-performance, scalable solutions for e-commerce, but also allows the applications to reach other platforms through the use of XML. This chapter serves as a high-level survey into the classes that make up ADO.NET and serves to familiarize you with the System.Xml library. In the next chapter, we delve into building software as services. We will make use of ADO.NET as the data-access and exchange mechanism in our software services.

CHAPTER 6

Web Services

Web Services allow access to software components through standard web protocols such as HTTP and SMTP. Using the Internet and XML, we can now create software components that communicate with others, regardless of language, platform, or culture. Until now, software developers have progressed toward this goal by adopting proprietary componentized software methodologies, such as DCOM; however, because each vendor provides its own interface protocol, integration of different vendors' components is a nightmare. By substituting the Internet for proprietary transport formats and adopting standard protocols such as SOAP, Web Services help software developers create building blocks of software, which can be reused and integrated regardless of their location.

In this chapter, we describe the .NET Web Services architecture and provide examples of a Web Service provider and several Web Service consumers.

Web Services in Practice

You may have heard the phrase "software as services" and wondered about its meaning. The term *service*, in day-to-day usage, refers to what you get from a service provider. For example, you bring your dirty clothing to the cleaner to use its cleaning *service*. Software, on the other hand, is commonly known as an application, either off-the-shelf, or a custom application developed by a software firm. You typically buy the software (or in our case, build the software). It usually resides on some sort of media such as floppy diskette or CD and is sold in a shrink-wrapped package through retail outlets.

How can software be viewed as services? The example we are about to describe might seem far-fetched; however, it is possible with current technology. Imagine the following. As you grow more attached to the Internet, you might choose to replace your computer at home with something like an

Internet Device, specially designed for use with the Internet. Let's call it an iDev. With this device, you can be on the Internet immediately. If you want to do word processing, you can point your iDev to a Microsoft Word service somewhere in Redmond and type away without the need to install word processing software. When you are done, the document can be saved at an iStore server where you can later retrieve it. Notice that for you to do this, the iStore server must host a software service to allow you to store documents. Microsoft would charge you a service fee based on the amount of time your word processor is running and which features you use (such as the grammar and spell checkers). The iStore service charges vary based on the size of your document and how long it is stored. Of course, all these charges won't come in the mail, but rather through an escrow service where the money can be piped from and to your bank account or credit card.

This type of service aims to avoid the need to upgrade your Microsoft Word application. If you get tired of Microsoft Word, you can choose to use a different software service from another company. Of course, the document that you store at the iStore server is already in a standard data format. Since iStore utilizes the iMaxSecure software service from a company called iNNSA (Internet Not National Security Agency), the security of your files is assured. And because you use the document storage service at iStore, you also benefit from having your document authenticated and decrypted upon viewing, as well as encrypted at storing time.

All of these things can be done today with Web Services.

In fact, Microsoft has launched a version of the "software as service" paradigm with its Passport authentication service. Basically, it is a centralized authentication service that you can incorporate into your web sites. At sites using the Passport authentication service, it's no longer necessary to memorize or track numerous username/password pairs.

Recently, Microsoft also announced .NET My Services (formerly code-named "HailStorm"), a set of user-centric Web Services, including identification and authentication, email, instant messaging, automated alert, calendar, address book, and storage. As you can see, most of these are well-known services that are provided separately today. Identification and authentication is the goal of the Passport project. Email might map to Hotmail or any other web-based email services. Instant messaging and automated alert should be familiar to you if you use MSN Messenger Service or AOL Instant Messenger. A calendar and address book are usually bundled together with the web-based email service. Consolidating these user-centric services and exposing them as Web Services would allow the user to publish and manage his own information.

A .NET My Services customer can also control access permission to the data to allow or restrict access to content. These services also allow other users, organizations, and smart devices to communicate and retrieve information about us. For example, how many times have you been on the road with your mobile phone and wanted your contact list from Outlook? Your mobile phone should be able to communicate with your address book Web Service to get someone's phone number, right? Or better yet, if your car broke down in the middle of nowhere, you should be able to use your mobile phone to locate the nearest mechanic. The user is in control of what information is published and to whom the information will be displayed. You would probably have it set up so that only you can access your address book, while the yellow pages Web Service that publishes the nearest mechanic shop to your stranded location would be publicly accessible to all.

Currently, users store important data and personal information in many different places. With .NET My Services, information will be centrally managed. For example, your mechanic might notify you when it's time for your next major service. Or when you move and change your address, instead of looking up the list of contacts you wish to send the update to, .NET My Services will help you publish your update in one action.

The potential for consumer-oriented and business-to-business Web Services like .NET My Services is great, although there are serious and well-founded concerns about security and privacy. In one form or another, though, Web Services are here to stay, so let's dive in and see what's underneath.

Web Services Framework

Web Services combine the best of both distributed componentization and the World Wide Web, extending distributed computing to broader ranges of client applications. The best thing is that this is done by seamlessly marrying and enhancing existing technologies.

Web Services Architecture

Web Services are distributed software components accessible through standard web protocols. The first part of the definition is similar to COM/DCOM components. However, it is the second part that distinguishes Web Services from the crowd. Web Services enable software to interoperate with a much broader range of clients. While COM-aware clients can understand only COM components, Web Services can be consumed by any application that understands how to parse an XML-formatted stream transmitted through

HTTP channels. XML is the key technology used in Web Services and is used in the following areas of the Microsoft .NET Web Services framework:

Web Service wire formats
> The technology enabling universal understanding of how to perform data exchanges between the service provider and consumer; the format of data for the request and response.

Web Service description in WSDL (Web Services Description Language)
> The language describing how the service can be used. Think of this as the instructions on the washing machine at the laundromat telling you where to put quarters, what buttons to push, etc.

Web Service discovery
> The process of advertising or publishing a piece of software as a service and allowing for the discovery of this service.

Figure 6-1 depicts the architecture of web applications using Windows DNA, while Figure 6-2 shows .NET-enabled web applications architecture. As you can see, communication between components of a web application does not have to be within an intranet. Furthermore, intercomponent communication can also use HTTP/XML.

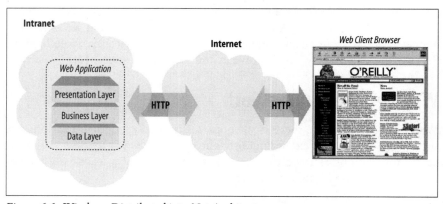

Figure 6-1. Windows Distributed interNet Architecture

Web Services Wire Formats

You may have heard the phrase "DCOM is COM over the wire." Web Services are similar to DCOM except that the wire is no longer a proprietary communication protocol. With Web Services, the wire formats rely on more open Internet protocols such as HTTP or SMTP.

A Web Service is more or less a component running on the web server, exposed to the world through standard Internet protocols. Microsoft .NET

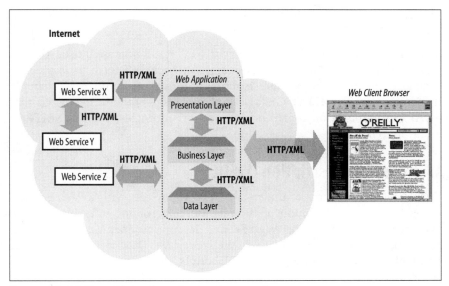

Figure 6-2. NET-enabled web application framework

Web Services currently supports three protocols: HTTP GET, HTTP POST, and SOAP (Simple Object Access Protocol), explained in the next sections. Because these protocols are standard protocols for the Web, it is very easy for the client applications to use the services provided by the server.

HTTP GET and HTTP POST

As their names imply, both HTTP GET and HTTP POST use HTTP as their underlying protocol. The GET and POST methods of the HTTP protocol have been widely used in ASP (Active Server Pages), CGI, and other server-side architectures for many years now. Both of these methods encode request parameters as name/value pairs in the HTTP request. The GET method creates a query string and appends it to the script's URL on the server that handles the request. For the POST method, the name/value pairs are passed in the body of the HTTP request message.

SOAP

Similar to HTTP GET and HTTP POST, SOAP serves as a mechanism for passing messages between the clients and servers. In this context, the clients are Web Services consumers, and the servers are the Web Services. The clients simply send an XML-formatted request message to the server to get the service. The server responds by sending back yet another XML-formatted message. The SOAP specification describes the format of these XML requests and responses. It is simple, yet it is extensible, because it is based on XML.

SOAP is different than HTTP GET and HTTP POST because it uses XML to format its payload. The messages being sent back and forth have a better structure and can convey more complex information compared to simple name/value pairs in HTTP GET/POST protocols. Another difference is that SOAP can be used on top of other transport protocols, such as SMTP in addition to HTTP.

Web Services Description (WSDL)

For Web Service clients to understand how to interact with a Web Service, there must be a description of the method calls, or the interface that the Web Service supports. This Web Service description document is found in an XML schema called *WSDL* (Web Services Description Language). Remember that type libraries and IDL scripts are used to describe a COM component. Both IDL and WSDL files describe an interface's method calls and the list of in and out parameters for the particular call. The only major difference between the two description languages is that all descriptions in the WSDL file are done in XML.

In theory, any WSDL-capable SOAP client can use the WSDL file to get a description of your Web Service. It can then use the information contained in that file to understand the interface and invoke your Web Service's methods.

WSDL Structure

The root of any Web Service description file is the <definitions> element. Within this element, the following elements provide both the abstract and concrete description of the service:

Types
> A container for datatype definitions.

Message
> An abstract, typed definition of the data being exchanged between the Web Service providers and consumers. Each web method has two messages: input and output. The input describes the parameters for the web method; the output describes the return data from the web method. Each message contains zero or more <part> parameters. Each parameter associates with a concrete type defined in the <types> container element.

Port type
> An abstract set of operations supported by one or more endpoints.

Operation

An abstract description of an action supported by the service. Each operation specifies the input and output messages defined as `<message>` elements.

Binding

A concrete protocol and data-format specification for a particular port type. Similar to port type, the binding contains operations, as well as the input and output for each operation. The main difference is that with binding, we are now talking about actual transport type and how the input and output are formatted.

Service

A collection of network endpoints—ports. Each of the Web Service wire formats defined earlier constitutes a port of the service (HTTP GET, HTTP POST, and SOAP ports).

Port

A single endpoint defined by associating a binding and a network address. In other words, it describes the protocol and data-format specification to be used as well as the network address of where the Web Service clients can bind to for the service.

The following shows a typical WSDL file structure:

```
<definitions name="" targetNamespace="" xmlns:...>

    <types>...</types>

    <message name="">...</message>
    ...

    <portType name="">
      <operation name="">
        <input message="" />
        <output message="" />
      </operation>
      ...
    </portType>
    ...

    <binding name="">
      <protocol:binding ...>
      <operation name="">
        <protocol:operation ...>
        <input>...</input>
        <output>...</output>
      </operation>
      ...
    </binding>
    ...
```

```
<service name="">
  <port name="" binding="">
    <protocol:address location="" />
  </port>
  ...
</service>
</definitions>
```

The <types> element contains physical type descriptions defined in XML Schema (XSD). These types are being referred to from the <message> elements.

For each of the web methods in the Web Service, there are two messages defined for a particular port: input and output. This means if a Web Service supports all three protocols: SOAP, HTTP GET, and HTTP POST, there will be six <message> elements defined, one pair for each port. The naming convention used by the Microsoft .NET autogenerated WSDL is:

```
MethodName + Protocol + {In, Out}
```

For example, a web method called GetBooks( ) has the following messages:

```
<message name="GetBooksSoapIn">...</message>
<message name="GetBooksSoapOut">...</message>
<message name="GetBooksHttpGetIn">...</message>
<message name="GetBooksHttpGetOut">...</message>
<message name="GetBooksHttpPostIn">...</message>
<message name="GetBooksHttpPostOut">...</message>
```

For each protocol that the Web Service supports, there is one <portType> element defined. Within each <portType> element, all operations are specified as <operation> elements. The naming convention for the port type is:

```
WebServiceName + Protocol
```

To continue our example, here are the port types associated with the Web Service that we build later in this chapter, PubsWS:

```
<portType name="PubsWSSoap">
  <operation name="GetBooks">
    <input message="GetBooksSoapIn" />
    <output message="GetBooksSoapOut" />
  </operation>
</portType>

<portType name="PubsWSHttpGet">
  <operation name="GetBooks">
    <input message="GetBooksHttpGetIn" />
    <output message="GetBooksHttpGetOut" />
  </operation>
</portType>

<portType name="PubsWSHttpPost">
  <operation name="GetBooks">
    <input message="GetBooksHttpPostIn" />
```

```
    <output message="GetBooksHttpPostOut" />
  </operation>
</portType>
```

We have removed namespaces from the example to make it easier to read.

While the port types are abstract operations for each port, the bindings provide concrete information on what protocol is being used, how the data is being transported, and where the service is located. Again, there is a <binding> element for each protocol supported by the Web Service:

```
<binding name="PubsWSSoap" type="s0:PubsWSSoap">
  <soap:binding transport="http://schemas.xmlsoap.org/soap/http"
                style="document" />
  <operation name="GetBooks">
    <soap:operation soapAction="http://tempuri.org/GetBooks"
                    style="document" />
    <input>
      <soap:body use="literal" />
    </input>
    <output>
      <soap:body use="literal" />
    </output>
  </operation>
</binding>

<binding name="PubsWSHttpGet" type="s0:PubsWSHttpGet">
  <http:binding verb="GET" />
  <operation name="GetBooks">
    <http:operation location="/GetBooks" />
    <input>
      <http:urlEncoded />
    </input>
    <output>
      <mime:mimeXml part="Body" />
    </output>
  </operation>
</binding>

<binding name="PubsWSHttpPost" type="s0:PubsWSHttpPost">
  <http:binding verb="POST" />
  <operation name="GetBooks">
    <http:operation location="/GetBooks" />
    <input>
      <mime:content type="application/x-www-form-urlencoded" />
    </input>
    <output>
      <mime:mimeXml part="Body" />
    </output>
  </operation>
</binding>
```

For SOAP protocol, the binding is <soap:binding>, and the transport is SOAP messages on top of HTTP protocol. The <soap:operation> element defines the HTTP header soapAction, which points to the web method. Both input and output of the SOAP call are SOAP messages.

For the HTTP GET and HTTP POST protocols, the binding is <http:binding> with the verb being GET and POST, respectively. Because the GET and POST verbs are part of the HTTP protocol, there is no need for the extended HTTP header (like soapAction for SOAP protocol). The only thing we need is the URL that points to the web method; in this case, the <soap:operation> element contains the attribute location, which is set to /GetBooks.

The only real difference between the HTTP GET and POST protocols is the way the parameters are passed to the web server. HTTP GET sends the parameters in the query string, while HTTP POST sends the parameters in the form data. This difference is reflected in the <input> elements of the operation GetBooks for the two HTTP protocols. For the HTTP GET protocol, the input is specified as <http:urlEncoded />, whereas for the HTTP POST protocol, the input is <mime:content type="application/x-www-form-urlencoded" />.

Looking back at the template of the WSDL document, we see that the only thing left to discuss is the <service> element, which defines the ports supported by this Web Service. For each of the supported protocol, there is one <port> element:

```
<service name="PubsWS">

  <port name="PubsWSSoap" binding="s0:PubsWSSoap">
    <soap:address
      location="http://.../PubsWs.asmx" />
  </port>

  <port name="PubsWSHttpGet" binding="s0:PubsWSHttpGet">
    <http:address
      location="http://.../PubsWs.asmx" />
  </port>

  <port name="PubsWSHttpPost" binding="s0:PubsWSHttpPost">
    <http:address
      location="http://.../PubsWs.asmx" />
  </port>

</service>
```

Even though the three different ports look similar, their binding attributes associate the address of the service with a binding element defined earlier. Web Service clients now have enough information on where to access the service, through which port to access the Web Service method, and how the communication messages are defined.

Although it is possible to read the WSDL and manually construct the HTTP* conversation with the server to get to a particular Web Service, there are tools that autogenerate client-side proxy source code to do the same thing. We show such a tool in "Web Services Consumers" later in this chapter.

Web Services Discovery

Even though advertising of a Web Service is important, it is optional. Web services can be private as well as public. Depending on the business model, some business-to-business (B2B) services would not normally be advertised publicly. Instead, the Web Service owners would provide specific instructions on accessing and using their service only to the business partner.

To advertise Web Services publicly, authors post discovery files on the Internet. Potential Web Services clients can browse to these files for information about how to use the Web Services—the WSDL. Think of it as the yellow pages for the Web Service. All it does is point you to where the actual Web Services reside and to the description of those Web Services.

The process of looking up a service and checking out the service description is called *Web Service discovery*. There are two ways of advertising the service: static and dynamic. In both of these, XML conveys the locations of Web Services.

Static discovery

Static discovery is easier to understand because it is explicit in nature. If you want to advertise your Web Service, you must explicitly create the *.disco* discovery file and point it to the WSDL.† All *.disco* files contain a root element discovery as shown in the following code sample. Note that discovery is in the namespace http://schemas.xmlsoap.org/disco/, which is referred to as disco in this sample.

```
<?xml version="1.0" ?>
<disco:discovery xmlns:disco="http://schemas.xmlsoap.org/disco/">
</disco:discovery>
```

Inside the discovery element, there can be one or more of contractRef or discoveryRef elements. Both of these elements are described in the

---

* Current Microsoft .NET SOAP implementation runs on top of HTTP.

† If you use Visual Studio .NET to create your Web Service, the discovery file is created automatically.

namespace http://schemas.xmlsoap.org/disco/scl/. The contractRef tag is used to reference an actual Web Service URL that would return the WSDL or the description of the actual Web Service contract. The discoveryRef tag, on the other hand, references another discovery document.

This XML document contains a link to one Web Service and a link to another discovery document:

```
<?xml version="1.0" ?>
<disco:discovery
        xmlns:disco="http://schemas.xmlsoap.org/disco/"
        xmlns:scl="http://schemas.xmlsoap.org/disco/scl/">
<scl:contractRef ref="http://yourWebServer/yourWebService.asmx?WSDL"/>
<scl:discoveryRef ref="http://yourBrotherSite/hisWebServiceDirectory.disco"/>
</disco:discovery>
```

This sample *disco* file specifies two different namespaces: disco, which is a nickname for the namespace http://schemas.xmlsoap.org/disco/; and scl, short for http://schemas.xmlsoap.org/disco/scl/. The contractRef element specifies the URL where *yourWebService* WSDL can be obtained. Right below that is the discoveryRef element, which links to the discovery file on *yourBrotherSite* web site. This linkage allows for structuring networks of related discovery documents.

Dynamic discovery

As opposed to explicitly specifying the URL for all Web Services your site supports, you can enable *dynamic discovery*, which enables all Web Services underneath a specific URL on your web site to be listed automatically. For your web site, you might want to group related Web Services under many different directories and then provide a single dynamic discovery file in each of the directory. The root tag of the dynamic discovery file is *dynamicDiscovery* instead of *discovery*.

```
<?xml version="1.0" encoding="utf-8"?>
<dynamicDiscovery xmlns="urn://schemas-dynamic:disco.2000-03-17" />
```

You can optionally specify exclude paths so that the dynamic mechanism does not have to look for Web Services in all subdirectories underneath the location of the dynamic discovery file. Exclude paths are in the following form:

```
<exclude path="pathname" />
```

If you run IIS as your web server, you'd probably have something like the following for a dynamic discovery file:[*]

```
<?xml version="1.0" encoding="utf-8"?>
<dynamicDiscovery xmlns="urn://schemas-dynamic:disco.2000-03-17">
```

---

[*] VS.NET uses *vsdisco* as the extension for its dynamic discovery files.

```
        <exclude path="_vti_cnf" />
        <exclude path="_vti_pvt" />
        <exclude path="_vti_log" />
        <exclude path="_vti_script" />
        <exclude path="_vti_txt" />
        <exclude path="Web References" />
    </dynamicDiscovery>
```

Discovery setting in practice

A combination of dynamic and static discovery makes a very flexible configuration. For example, you can provide static discovery documents at each of the directories that contain Web Services. At the root of the web server, provide a dynamic discovery document with links to all static discovery documents in all subdirectories. To exclude Web Services from public viewing, provide the exclude argument to XML nodes to exclude their directories from the dynamic discovery document.

UDDI

Universal Description, Discovery, and Integration (UDDI) Business Registry is like a yellow pages of Web Services. It allows businesses to publish their services and locate Web Services published by partner organizations so that they can conduct transactions quickly, easily, and dynamically with their trading partner.

Through UDDI APIs, businesses can find services over the web that match their criteria (e.g., cheapest fare), that offer the service they request (e.g., delivery on Sunday), and so on. Currently backed by software giants such as Microsoft, IBM, and Ariba, UDDI is important to Web Services because it enables access to businesses from a single place.

The System.Web.Services Namespace

Now that we have run through the basic framework of Microsoft .NET Web Services, let us take a look inside what the .NET SDK provides us in the System.Web.Services namespace.

There are only a handful of classes in the System.Web.Services namespace and the most important ones for general use are:

WebService
    The base class for all Web Services.

WebServiceAttribute
    An attribute that can be associated with a Web Service–derived class.

WebMethodAttribute

An attribute that can be associated with public methods within a Web Service–derived class.

The two essential classes for creating Web Services are the WebService base class and WebMethodAttribute. We make use of these classes in the next section, where we implement a Web Service provider and several Web Service consumers. WebService is the base class from which all Web Services inherit. It provides properties inherent to legacy ASP programming such as Application, Server, Session, and a new property, Context, which now includes Request and Response.

The WebMethodAttribute class allows you to apply attributes to each public method of your Web Service. Using this class, you can assign specific values to the following attributes: description, session state enabling flag, message name, and transaction mode. See the following section for an example of attribute setting in C# and VB.

The WebServiceAttribute class is used to provide more attributes about the Web Service itself. You can display a description of the Web Service, as well as the namespace to which this Web Service belongs.

Web Services Provider

In this section, we describe how to develop a Web Service, first from the point of view of service providers and then of the consumers. Web Services providers implement Web Services and advertise them so that the clients can discover and make use of the services. Because Web Services run on top of HTTP, there must be a web server application of some sort on the machine that hosts the Web Services. This web server application can be Microsoft Internet Information Services (IIS), Apache, or any other program that can understand and process the HTTP protocol. In our examples, we use Microsoft IIS, since that is the only web server currently supported by .NET.

Web Service Provider Example

We will be building a Web Service called *PubsWS* to let consumers get information from the sample *Pubs* database. All data access will be done through ADO.NET, so read Chapter 5 before attempting the examples.

Creating a Web Service is a three-step process.

1. Create a new *asmx* file for the Web Service. This must contain the <% webservice ... %> directive, as well as the class that provides the Web Service implementation. To the Web Service clients, this *asmx* file is the

entry point to your Web Service. You need to put this in a virtual directory that has the executescripts permission turned on.

2. Inherit from the WebService class of the System.Web.Services namespace. This allows the derived class to access all the normal ASP objects exposed in the WebService base class. From this point, you can use these ASP objects as if you were developing an ASP-based application.* It is highly recommended that you specify a namespace for your Web Service before publishing it publicly because the default namespace, *http://tempuri.org/*, will not uniquely identify your Web Service from other Web Services. To do this, tag the Web Service class with the Namespace attribute, specifying your own namespace.

3. Tag the public methods with WebMethod attributes to make *web methods*—public methods of a distributed component that are accessible via the Web. You don't have to tag a method as WebMethod unless you want that method to be published as a web method.

The following C# code demonstrates a simple Web Service† that exposes four methods to *Internet* clients. We emphasize "Internet" because anyone that can access this *asmx* file on the web server can access these methods, as opposed to your COM component, which can be accessed only by COM clients:

```
<%@ WebService Language="C#" Class="PubsWS.PubsWS" %>

namespace PubsWS
{
  using System;
  using System.Data;
  using System.Data.OleDb;
  using System.Web;
  using System.Web.Services;

  [WebService(Namespace="http://Oreilly/DotNetEssentials/")]
  public class PubsWS : WebService
  {
    private static string m_sConnStr =
"provider=sqloledb;server=(local);database=pubs; Integrated Security=SSPI";
```

---

* Access to the Request and Response objects through the Context property of the WebService class.

† For security reasons, the current release of ASP.NET runs as the account ASPNET. If you are using integrated security to access database resources, you must grant database access to the ASP-NET account. You can also enable impersonation in the *web.config* or *machine.config* file:

```
<system.web>
  <identity impersonate="true" userName="" password=""/>
</system.web>
```

If you set impersonate to true but leave userName and password blank, the application will run as *MachineName*\IUSR_MachineName, so make sure to grant this user (or whatever userName you specify) database access.

```csharp
[WebMethod(Description="Returns a DataSet containing all authors.")]
public DataSet GetAuthors()
{
  OleDbDataAdapter oDBAdapter;
  DataSet oDS;

  oDBAdapter = new OleDbDataAdapter("select * from authors",
                                    m_sConnStr);
  oDS = new DataSet();
  oDBAdapter.Fill(oDS, "Authors");
  return oDS;
}

[WebMethod]
public DataSet GetAuthor(string sSSN)
{
  OleDbDataAdapter oDBAdapter;
  DataSet oDS;

  oDBAdapter = new OleDbDataAdapter(
               "select * from authors where au_id ='"
               + sSSN + "'", m_sConnStr);
  oDS = new DataSet();
  oDBAdapter.Fill(oDS, "SelectedAuthor");
  return oDS;
}

[WebMethod(MessageName="GetBooksByAuthor",
           Description="Find books by author's SSN.")]
public DataSet GetBooks(string sAuthorSSN)
{
  OleDbDataAdapter oDBAdapter;
  DataSet oDS;

  oDBAdapter = new OleDbDataAdapter(
                   "select * from titles inner join titleauthor on " +
                   "titles.title_id=titleauthor.title_id " +
                   "where au_id='" + sAuthorSSN + "'", m_sConnStr);
  oDS = new DataSet();
  oDBAdapter.Fill(oDS, "Books");
  oDBAdapter = new OleDbDataAdapter("select * from authors " +
                   "where au_id='" + sAuthorSSN + "'", m_sConnStr);
  oDBAdapter.Fill(oDS, "Author");

  return oDS;
}

[WebMethod]
public DataSet GetBooks()
{
  OleDbDataAdapter oDBAdapter;
  DataSet oDS;
```

```
        oDBAdapter = new OleDbDataAdapter("select * from titles" ,
                                           m_sConnStr);
        oDS = new DataSet( );
        oDBAdapter.Fill(oDS, "Books");
        return oDS;
    }

  } // end PubsWS
}
```

If you are familiar with ASP, you may recognize the usage of the @ symbol in front of keyword WebService. This WebService directive specifies the language of the Web Service so that ASP.NET can compile the Web Service with the correct compiler. This directive also specifies the class that implements the Web Service so it can load the correct class and employ reflection to generate the WSDL for the Web Service.

Because *PubsWS* also uses ADO.NET's OLE DB provider for its data-access needs, we have to add a reference to System.Data and System.Data.OleDb, in addition to the System, System.Web, and System.Web.Services namespaces.

Class PubsWS inherits from WebService with the colon syntax that should be familiar to C++ or C# developers:

```
public class PubsWS : WebService
```

The four methods that are tagged with WebMethod attributes are GetAuthors(), GetAuthor(), GetBooks(*string*), and GetBooks(). In C#, you can tag public methods with a WebMethod attribute using the [ ] syntax. In VB, you must use <>. For example, in VB, the second method would be declared as:

```
<WebMethod( )> Public Function GetAuthor(sSSN As String) As DataSet
```

By adding [WebMethod] in front of your public method, you make the public method callable from any Internet client. What goes on behind the scenes is that your public method is associated with an *attribute*, which is implemented as a WebMethodAttribute class. WebMethodAttribute has six properties:

BufferResponse (boolean)
  Controls whether or not to buffer the method's response.

CacheDuration
  Specifies the length of time in seconds to keep the method response in cache; the default is not to hold the method response in cache (0 seconds).

Description
  Provides additional information about a particular web method.

EnableSession (boolean)

Enables or disables session state. If you don't want to use session state for the web method, you could to disable this flag so the web server doesn't have to generate and manage session IDs for each user accessing this web method. It might improve performance. This flag is true by default.

MessageName

Distinguishes web methods with the same names. For example, if you have two different methods called GetBooks (one method retrieves all books while the other method retrieves only books written by a certain author) and you want to publish both of these methods as web methods, the system will have a problem trying to distinguish the two methods since their names are duplicated. You have to use the MessageName property to make sure all service signatures within the WSDL are unique. If the protocol is SOAP, MessageName is mapped to the SOAPAction request header and nested within the soap:Body element. For HTTP GET and HTTP POST, it is the PathInfo portion of the URI (as in *http://localhost// PubsWS/PubsWS.asmx/GetBooksByAuthor*).

TransactionOption

Can be one of five modes: Disabled, NotSupported, Supported, Required, and RequiresNew. Even though there are five modes, web methods can only participate as the root object in a transaction. This means both Required and RequiresNew result in a new transaction being created for the web method. The Disabled, NotSupported, and Supported settings result in no transaction being used for the web method. The TransactionOption property of a web method is set to Disabled by default.

To set up these properties, pass the property name and its value as a *name = value* pair:

```
[WebMethod(Description="Returns a DataSet containing all authors.")]
public DataSet GetAuthors()
```

You can separate multiple properties with a comma:

```
[WebMethod(MessageName="GetBooksByAuthor",
          Description="Find books by author's SSN.")]
public DataSet GetBooks(string sAuthorSSN)
```

Web.Config

If you set up your Web Services from scratch, you should also need to provide the configuration file (*web.config*) in the same directory as your *asmx* file. This configuration file allows you to control various application settings about the virtual directory. Here, we set the authentication mode to None to make our Web Services development and testing a little easier.

When you release your Web Services to the public, you should change this setting to Windows, Forms, or Passport instead of None:

```
<configuration>
  <system.web>
    <authentication mode="None" />
  </system.web>
</configuration>
```

The following list shows the different modes of authentication:

Forms

Basic Forms authentication is where unauthenticated requests are redirected to a login form.

Windows

Authentication is performed by IIS in one of three ways: basic, digest, or Integrated Windows Authentication.

Passport

Unauthenticated requests to the resource are redirected to Microsoft's centralized authentication service. When authenticated, a token is passed back and used by subsequent requests.

Discover files

After creating the Web Service, you can provide the supporting files to help in the discovery of the service. The static discovery disco file is as follows:[*]

```
<?xml version="1.0" ?>
<disco:discovery xmlns:disco="http://schemas.xmlsoap.org/disco/"
                 xmlns:scl="http://schemas.xmlsoap.org/disco/scl/">
<scl:contractRef ref="http://localhost/PubsWS/PubsWS.asmx?WSDL"/>
</disco:discovery>
```

Web Services Consumers

Now that you have successfully created a Web Service, let's take a look at how this Web Service is used by web clients. Web Services clients communicate with Web Services through standard web protocols. They send and receive XML-encoded messages to and from the Web Services. This means any application on any platform can access the Web Services as long as it uses standard web protocols and understands the XML-encoded messages. As mentioned earlier, there are three protocols that the web clients can employ to communicate with the servers (Web Services): HTTP GET, HTTP POST, and SOAP. We demonstrate next how to build client applications

---

[*] This code snippet assumes the virtual directory you set up is */PubsWS* on your local web server.

that utilize each of these protocols. These Web Services–client applications are done in both VB6 and .NET languages, such as C# and VB.NET, to demonstrate the cross-language/cross-platform benefits of Web Services. For example, you can replace the example in VB6 with Perl running on Unix, and the Web Services should still be serving.

HTTP GET Consumer

Let's look at how it is done using HTTP GET first, since it is the simplest. In the examples that follow, we use *localhost* as the name of the web server running the service and *PubsWS* as the virtual directory. If you have deployed the sample Web Service on a remote server, you'll need to substitute the name of the server and virtual directory as appropriate.

If you point your web browser at the Web Service URL (*http://localhost/PubsWS/PubsWS.asmx*), it will give you a list of supported methods. To find out more about these methods, click one of them. This brings up a default Web Service consumer. This consumer, autogenerated through the use of reflection, is great for testing your Web Services' methods.* It uses the HTTP GET protocol to communicate with the Web Service. This consumer features a form that lets you test the method (see Figure 6-3), as well as descriptions of how to access the method via SOAP, HTTP GET, or HTTP POST.

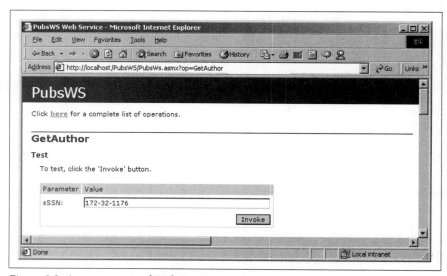

Figure 6-3. An autogenerated Web Services consumer

---

* A simple Reflection example can be found in the section "Attribute-Based Programming" in Chapter 4.

Here is the description of the GET request and response supplied by the default consumer:

The following is a sample HTTP GET request and response. The **placeholders** shown need to be replaced with actual values.

```
GET /PubsWS/PubsWS.asmx/GetAuthor?sSSN=string HTTP/1.1
Host: localhost

HTTP/1.1 200 OK
Content-Type: text/xml; charset=utf-8
Content-Length: length

<?xml version="1.0" encoding="utf-8"?>
<DataSet xmlns="http://Oreilly/DotNetEssentials/">
  <schema xmlns="http://www.w3.org/2001/XMLSchema">schema</schema>xml
</DataSet>
```

Using HTTP GET protocol, the complete URL to invoke the web method, along with parameters, can be the following:

```
http://localhost/PubsWS/PubsWS.asmx/GetAuthor?sSSN=172-32-1176
```

Here is the response, including HTTP response headers and the raw XML (note how the response includes the serialized schema and data from the DataSet object):

```
Cache-Control: private, max-age=0
Date: Tue, 08 May 2001 20:53:16 GMT
Server: Microsoft-IIS/5.0
Content-Length: 2450
Content-Type: text/xml; charset=utf-8
Client-Date: Tue, 08 May 2001 20:53:16 GMT
Client-Peer: 127.0.0.1:80

<?xml version="1.0" encoding="utf-8"?>
<DataSet xmlns="http://Oreilly/DotNetEssentials/">
  <xs:schema id="NewDataSet"
             xmlns=""
             xmlns:xs="http://www.w3.org/2001/XMLSchema"
             xmlns:msdata="urn:schemas-microsoft-com:xml-msdata">
    <xs:element name="NewDataSet" msdata:IsDataSet="true">
      <xs:complexType>
        <xs:choice maxOccurs="unbounded">
          <xs:element name="SelectedAuthor">
            <xs:complexType>
              <xs:sequence>
                <xs:element name="au_id" type="xs:string"
                            minOccurs="0" />
                <xs:element name="au_lname" type="xs:string"
                            minOccurs="0" />
```

```
                    <xs:element name="au_fname" type="xs:string"
                               minOccurs="0" />
                    <xs:element name="phone" type="xs:string"
                               minOccurs="0" />
                    <xs:element name="address" type="xs:string"
                               minOccurs="0" />
                    <xs:element name="city" type="xs:string"
                               minOccurs="0" />
                    <xs:element name="state" type="xs:string"
                               minOccurs="0" />
                    <xs:element name="zip" type="xs:string"
                               minOccurs="0" />
                    <xs:element name="contract" type="xs:boolean"
                               minOccurs="0" />
                </xs:sequence>
              </xs:complexType>
            </xs:element>
          </xs:choice>
        </xs:complexType>
      </xs:element>
    </xs:schema>
    <diffgr:diffgram
            xmlns:msdata="urn:schemas-microsoft-com:xml-msdata"
            xmlns:diffgr="urn:schemas-microsoft-com:xml-diffgram-v1">
      <NewDataSet xmlns="">
        <SelectedAuthor diffgr:id="SelectedAuthor1" msdata:rowOrder="0">
          <au_id>172-32-1176</au_id>
          <au_lname>White</au_lname>
          <au_fname>Johnson</au_fname>
          <phone>408 496-7223</phone>
          <address>10932 Bigge Rd.</address>
          <city>Menlo Park</city>
          <state>CA</state>
          <zip>94025</zip>
          <contract>true</contract>
        </SelectedAuthor>
      </NewDataSet>
    </diffgr:diffgram>
</DataSet>
```

HTTP POST Consumer

In the section "HTTP GET Consumer," we saw the automatic creation of a Web Services consumer by merely hitting the URL of the Web Services, *http: // localhost/PubsWS/PubsWS.asmx*. It is now time for us to see how a web client can use HTTP POST and SOAP to access a Web Service. This time around, we are going write a C# Web Service consumer.

The Microsoft .NET SDK has a rich set of tools to simplify the process of creating or consuming Web Services. We are going to use one of these tools, wsdl, to generate source code for the proxies to the actual Web Services:*

```
wsdl /l:CS /protocol:HttpPost http://localhost/PubsWS/PubsWS.asmx?WSDL
```

This command line creates a proxy for the PubsWS Web Service from the WSDL (Web Services Description Language) document from the URL *http://localhost/PubsWS/PubsWS.asmx?WSDL*. The proxy uses HTTP POST as its protocol to talk to the Web Service; it is generated as a C# source file. The wsdl tool can also take a WSDL file as its input instead of a URL pointing to the location where the WSDL can be obtained.

This C# proxy source file represents the proxy class for the PubsWS Web Service that the clients can compile against. This generated C# file contains a proxy class PubsWS that derives from HttpPostClientProtocol class. If you use the /protocol:HttpGet or /protocol:SOAP parameters, the PubsWS derives from either the HttpGetClientProtocol or SoapHttpClientProtocol class.

After generating the C# source file *PubsWS.cs*, we have two choices for how this proxy can be used. One way is to include this source file in the client application project using Visual Studio.NET. The project has to be a C# project if you choose this route. To make use of the proxy, you also have to add to your project any references that the proxy depends on. In this example, the necessary references for the proxy file are System.Web.Services, System.Web.Services.Protocols, System.Xml.Serialization, and System.Data.

The other way to use the proxy is more flexible. You can compile the C# source file into a dynamic link library (DLL) and then add a reference to this DLL to any project you want to create. This way you can even have a VB project use the DLL.

Below is the command line used to compile the C# proxy source into a DLL. Notice that the three references are linked to *PubsWS.cs* so that the resulting *PubsWS.DLL* is self-contained (type the entire command on one line):

```
csc /t:library
    /r:system.web.services.dll
    /r:system.xml.dll
    /r:system.data.dll
    PubsWS.cs
```

Regardless of how you choose to use the proxy, the client application code will still look the same. Consider the next two code examples containing C#

---

* *wsdl.exe* generates the proxy source code similar to the way IDL compilers generate source files for DCOM proxies. The only difference is that WSDL is the language that describes the interface of the software component, which is XML-based.

and VB code. For both languages, the first lines create an instance of the proxy to the Web Service, PubsWS. The second lines invoke the GetAuthors web method to get a DataSet as the result. The remaining lines bind the default view of the table Authors to the data grid, add the data grid to a form, and display the form. Note that these examples use the Windows Forms API, which we'll discuss in Chapter 8. Here is the C# Web Service client, *TestProxy.cs*:

```
using System;
using System.Drawing;
using System.Windows.Forms;
using System.Data;

public class TestProxy
{

  public static void Main( )
  {

    /* Create a proxy. */
    PubsWS oProxy = new PubsWS( );

    /* Invoke GetBooks( ) over HTTPPOST and get the data set. */
    DataSet oDS = oProxy.GetAuthors( );

    /* Create a data grid and connect it to the data set. */
    DataGrid dg = new DataGrid( );
    dg.Size = new Size(490, 270);
    dg.DataSource = oDS.Tables["Authors"].DefaultView;

    /* Set the properties of the form and add the data grid. */
    Form myForm = new Form( );
    myForm.Text = "DataGrid Sample";
    myForm.Size = new Size(500, 300);
    myForm.Controls.Add(dg);

    /* Display the form. */
    System.Windows.Forms.Application.Run(myForm);

  }

}
```

If you created the DLL as previously directed, you can compile this with the following command:

```
csc TestProxy.cs /r:PubsWS.dll
```

This creates the executable *TestProxy.exe*, which gets a DataSet using a HTTP POST call, and displays a data grid containing that dataset. Figure 6-4 shows the output of the C# client after obtaining the data from the PubsWS Web Service via HTTP POST protocol.

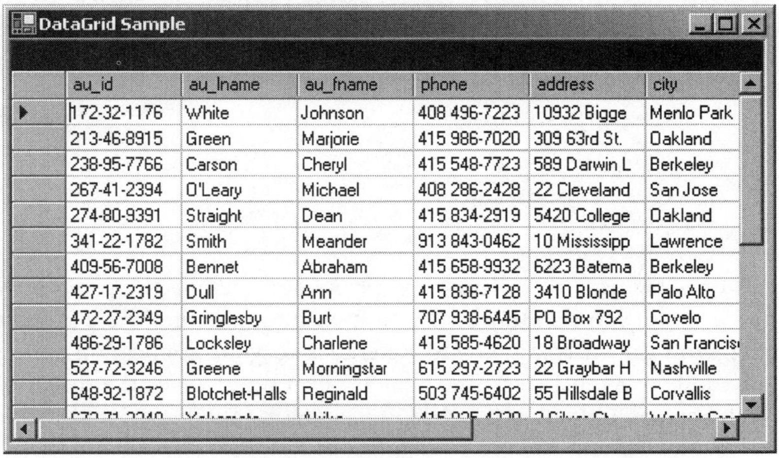

DataGrid Sample

au_id	au_lname	au_fname	phone	address	city
172-32-1176	White	Johnson	408 496-7223	10932 Bigge	Menlo Park
213-46-8915	Green	Marjorie	415 986-7020	309 63rd St.	Oakland
238-95-7766	Carson	Cheryl	415 548-7723	589 Darwin L	Berkeley
267-41-2394	O'Leary	Michael	408 286-2428	22 Cleveland	San Jose
274-80-9391	Straight	Dean	415 834-2919	5420 College	Oakland
341-22-1782	Smith	Meander	913 843-0462	10 Mississipp	Lawrence
409-56-7008	Bennet	Abraham	415 658-9932	6223 Batema	Berkeley
427-17-2319	Dull	Ann	415 836-7128	3410 Blonde	Palo Alto
472-27-2349	Gringlesby	Burt	707 938-6445	PO Box 792	Covelo
486-29-1786	Locksley	Charlene	415 585-4620	18 Broadway	San Francisc
527-72-3246	Greene	Morningstar	615 297-2723	22 Graybar H	Nashville
648-92-1872	Blotchet-Halls	Reginald	503 745-6402	55 Hillsdale B	Corvallis

Figure 6-4. C# Web Service client after calling GetAuthors()

Here is the VB Web Service client, *TestProxyVB.vb*:

```
imports System
imports System.Drawing
imports System.Windows.Forms
imports System.Data

Module TestProxyVB
  Sub Main( )
    ' Create a proxy.
    dim oProxy as PubsWS = new PubsWS( )

    ' Invoice GetBooks( ) over SOAP and get the data set.
    dim oDS as DataSet = oProxy.GetAuthors( )

    ' Create a data grid and connect it to the data set.
    dim dg as DataGrid = new DataGrid( )
    dg.Size = new Size(490, 270)
    dg.DataSource = oDS.Tables("Authors").DefaultView

    ' Set the properties of the form and add the data grid.
    dim myForm as Form = new Form( )
    myForm.Text = "DataGrid Sample"
    myForm.Size = new Size(500, 300)
    myForm.Controls.Add(dg)

    ' Display the form.
    System.Windows.Forms.Application.Run(myForm)
  End Sub
End Module
```

You can compile the VB Web Service client with this command (type the entire command on one line):

```
vbc TestProxyVB.vb
    /r:System.Drawing.dll
    /r:System.Windows.Forms.dll
    /r:System.Data.dll
    /r:PubsWS.dll
    /r:System.Web.Services.dll
    /r:System.dll
    /r:System.xml.dll
```

Instead of using `wsdl` to generate the proxy and include the proxy in your application, you can also rely on VS.NET to automate the whole process. In VS.NET, you can just add a Web Reference to your application. The process of adding a Web Reference to an application involves the discovery of the Web Service, obtaining the WSDL, generating the proxy, and including the proxy into the application.[*]

Non-.NET Consumers

This section shows how to develop non-.NET Web Service consumers using HTTP GET, HTTP POST, and SOAP protocols. Because we cannot just create the proxy class from the WSDL and compile it with the client code directly, we must look at the WSDL file to understand how to construct and interpret messages between the Web Service and the clients. We trimmed down the WSDL file for our PubsWS Web Service to show only types, messages, ports, operations, and bindings that we actually use in the next several Web Service–client examples. In particular, we will have our VB6 client access the following.

Web method	Protocol
GetBooks( )	HTTP GET protocol
GetAuthor(ssn)	HTTP POST protocol
GetBooksByAuthor(ssn)	SOAP protocol

As a reference, here is the simplified version of the WSDL file while you experiment with the VB6 client application:

```
<?xml version="1.0" encoding="utf-8"?>
<definitions xmlns:...
    xmlns:s0="http://Oreilly/DotNetEssentials/"
    targetNamespace="http://Oreilly/DotNetEssentials/" >
```

---

[*] You can find the proxy source file under *Web References\ReferenceName* as *reference.cs* (if you're working with C#). If you have not renamed the reference name, it is *localhost* by default.

```
<types>
    <!-- This datatype is used by the HTTP POST call -->
    <s:element name="GetAuthor">
      <s:complexType>
        <s:sequence>
          <s:element minOccurs="1" maxOccurs="1"
                     name="sSSN" type="s:string" />
        </s:sequence>
      </s:complexType>
    </s:element>
    <!-- This datatype is used by the HTTP POST call -->
    <s:element name="GetAuthorResponse">
      <s:complexType>
        <s:sequence>
          <s:element minOccurs="1" maxOccurs="1"
                     name="GetAuthorResult"">
            <s:complexType>
              <s:sequence>
                <s:element ref="s:schema" />
                <s:any />
              </s:sequence>
            </s:complexType>
          </s:element>
        </s:sequence>
      </s:complexType>
    </s:element>

    <!-- This datatype is used by the SOAP call -->
    <s:element name="GetBooksByAuthor">
      <s:complexType>
        <s:sequence>
          <s:element minOccurs="1" maxOccurs="1"
            name="sAuthorSSN" type="s:string" />
        </s:sequence>
      </s:complexType>
    </s:element>
    <!-- This datatype is used by the SOAP call -->
    <s:element name="GetBooksByAuthorResponse">
      <s:complexType>
        <s:sequence>
          <s:element minOccurs="1" maxOccurs="1"
                     name="GetBooksByAuthorResult"">
            <s:complexType>
              <s:sequence>
                <s:element ref="s:schema" />
                <s:any />
              </s:sequence>
            </s:complexType>
          </s:element>
        </s:sequence>
      </s:complexType>
    </s:element>
```

```
<!-- This datatype is used by the HTTP GET call -->
<s:element name="GetBooks">
  <s:complexType />
</s:element>
<!-- This datatype is used by the HTTP GET call -->
<s:element name="GetBooksResponse">
  <s:complexType>
    <s:sequence>
      <s:element minOccurs="1" maxOccurs="1"
                 name="GetBooksResult">
        <s:complexType>
          <s:sequence>
            <s:element ref="s:schema" />
            <s:any />
          </s:sequence>
        </s:complexType>
      </s:element>
    </s:sequence>
  </s:complexType>
</s:element>

<!-- This datatype is used by the HTTP GET/POST responses -->
<s:element name="DataSet">
  <s:complexType>
    <s:sequence>
      <s:element ref="s:schema" />
      <s:any />
    </s:sequence>
  </s:complexType>
</s:element>

</types>

<!-- These messages are used by the SOAP call -->
<message name="GetBooksByAuthorSoapIn">
  <part name="parameters" element="s0:GetBooksByAuthor" />
</message>
<message name="GetBooksByAuthorSoapOut">
  <part name="parameters" element="s0:GetBooksByAuthorResponse" />
</message>

<!-- These messages are used by the HTTP GET call -->
<message name="GetBooksHttpGetIn" />
<message name="GetBooksHttpGetOut">
  <part name="Body" element="s0:DataSet" />
</message>

<!-- These messages are used by the HTTP POST call -->
<message name="GetAuthorHttpPostIn">
  <part name="sSSN" type="s:string" />
</message>
<message name="GetAuthorHttpPostOut">
  <part name="Body" element="s0:DataSet" />
```

```
  </message>

<!-- SOAP port -->
<portType name="PubsWSSoap">
  <operation name="GetBooks">
    <documentation>Find books by author's SSN.</documentation>
    <input name="GetBooksByAuthor"
           message="sO:GetBooksByAuthorSoapIn" />
    <output name="GetBooksByAuthor"
            message="sO:GetBooksByAuthorSoapOut" />
  </operation>
</portType>

<!-- HTTP GET port -->
<portType name="PubsWSHttpGet">
  <operation name="GetBooks">
    <input message="sO:GetBooksHttpGetIn" />
    <output message="sO:GetBooksHttpGetOut" />
  </operation>
</portType>

<!-- HTTP POST port -->
<portType name="PubsWSHttpPost">
  <operation name="GetAuthor">
    <input message="sO:GetAuthorHttpPostIn" />
    <output message="sO:GetAuthorHttpPostOut" />
  </operation>
</portType>

<!-- SOAP binding -->
<binding name="PubsWSSoap" type="sO:PubsWSSoap">
  <soap:binding
        transport="http://schemas.xmlsoap.org/soap/http"
        style="document" />
  <operation name="GetBooks">
    <soap:operation
         soapAction="http://Oreilly/DotNetEssentials/GetBooksByAuthor"
         style="document" />
    <input name="GetBooksByAuthor">
      <soap:body use="literal" />
    </input>
    <output name="GetBooksByAuthor">
      <soap:body use="literal" />
    </output>
  </operation>
</binding>

<!-- HTTP GET binding -->
<binding name="PubsWSHttpGet" type="sO:PubsWSHttpGet">
  <http:binding verb="GET" />
  <operation name="GetBooks">
    <http:operation location="/GetBooks" />
```

```
      <input>
        <http:urlEncoded />
      </input>
      <output>
        <mime:mimeXml part="Body" />
      </output>
    </operation>
  </binding>

  <!-- HTTP POST binding -->
  <binding name="PubsWSHttpPost" type="s0:PubsWSHttpPost">
    <http:binding verb="POST" />
    <operation name="GetAuthor">
      <http:operation location="/GetAuthor" />
      <input>
        <mime:content type="application/x-www-form-urlencoded" />
      </input>
      <output>
        <mime:mimeXml part="Body" />
      </output>
    </operation>
  </binding>

  <!-- The whole Web Service and address bindings -->
  <service name="PubsWS">

    <port name="PubsWSSoap" binding="s0:PubsWSSoap">
      <soap:address location="http://localhost/PubsWS/PubsWS.asmx" />
    </port>

    <port name="PubsWSHttpGet" binding="s0:PubsWSHttpGet">
      <http:address location="http://localhost/PubsWS/PubsWS.asmx" />
    </port>

    <port name="PubsWSHttpPost" binding="s0:PubsWSHttpPost">
      <http:address location="http://localhost/PubsWS/PubsWS.asmx" />
    </port>

  </service>

</definitions>
```

In both the HTTP GET and HTTP POST protocols, you pass parameters to the Web Services as name/value pairs. With the HTTP GET protocol, you must pass parameters in the query string, whereas the HTTP POST protocol packs the parameters in the body of the request package. To demonstrate this point, we will construct a simple VB client using both HTTP GET and HTTP POST protocols to communicate with the PubsWS Web Service.

Let's first create a VB6 standard application. We need to add a reference to Microsoft XML, v3.0 (*msxml3.dll*), because we'll use the XMLHTTP object

---

to help us communicate with the Web Services. For demonstrative purposes, we will also use the Microsoft Internet Controls component (*shdocvw.dll*) to display XML and HTML content.

First, add two buttons on the default form, form1, and give them the captions GET and POST, as well as the names cmdGet and cmdPost, respectively. After that, drag the WebBrowser object from the toolbar onto the form, and name the control myWebBrowser. If you make the WebBrowser navigate to about:blank initially, you will end up with something like Figure 6-5.

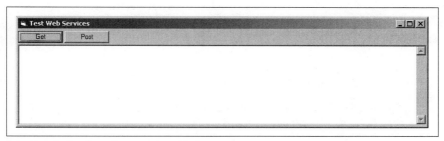

Figure 6-5. VB client form to test Web Services

Now all we need is some code similar to the following to handle the two buttons' click events:

```
Private Sub cmdGet_Click( )
    Dim oXMLHTTP As XMLHTTP
    Dim oDOM As DOMDocument
    Dim oXSL As DOMDocument

    ' Call the Web Service to get an XML document
    Set oXMLHTTP = New XMLHTTP
    oXMLHTTP.open "GET",_
                  "http://localhost/PubsWS/PubsWS.asmx/GetBooks", _
                  False
    oXMLHTTP.send
    Set oDOM = oXMLHTTP.responseXML

    ' Create the XSL document to be used for transformation
    Set oXSL = New DOMDocument
    oXSL.Load App.Path & "\templateTitle.xsl"

    ' Transform the XML document into an HTML document and display
    myWebBrowser.Document.Write CStr(oDOM.transformNode(oXSL))
    myWebBrowser.Document.Close

    Set oXSL = Nothing
    Set oDOM = Nothing
    Set oXMLHTTP = Nothing
End Sub
```

```
Private Sub cmdPost_Click( )
  Dim oXMLHTTP As XMLHTTP
  Dim oDOM As DOMDocument
  Dim oXSL As DOMDocument

  ' Call the Web Service to get an XML document
  Set oXMLHTTP = New XMLHTTP
  oXMLHTTP.open "POST", _
                "http://localhost/PubsWS/PubsWS.asmx/GetAuthor", _
                False
  oXMLHTTP.setRequestHeader "Content-Type", _
                            "application/x-www-form-urlencoded"
  oXMLHTTP.send "sSSN=172-32-1176"
  Set oDOM = oXMLHTTP.responseXML

  ' Create the XSL document to be used for transformation
  Set oXSL = New DOMDocument
  oXSL.Load App.Path & "\templateAuthor.xsl"

  ' Transform the XML document into an HTML document and display
  myWebBrowser.Document.Write oDOM.transformNode(oXSL)
  myWebBrowser.Document.Close

  Set oXSL = Nothing
  Set oDOM = Nothing
  Set oXMLHTTP = Nothing
End Sub
```

The two subroutines are similar in structure, except that the first one uses the HTTP GET protocol and the second one uses the HTTP POST protocol to get to the PubsWS Web Service. Let's take a closer look at what the two subroutines do.

For the HTTP GET protocol, we use the XMLHTTP object to point to the URL for the web method, as specified in the WSDL. Since the GetBooks web method does not require any parameters, the query string in this case is empty. The method is invoked synchronously because the async parameter to XMLHTTP's open method is set to false. After the method invocation is done, we transform the XML result using *templateTitle.xsl* and display the HTML on the myWebBrowser instance on the form. Figure 6-6 displays the screen of our Web Services testing application after invoking the GetBooks web method at URL *http://localhost/PubsWS/ PubsWS.asmx/* through HTTP GET protocol.

For the HTTP POST protocol, we also point the XMLHTTP object to the URL for the web method—in this case, method GetAuthor. Because this is a POST request, we have to specify in the HTTP header that the request is coming over as a form by setting the Content-Type header variable to

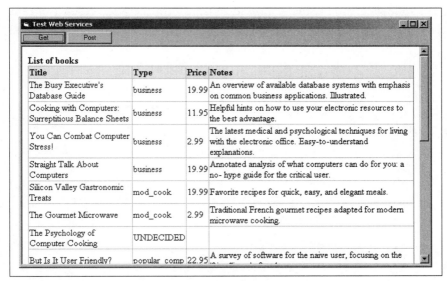

Figure 6-6. VB client form after calling GetBooks

application/x-www-form-urlencoded. If this variable is not set, XMLHTTP by default passes the data to the server in XML format.

Another difference worth noticing is that the GetAuthor method requires a single parameter, which is the SSN of the author as a string. Since this is a post request, we are going to send the name/value pair directly to the server in the body of the message. Because the Content-Type header has been set to application/x-www-form-urlencoded, the server will know how to get to the parameters and perform the work requested. This time, we use *templateAuthor.xsl* to transform the XML result to HTML and display it. Figure 6-7 shows our application after invoking the GetAuthor web method of PubsWS Web Service through HTTP POST protocol.

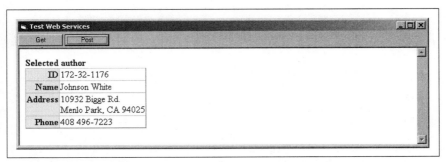

Figure 6-7. VB client form after calling GetAuthor

The following code is the XSL used to transform the XML result from the GetBooks web method call to HTML to be displayed on the web browser instance on the VB form:

```
<html version="1.0" xmlns:xsl="http://www.w3.org/TR/WD-xsl">
<head><title>A list of books</title></head>
<style>
.hdr { background-color=#ffeedd; font-weight=bold; }
</style>
<body>
<B>List of books</B>
<table style="border-collapse:collapse" border="1">
<tr>
  <td class="hdr">Title</td>
  <td class="hdr">Type</td>
  <td class="hdr">Price</td>
  <td class="hdr">Notes</td>
</tr>
<xsl:for-each select="//Books">
<tr>
  <td><xsl:value-of select="title"/></td>
  <td><xsl:value-of select="type"/></td>
  <td><xsl:value-of select="price"/></td>
  <td><xsl:value-of select="notes"/></td>
</tr>
</xsl:for-each>
</table>
</body>
</html>
```

Here is the XSL used to transform the XML result from the GetAuthor web method call to HTML to be displayed on the web browser instance on the VB form:

```
<html version="1.0" xmlns:xsl="http://www.w3.org/TR/WD-xsl">
<head><title>Selected author</title></head>
<STYLE>
.hdr { background-color:'#ffeedd';
       text-align:'right'; vertical-align:'top';
       font-weight=bold; }
</STYLE>
<body>
<B>Selected author</B>
<xsl:for-each select="//SelectedAuthor">
<table style="border-collapse:'collapse'" border="1">
<tr><td class="hdr">ID</td>
    <td><xsl:value-of select="au_id"/></td></tr>
<tr><td class="hdr">Name</td>
    <td><xsl:value-of select="au_fname"/>
        <xsl:value-of select="au_lname"/></td></tr>
<tr><td class="hdr">Address</td>
    <td><xsl:value-of select="address"/><br>
        <xsl:value-of select="city"/>,
```

```
    <xsl:value-of select="state"/>
      <xsl:value-of select="zip"/></br></td></tr>
<tr><td class="hdr">Phone</td>
    <td><xsl:value-of select="phone"/></td></tr>
</table>
</xsl:for-each>
</body>
</html>
```

We can also use SOAP protocol to access the Web Service. Because the Web Service is exposed through HTTP and XML, any clients on any platform can access the service as long as they conform to the specification of the service. Again, this specification is the WSDL file. By inspecting the WSDL file—specifically, the SOAP section—we can use XMLHTTP again to communicate in SOAP dialog. Let's see how this can be done.

Let's go back to the example of consumer Web Services using VB6 and XMLHTTP. Add another button on the form, and call it cmdSOAP with caption SOAP. This time, we will ask the Web Service to return all books written by a particular author:

```
Private Sub cmdSOAP_Click()
  Dim oXMLHTTP As XMLHTTP
  Dim oDOM As DOMDocument
  Dim oXSL As DOMDocument

  ' Call the Web Service to get an XML document
  Set oXMLHTTP = New XMLHTTP
  oXMLHTTP.open "POST", "http://localhost/PubsWS/PubsWS.asmx", False

  Dim sBody As String

  sBody = "" & _
  "<soap:Envelope" & _
  " xmlns:xsi=""http://www.w3.org/2001/XMLSchema-instance""" & _
  " xmlns:xsd=""http://www.w3.org/2001/XMLSchema""" & _
  " xmlns:soap=""http://schemas.xmlsoap.org/soap/envelope/"">" & _
  "<soap:Body>" & _
  "<GetBooksByAuthor xmlns=""http://Oreilly/DotNetEssentials/"">" & _
  "<sAuthorSSN>213-46-8915</sAuthorSSN>" & _
  "</GetBooksByAuthor>" & _
  "</soap:Body>" & _
  "</soap:Envelope>"

  oXMLHTTP.setRequestHeader "Content-Type", "text/xml"
  oXMLHTTP.setRequestHeader "SOAPAction",
                    "http://Oreilly/DotNetEssentials/GetBooksByAuthor"

  oXMLHTTP.send sBody

  Set oDOM = oXMLHTTP.responseXML
```

```
' Create the XSL document to be used for transformation
Set oXSL = New DOMDocument
oXSL.Load App.Path & "\templateAuthorTitle.xsl"

' Transform the XML document into an HTML document
myWebBrowser.Document.Write oDOM.transformNode(oXSL)
myWebBrowser.Document.Close

Set oXSL = Nothing
Set oDOM = Nothing
Set oXMLHTTP = Nothing
End Sub
```

This method is structurally similar to the ones used for HTTP GET and HTTP POST; however, it has some very important differences. In SOAP, you have to set the Content-Type to text/xml instead of application/x-www-form-urlencoded as for the HTTP POST. By this time, it should be clear to you that only HTTP POST and SOAP care about the Content-Type because they send the data in the body of the HTTP request. The HTTP GET protocol does not really care about the Content-Type because all of the parameters are packaged into the query string. In addition to the difference in format of the data content, you also have to refer to the WSDL to set the SOAPAction header variable to the call you want. Looking back at the SOAP section of the WSDL, if you want to call the GetBooks(sAuthorSSN) method of the Web Service, you will set the SOAPAction header variable to http://Oreilly/DotNetEssentials/GetBooksByAuthor. On the other hand, if you want to call the GetBooks() method instead, the SOAPAction variable has to be set to http://Oreilly/DotNetEssentials/GetBooks. The reason the namespace is http://Oreilly/DotNetEssentials/ is because we set it up as the attribute of the PubsWS Web Service class.

After setting up the header variables, pass the parameters to the server in the body of the message. While HTTP POST passes the parameters in name/value pairs, SOAP passes the parameters in a well-defined XML structure:

```
<soap:Envelope ...namespace omitted...">
  <soap:Body>
    <GetBooksByAuthor xmlns="http://Oreilly/DotNetEssentials/">
      <sAuthorSSN>213-46-8915</sAuthorSSN>
    </GetBooksByAuthor>
  </soap:Body>
</soap:Envelope>
```

Both the SOAP request and response messages are packaged within a Body inside an Envelope. With the previously specified request, the response SOAP message looks like this:

```
<?xml version="1.0"?>
<soap:Envelope ...namespace omitted...>
```

```
<soap:Body>
  <GetBooksByAuthorResult xmlns="http://Oreilly/DotNetEssentials/">
    <result>
      <xsd:schema id="NewDataSet" ...>

        <... content omitted ...>

      </xsd:schema>
      <NewDataSet xmlns="">
        <Books>
          <title_id>BU1032</title_id>
          <title>The Busy Executive's Database Guide</title>
        <... more ...>
        </Books>
        <Books>
          <title_id>BU2075</title_id>
          <title>You Can Combat Computer Stress!</title>
          <... more ...>
        </Books>
        <Author>
          <au_id>213-46-8915</au_id>
          <au_lname>Green</au_lname>
          <au_fname>Marjorie</au_fname>
          <phone>415 986-7020</phone>
          <address>309 63rd St. #411</address>
          <city>Oakland</city>
          <state>CA</state>
          <zip>94618</zip>
          <contract>True</contract>
        </Author>
      </NewDataSet>
    </result>
  </GetBooksByAuthorResult>
</soap:Body>
</soap:Envelope>
```

Figure 6-8 shows the result of the test form after invoking the GetBooks-ByAuthor web method using the SOAP protocol.

Figure 6-8. VB client form after calling GetBooksByAuthor

The XSL stylesheet used for transformation of the resulting XML to HTML is included here for your reference. Notice that since GetBooksByAuthor returns two tables in the dataset, author and books, we can display both the author information and the books that this author wrote.

```html
<html version="1.0" xmlns:xsl="http://www.w3.org/TR/WD-xsl">
<head><title>A list of books</title></head>
<style>
.hdr { background-color=#ffeedd; font-weight=bold; }
</style>
<body>
<B>List of books written by
  <I><xsl:value-of select="//Author/au_fname"/>
     <xsl:value-of select="//Author/au_lname"/>
     (<xsl:value-of select="//Author/city"/>,
     <xsl:value-of select="//Author/state"/>)
  </I>
</B>
<table style="border-collapse:collapse" border="1">
<tr>
  <td class="hdr">Title</td>
  <td class="hdr">Type</td>
  <td class="hdr">Price</td>
  <td class="hdr">Notes</td>
</tr>
<xsl:for-each select="//Books">
<tr>
  <td><xsl:value-of select="title"/></td>
  <td><xsl:value-of select="type"/></td>
  <td><xsl:value-of select="price"/></td>
  <td><xsl:value-of select="notes"/></td>
</tr>
</xsl:for-each>
</table>
</body>
</html>
```

As you can see, we can easily have any type of Web Service clients accessing .NET Web Services. The clients to the Web Services need to know how to communicate only in HTTP and understand the Web Services Description Language (WSDL) to communicate with the server. By the same token, we can also develop Web Services in any language and on any platform as long as we adhere to the specification of WSDL.

Web Services and Security

This section demonstrates how to incorporate security into your Web Service. We will do so in two ways: system security and application security. System-level security allows for restricting access to the Web Services from unauthorized clients. It is done in a declarative fashion, whereas application-level security is more flexible. With system-level security, you will most likely have the list of authorized clients' IP addresses that you will let access your Web Service through the use of some configuration-management tools. With application-level security, you will incorporate the authentication into your Web Service, thus providing a more flexible configuration.

System Security

Because Web Services communication is done through HTTP, you can apply system-level security on Web Services just as you do for other web pages or resources on your web site.

There are a number of different ways you can secure your Web Services. For a B2B solution, you can use the IIS Administration Tool to restrict or grant permission to a set of IP addresses, using the Internet Protocol Security (IPSec) to make sure that the IP address in the TCP/IP header is authenticated. When you rely only on the client to provide the IP in the TCP/IP header, hackers can still impersonate other host IPs when accessing your Web Services. IPSec authenticates the host addresses using the Kerberos authentication protocol. You can also use a firewall to restrict access to your Web Services for your partner companies. For a business-to-consumer (B2C) scenario, you can take advantage of the authentication features of the HTTP protocol.

To show how to use the authentication feature of the HTTP protocol to secure your Web Services, let's revisit the example Web Service we have in this chapter, PubsWS. All we have to do to secure PubsWS Web Service is go to the IIS Admin Tool and choose to edit the File Security properties for the *PubsWS.asmx*. Instead of keeping the default setting, which leaves this file accessible to all anonymous users, we change this setting to "Basic Authentication" only, which means unchecking "Anonymous Access" and checking only "Basic Authentication" in the Authenticated Access frame. After this change, only users that pass the authentication can make use of the Web Service.

For real-life situations, of course, we are not going to use just the Basic Authentication method, because it sends the username and password in clear text through the HTTP channel. We would choose other methods, such as Secure Sockets Layer (SSL) underneath Basic Authentication, so that the data passed back and forth is secure. Available methods include:

Basic Authentication
> Sends the username and password to the web server in clear text. IIS authenticates the login against the database of users for the domain.

Basic over SSL Authentication
> Similar to Basic Authentication, except that the username and password are sent with Secure Sockets Layer (SSL) encryption.

Digest Authentication
> Uses a hashing technique, as opposed to SSL encryption, to send client credentials securely to the server.

Integrated Windows Authentication
> Good for intranet scenarios only. Uses the login information of the client for authentication.

Client Certificates Authentication
> Requires each of the clients to obtain a certificate that is mapped to a user account. The use of client-side digital certificates is not widespread at this time.

Application Security

A less systematic way of securing your Web Services involves taking security into your own hands. You can program your Web Services so that all of their methods require an access token, which can be obtained from the Web Service after sending in the client's username and password. The client credentials can be sent to the server through SSL, which eliminates the risk of sending clear-text passwords across the wire. Through this SSL channel, the server returns an access token to the caller, who can use it to invoke all other Web Service methods. Of course, all of the other web methods that you publish have to have one parameter as the token. A simple pseudocode example of a bank account Web Service can be as follows:

```
Web Service Bank Account
  Web Methods:
    Login(user id, password) returns access token or nothing
    Deposit(access token, account number, amount, balance) returns boolean
    Withdraw(access token, account number, amount, balance) returns boolean
```

The only method that should be on SSL is the Login method. Once the token is obtained, it can be used for other web methods. Of course, you should be able to make sure that subsequent calls using this token are coming from the same IP as the Login( ) call. You can also incorporate an expiration timestamp on this access token to ensure that the token only exists in a certain time frame until a renewal of the access token is needed.

The Microsoft .NET Cryptographic Services can be very useful if you choose this route. DES, RC2, TripleDES, and RSA encryption/decryption algorithms are supported along with hashing methods such as SHA and MD5.

These implementations in the .NET library enable developers to avoid low-level grunt work and focus on the application logic.

Summary

In this chapter, we've introduced you to the new paradigm of applications—the enterprise application. You are no longer restricted to homogeneous platforms for implementing your solutions. With Microsoft Web Services, your solutions can span many different platforms because the communication between Web Services is done through standard Internet protocols such as HTTP and XML. The distributed components in Windows DNA with which you may be familiar are now replaced by Web Services. Using Web Services as components in a distributed environment allows for a heterogeneous system. The Web Services in your system can not only be implemeneted in different languages, but they can even be on different platforms. Because of this greater interoperability, Web Services are eminently suitable for business-to-business (B2B) integration.

CHAPTER 7

Web Forms

This chapter introduces the next technology for providing dynamic and interactive web pages. ASP.NET takes ASP a step further to simplify the development process of web pages and enhance scalability of web applications. First, we review the conventional way of developing web applications using ASP to uncover some of the pitfalls that ASP.NET overcomes. We then discuss the benefits of ASP.NET and provide a high-level survey of the classes in the ASP.NET, such as control and page, as well as the complete syntax of ASP.NET Web Forms. To wrap up the chapter, we discuss the many aspects of ASP.NET development: how ASP.NET supports Web Services development, how to use custom server controls, and how session management has been improved to provide more scalable web solutions. This overview chapter is designed to provide experienced developers with a solid introduction to ASP.NET and Web Forms; for additional in-depth information, see *Programming ASP.NET* by Liberty and Hurwitz (O'Reilly) and *ASP.NET in a Nutshell* by Duthie and Mani (O'Reilly).

ASP

Microsoft Active Server Pages (ASP) is a server-side scripting technology enabling dynamic web pages. An ASP page contains HTML markup and server-side scripts that generate HTML content dynamically. The server-side scripts run when a request for the ASP page arrives at the web server. Inputs to the ASP page come from the client browsers through HTTP POST and GET methods. ASP provides an object model to simplify developers' tasks. Besides objects from the ASP object model like Application, Server, Request, Response, and Session, developers can use any COM components on the server.

If you've already been developing web applications using ASP, you probably agree that it is very easy to end up with intertwined, possibly conflicting

HTML markups and server-side scripts. The poor encapsulation model of ASP pages makes them difficult to manage and reuse. Attempts have been made to improve upon this model, including server-side include files and parameterized functions in scripts; however, these attempts come with trade-offs such as time, the management of a network of include files, the performance impact of having nested includes, as well as object ID and variable-scope management.

Developers that deal with cross-browser web applications also run into problems generating HTML according the client's browser capability. Most of the time, we end up generating only the simplest HTML tags and client-side scripts, which can be understood by many browsers, and foregoing the features of the more advanced browsers. The resulting web application can be only as good as the worst browser it supports. Sometimes, we also attempt to generate different HTML markups for different browsers to take advantage of browser-specific features, resulting in much better client-side experience; however, this involves much more development time and effort.

Since scripting in ASP is available only to late-bound languages such as VBScript and JavaScript, type-safety is not an option. In addition, server-side scripts in ASP pages get reinterpreted each time the page is accessed, which is not ideal for performance.

Form-state maintenance in an ASP-based application is also labor-intensive—developers must do everything manually, including reposting data, using hidden fields, and session variables. At times, web applications are configured to run in web farm environments where there is more than one web server available to the client. Maintaining session states becomes much harder in these scenario because it is not guaranteed that the client would return to the same server for the next request. Basically, the developers have to save states manually to SQL Server or other external storage.

While ASP is a great technology to build dynamic web pages, it has room for improvement. ASP.NET evolved from ASP and overcomes most, if not all, of its shortfalls.

ASP.NET

Visual Basic developers have long enjoyed the ease of programming with forms and controls. Writing a VB form-based application is as simple as dragging some controls onto a form and writing some event-handling functions. This is one of the reasons VB has attracted lots of programmers interested in speed of development. Microsoft wisely built this feature into ASP.NET.

ASP.NET simplifies web page development with form-based programming. In ASP.NET, these forms are called *Web Forms* and are analogous to VB forms, replacing ASP pages. Similar to VB, Web Forms programming is also event based. We don't have to write in-line ASP scripts and rely on the top-down parsing interpretation as in ASP programming. To match the rich set of ActiveX controls that VB programmers love in their toolset, ASP.NET equips ASP programmers with *server controls*. To further enhance the productivity of developers, ASP.NET's Web Forms also allow for the separation of the application logic and the presentation layer.

ASP.NET evolves from the ASP programming model with the following additional benefits:

- Clean separation between the application logic (server-side code) and the presentation layer (HTML markup)—no more spaghetti code
- A rich set of server controls that automatically render HTML suitable for any clients and that additionally manage their states
- Enhanced session-state management
- An event-based programming model on the server side, which is simpler and more intuitive
- Application logic that can be written in any Microsoft .NET language (VB, C#, Managed C++, etc.); application server-side code is compiled for better performance
- Visual Studio.NET as a RAD tool, which simplifies the development process of Web Forms

The System.Web.UI Namespace

Before getting into developing your favorite *Hello, World!* application in ASP. NET, it's important that you become familiar with the underlying structure of ASP.NET. This section describes some of the most important classes packaged in the System.Web.UI namespace in the ASP.NET framework.

The System.Web.UI namespace defines classes and interfaces used in constructing and rendering elements on a Web Form. The most important class in the System.Web.UI is the Control class, which defines properties, methods, and events that are common in all server controls in the Web Forms framework. Another important class in this namespace is Page, which is a derivative of the Control class. All ASP.NET web pages are instances of derivatives of the Page class. To have an extensible framework, the System.Web. UI namespace also includes the UserControl class, which is similar to the Page class except that it is mainly used as the base class for user controls. We will make use of the UserControl and Page classes in "ASP.NET Application Development" and "Custom Server Controls" later in this chapter.

Control Class

The Control class is the root of all controls. For example, a text box is a control; a button or a combo box is also a control. The Control class basically encapsulates common functionalities and properties of all user-interface widgets. As you get deeper into ASP.NET development, everything you see is a Control derivative of some sort.

Control's properties

The Control class has the following important properties: Controls, ID, Parent, EnableViewState, Visible, Context, and ViewState. We will go over each of these properties briefly to show you what the Control class is made up of and how deriving from Control class would create a model that is consistent and easy to work with.

The Controls property represents the children of the control instance; the Parent property defines the parent of the control. These properties enable a hierarchy of controls on a web page. The ID property allows the control to be accessed programmatically by just using the ID and the dot notation to get to the object's properties and methods, i.e., MyObjectId.propertyname. It also allows us to write event handlers for events raised by this control.

The EnableViewState flag indicates whether the control will maintain its view state, as well as all view states of its child controls. If this flag is set to true, the control will remember its previous view state when the page posts back to itself.* For example, if EnableViewState is set to true, the user's previous selection or form-field data are preserved automatically when the user performs some operation that requires a postback. When the page is sent back to the browser, the user can just continue filling in the form as if he never left it. This is how all derivatives of the Control class maintain their states between requests and free developers from the plumbing works with hidden form fields.

The Context property enables us to get to information about the current HTTP request, such as the Application, Server, Session, Request, and

---

* *Postback* is the condition when an ASP page posts the data back to itself for processing. In conventional ASP programming, the state of the fields in the form have to be managed manually. In ASP.NET, we can have these field states managed automatically with a simple EnableViewState flag.

Response objects. ASP developers should be familiar with these intrinsic objects. You will likely use the Context property when you are processing the web page's OnLoad event to get to application- or session-level variables and request parameters to set up your page. Through the Context property, you can also get other information, such as cached resources, including database connections, for performance improvement; the trace property, for debugging purposes; and the user property, for security validation.

The ViewState property is an instance of the StateBag class, which is used to store name/value pairs of information that can be made accessible across multiple requests for the same web page. These name/value pairs are instances of the StateItem class.

Control class methods

The list of methods for the Control class is much longer than what we've covered in this section; however, this short list is probably all you need to know to get started with the Control class:

DataBind method
> Binds the control to a data source. This method is used in conjunction with the data-binding expression syntax on the Web Form. When this method is called, all data-binding tags, <%# %>, are re-evaluated so that the new data is bound to the appropriate tag location.

CreateChildControls method
> Called before any compositional custom control is rendered. A compositional custom control is similar to an ActiveX control: it composes other controls. You would not use this method simply to use the control. When developing custom controls, this method can be overridden so that custom-control developers can create and layout child controls prior to rendering the control, whether for the first time or for postbacks.

Render method
> Similar to the CreateChildControls, primarily used to develop custom controls. Control developers override this method to render the control content through the provided HtmlTextWriter parameter.
>
> We will revisit the Render and CreateChildControls methods when we show you how to create custom controls in "Custom Server Controls" later in this chapter.

SaveViewState and LoadViewState methods
> Save and reload the state for the control. Server controls maintain their state between requests via these methods.

Page Class

As mentioned earlier, the Page class is actually a derivative* of the Control class. This means it inherits all properties, methods, and events exposed by the Control class. In addition to the inherited things, the Page class defines more specific properties, methods, and events for a web page in the ASP.NET framework.

If you've done ASP development, you already know that Application, Request, Response, Server, and Session are intrinsic objects that you can access while scripting your ASP page. With ASP.NET, these objects are actually properties of the Page class. In addition to these familiar objects, the Page class also exposes other properties such as Cache, ErrorPage, IsPostBack, IsValid, Trace, and Validators.

Page class properties and methods

This list is not complete; however, it includes some of the more important features that we want to introduce:

Cache property
> Points to a Cache object of the Context for the current page. Here, resources such as database connections are stored for reuse without having to recreate the connection, given that the cache item is not yet expired.

ErrorPage property
> Specifies the page to display when an error occurs. You can also specify the error page by using the @Page directive as shown in the "Web Form Syntax" section in this chapter.

IsPostBack property
> Indicates whether the page request is an original request or a postback, since the interaction between the user and the server controls requires a postback to the current page. If IsPostBack is true, you should not redo all your page initialization to improve performance.

Validators property
> Groups together server controls that can validate themselves inside the Validators property of the Page. (In ASP.NET, a web page usually consists of a number of server controls.) This is so that when the Page needs to validate itself, it can delegate the validation to all of these controls and then set the IsValid property to the appropriate value.

---

* The Page class derives from TemplateControl, which derives from the Control class.

Trace property

References a TraceContext object, through which you can issue warning or error messages. Tracing can be switched on or off at anytime from the web.config setting. *web.config* is an XML-based text file that stores the runtime configuration for an ASP.NET application. Changes to this file take effect immediately, unlike *global.asa* in ASP development. The main configuration file is at the root of your web application; however, you can have a configuration file for each subdirectory in your web application. The closest configuration file overrides the settings of distant configuration files. Being able to switch off tracing in a configuration file like this is much better than doing so manually in ASP development, where you must go through all ASP files to remove all instances of Response.Write debugging messages when you are ready to deploy your application.

LoadControl method

Loads server controls into the page programmatically. You can also have static server control declared on the page using the server-side object syntax as described in the "Web Form Syntax" section later in this chapter.

MapPath method

Maps a virtual path to a physical path for file I/O. This should be familiar to ASP developers.

Validate method

Works with the Server Validation Controls on the page to validate data on the page. If any of the server controls fail to validate, this method returns false, and the failed server-validation control renders the error message to the user.

CreateHtmlTextWriter method

Produces an HtmlTextWriter object to write HTML to the response stream. This is similar to ASP's Response.Write method; however, the HtmlTextWriter object is much smarter than the raw Write method. It helps you write well-formed HTML.

SavePageStateToPersistenceMedium and LoadPageStateFromPersistence-Medium methods

By default, save and load view state for all controls as hidden fields on the page. If you don't want this setting, you can override the Save-PageStateFromPersistenceMedium method to save the view state anywhere other than hidden fields. You will also have to override the LoadPageStateFromPersistenceMedium method to have the saved view states loaded back onto the page prior to rendering.

UserControl Class

The UserControl class is similar to the Page class (see the previous section) with the omission of page-specific properties or methods such as ErrorPage, IsValid, User, Validators, MapPath, Validate, and CreateHtmlTextWriter.

The UserControl class is typically used as the base class for custom controls. We can also build custom controls by inheriting directly from the Control class; however, it's better to start from UserControl because it is not as raw as the Control class. If you find that UserControl supports a number of properties and methods that you don't really want in your custom control, you might choose to inherit the raw Control class instead. We show you how to create custom controls in the "Custom Server Controls" section later in this chapter.

System.Web.UI.HtmlControls Namespace

If you've done any client-side DHTML scripting, you know how all HTML tags are mapped to scriptable objects. ASP.NET brings this mapping to the server side. Before the web page is rendered and sent back the client, you can access and manipulate each of the objects on the page.

ASP.NET maps HTML tags with objects in the hierarchy of server-side classes defined in the System.Web.UI.HtmlControls namespace. These server objects are called *HtmlControls* because they closely map to standard HTML elements.

For example, here is a simple HTML page that relies on client-side scripting to change the output page dynamically. (This page won't run on browsers that do not support VBScript client-side scripting or browsers that have client-side scripting turned off.)

```
<html>
<head>
  <script language=vbscript>
  sub cmd1_onclick( )
    txtMessage.InnerHtml = _
        "(Client-side) Your name is: " & frm1.txtName.value
  end sub
  </script>
</head>
<body>
  <form id=frm1>
    Enter Name: <input id="txtName" type="text" size="40">
    <input type=button id="cmd1" value="Click Me">
    <span id="txtMessage"></span>
  </form>
</body>
</html>
```

We will convert this page so that it relies on server control instead of the IE Document Object Model. Since the output of the page is controlled from the server side, the page works regardless of what kind of browser you are using. One drawback to this is that all interaction with the page requires a post-back to the server.

To take advantage of server controls mapping, all you have to do is to add the id and runat attributes, and your server-side script will be able to access and manipulate the server controls:

```
<html>
<head>
  <script id="scr1" language="c#" runat="server">
    void svr_cmd1_onclick(Object o, EventArgs e)
    {
      txtMessage.InnerHtml =
          "(Server-side) Your name is: " + txtName.Value;
    }
  </script>
</head>
<body>
  <form id="frm1" runat="server">
    Enter Name: <input id="txtName" type="text" size="40" runat="server">
    <input type="button" id="cmd1" value="Click Me"
        onserverclick="svr_cmd1_onclick" runat="server">
    <span id="txtMessage" runat="server"></span>
  </form>
</body>
</html>
```

By adding the runat="server" attribute to the HTML form and its controls, you have exposed an HtmlForm object, an HtmlInputText object, an Html-InputButton object, and an HtmlGenericControl object (the span) to your server-side script, as depicted in Figure 7-1. As you can see in the previous script, you can manipulate the HtmlGenericControl object's txtMessage to set its InnerHtml property.

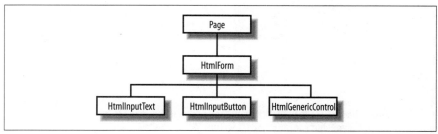

Figure 7-1. Server-side scriptable objects for the code example

---

Even though the results of the two simple examples appear to be the same, they are drastically different from the technical point of view. Client-side scripting, as the name implies, runs in the client browser process. On the other hand, when we have controls tagged to run on the server, we can have accesses to other server resources.

Most classes in the System.Web.UI.HtmlControls namespace are derivatives of the HtmlControl class, which in turn derives from the Control class of the System.Web.UI namespace. See Figure 7-2 for a graphical presentation of the hierarchy. The HtmlControl class serves as the base class for these HtmlControls because most HTML elements share common characteristics that are defined in this HtmlControl base class. They share properties such as ID, Disabled, Value, Style, and TagName. Because these HtmlControls ultimately are derivatives of the Control class, they also have methods and events that the Control class exposes.

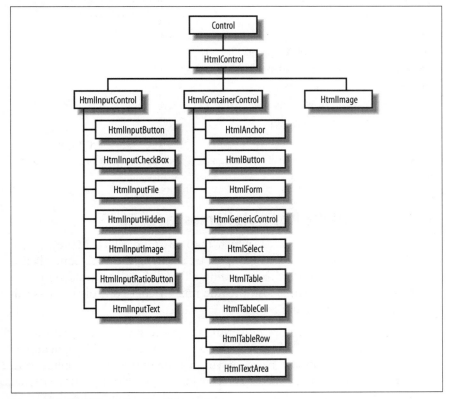

Figure 7-2. HtmlControls object hierarchy

Table 7-1 maps the HtmlControls to standard HTML tags. This means when you have an HTML tag that is flagged to run on the server side with `runat="server"`, ASP.NET creates an appropriate HtmlControl that you can program against.

Table 7-1. HtmlControls mapping to HTML tags

HTMLControl	Description	HTML tag
HtmlImage	Image tag	`<img>`
HtmlInputFile	File selector	`<input type="file">`
HtmlInputHidden	Used for hidden form fields	`<input type="hidden">`
HtmlInputImage	Image input	`<input type="image">`
HtmlInputRadioButton	Radio button	`<input type="radio">`
HtmlInputText	Standard text input	`<input type="text">`
HtmlInputButton	Standard HTML but_ ton	`<input type="button">`
HtmlInputCheckBox	Standard HTML checkbox	`<input type="checkbox">`
HtmlForm	Form tag	`<form>`
HtmlGenericControl	Miscellaneous generic HTML tags	`<span, div, etc.>`
HtmlSelect	Standard HTML drop-down control	`<select>`
HtmlTable	Standard HTML table	`<table>`
HtmlTableCell	A cell in a table row	`<td>`
HtmlTableRow	A row in a table	`<tr>`
HtmlTextArea	Multiline text area	`<textarea rows=n cols=n>`
HtmlAnchor	Standard HTML hyperlink control	`<a href=...>` or `<a name=...>`
HtmlButton	HTML button	`<button>`

System.Web.UI.WebControls Namespace

While providing HtmlControls, which map to standard HTML elements, ASP.NET also provides another group of UI controls, the WebControl class (see Figure 7-3). In addition to providing all traditional controls similar to HtmlControls, WebControls also provide much richer controls such as calendars, grids, and validators.

WebControls are richer, more powerful, and more flexible than HtmlControls. It seems that it is the natural choice for new ASP.NET applications; however, HtmlControls are better if you are migrating ASP applications. Another thing that might make you consider using HtmlControls is that with it, your client-side scripts can still access and manipulate the objects.

Most classes in this namespace are based on WebControl, which is again a derivative of the Control class. The WebControl class provides the common properties and methods inherited by all of its descendants, including access key, tab index, tool tip, color, font, and border setting.

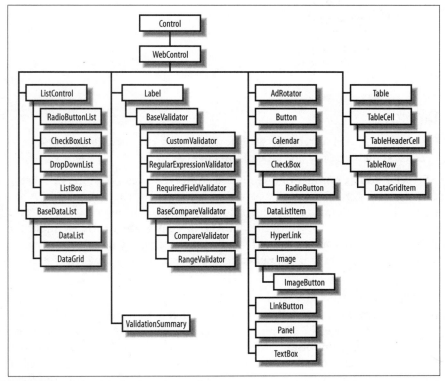

Figure 7-3. WebControls object hierarchy

Web Form Syntax

Similar to Active Server Pages, Web Forms are text files consisting of HTML tags and other controlling tags such as directives and script blocks. The default extension for web forms is *aspx*; however, you can use the IIS administration tool to map other file extensions explicitly with *aspnet_isapi.dll* to have them parsed and compiled when accessed, as if they were ASP.NET resources.

There are ten different syntax elements in ASP.NET; because most of them are carried over from ASP, we list here the familiar ones and discuss only those that are important in ASP.NET:

Directives
Code declaration blocks

Code rendering blocks
HTML control syntax
Custom control syntax
Data-binding expressions
Server-side object tags
Server-side include directives
Server-side comments
Literal text

Directives

Previously, all ASP directives were formatted as <%@ [*attribute=value*]+ %> because there was only one type of directive.*

ASP.NET adds a number of directives to ASP.NET files. With the new list of directives—Page, Control, Import, Implements, Register, Assembly, OutputCache and Reference—the syntax for directive is now <%@ directive [*attribute=value*]+ %>. All of the old ASP directives are attributes under the Page directive. If you use the old syntax by omitting the directive name, the attribute/value pairs will be applied to the default directive, which is Page.

@ Page

In addition to containing all previous ASP directives (CodePage, EnableSessionState, Language, LCID, and Transaction), the ASP.NET Page directive also supports the important attributes ErrorPage, Inherits, Src, and EnableViewState, which we will make use of in this chapter. The complete list of all attributes for the Page directive can be found in the .NET Framework Developers' Guide.

```
<@ Page Language="VB" ErrorPage="URL" EnableViewState="true">
```

@ Control

Similar to the way the Page directive is used for an ASP.NET page (an .aspx file), the Control directive is used for an ASP.NET control (an .ascx file). (We get into developing ASP.NET controls in the "Custom Server Controls" section later in this chapter.)

---

* As noted in the Preface, the plus sign here indicates one or more instances of the preceding term in brackets.

@ Import

We can use the Import directive to add namespace references to the current page. Your code can access all classes and interfaces of imported namespaces. For example, if you want to use ADO.NET, you would include the following code:

```
<%@ Import Namespace="System.Data" %>
<%@ Import Namespace="System.Data.OleDb" %>
```

A number of namespaces are automatically imported into all ASP.NET pages to simplify the developers' task:

System
System.Collections
System.Collections.Specialized
System.Configuration
System.IO
System.Text
System.Text.RegularExpressions
System.Web
System.Web.Caching
System.Web.Security
System.Web.SessionState
System.Web.UI
System.Web.UI.HtmlControls
System.Web.UI.WebControls

@Implements

Because an *aspx* file is basically a Page class derivative, it too can also implement an interface. The @Implements directive is used to declare that the *aspx* implements the specified interface. For example, the following line declares that the page implements the IPostBackEventHandler interface:

```
<%@ Implements Interface="System.Web.UI.IPostBackEventHandler" %>
```

@ Register

This directive registers custom server controls for use in the current page by specifying the aliases to be used as prefixes for class names. It is used in conjunction with the custom server-control elements to provide a concise way of specifying server-control names. The following line of code registers a custom control to be used in this page:

```
<%@ Register Tagprefix="Ch07"
             TagName="MyCustomControl
             Src="MyCustomControl.ascx" %>
```

The name of the control is `MyCustomControl`; the prefix used when declaring the control is `Ch07`; the source for the control is in `MyCustomControl.ascx`. (We demonstrate this when we develop our ASP.NET controls later in this chapter.)

@ Assembly

The Assembly directive specifies the assembly to which the current page belongs. This effectively makes all the classes and interfaces belonging to the assembly accessible to the current page. For example, the following line of code specifies that the current page belong to the Ch07 assembly:

```
<%@ Assembly Name="Ch07" %>
```

This means that code in this page can access anything in the Ch07 assembly.

@ OutputCache

You can use the OutputCache directive to control the output-caching duration for the current page. This is similar to setting up the expiration for the response object in ASP programming. The Duration attribute of the OutputCache directive defines the time in seconds until the page expires.

@Reference

The @Reference directive is used to add a reference to a page or a control to this *aspx* page.

Code Declaration Blocks

As in ASP, *code declaration blocks* define the code to be parsed and run for the page. In these blocks, the runat attribute specifies whether the code block is client-side or server-side code. For server-side programming, set this attribute to server. If you ignore the runat attribute, IIS will interpret the code block as client-side code, which is used for Dynamic HTML (DHTML).

```
<script runat="server" [language="codelanguage"]>
  Code
</script>
```

For both client-side and server-side code declaration blocks, you can also use the src attribute to point to an external source file containing the code. This is to help separate the code from the HTML content of the page. The value for src can be a relative path or a URL to a source file. The URL can be on the same or a different web server.

```
<script runat="server"
  [language="codelanguage"]
  [src="externalfilename"] />
```

Code Rendering Blocks

There are no changes to this syntax versus that in ASP. Inline code or inline expressions specified in these code rendering blocks are executed when the page is rendered. All these blocks are enclosed between the tags <% and %>. The language used in these tags is specified in the language attribute of the Page directive.

HTML-Control Syntax

HTML controls are very similar to standard HTML elements, with the exception of the id and the runat attributes. If you've developed web applications with DHTML, you should be familiar with the id attribute of an HTML element and how to programmatically reference the client-side control representing the HTML element. The difference in this case is that the control is not on the client side but on the server side. For example, the following code represents an HTML server button control:

```
<input id="cmd1" runat="server"
   type="button" value="Click Me" />
```

All HTML server controls must be inside a <form runat="server"> control because web forms use the POST method to maintain the controls' states.

When encountering an HTML element tagged with id and the runat attribute set to server, ASP.NET creates the appropriate scriptable server HtmlControl object. For example, the previous HTML snippet generates a server HtmlControl of type HtmlInputButton that has an id of cmd1.

You can bind an event handler to this control's event to handle notification from this control, such as the onclick event. There are two ways to bind an event handler to a control's event, the declarative way and the programmatic way. The declarative is done inside the HTML element tag as an attribute/value pair. The attribute is the name of the event, and the value is the name of the event-handling function. For example, to handle the onclick event, add this to the previous HTML tag:

```
onserverclick="handleServerClick"
```

The programmatic way to bind an event to the handler involves a line of code that assigns a delegate to the event property of the control. In C#, the code to bind the ServerClick event of the button to the event handler handleServerClick is:

```
cmd1.ServerClick += new System.EventHandler(handleServerClick);
```

If you've used client-side DHTML in your web applications, event binding should be nothing new to you, except for some subtle differences. The first difference is obvious: the event handler runs on the server before the page is sent back to the browser, instead of running on the client side. The other difference is that all event-handler functions for server-side have to have two parameters: Sender and Event. The Sender parameter is of type object, indicating the source element that caused the event to happen; the Event parameter is of type EventArgs, which is the actual event fired. In DHTML scripting, we would inspect the window.event object to find out which element was the source of the event and other event information.

Custom-Control Syntax

Similar to HTML Server Controls, *custom controls* also have id and runat attributes; however, custom controls are not standard HTML elements. To insert a custom control into a page, use the following syntax:

```
<tagprefix:tagname id="controlID" runat="server" eventname=
    "eventHandler" />
```

Notice that all custom controls' tags have a tag prefix, which is an alias to the namespace in which the control is defined. See the Register directive earlier in this chapter for information on registering namespaces' aliases. Binding events to their handlers for custom controls is the same as for HTML controls. Even though we show the two ways of binding events, it is preferable to bind events using the second method because it cleanly separates the HTML tags from the code behind the screen.

All web controls mentioned in the WebControls namespace can be inserted in the same manner (these controls have the prefix asp). For example, you can have the following tags in your *aspx* page:

```
<asp:TextBox id=txt1 runat=server></asp:TextBox>
<asp:Button id=cmd1 runat=server Text="Web Button"></asp:Button>
<asp:Label id=label1 runat=server></asp:Label>
```

These tags result in three objects generated from the three classes: TextBox, Button, and Label, from the System.Web.UI.WebControls namespace. In your server script, you can access and manipulate these objects to render your page appropriately.

Data-Binding Expressions

Data-binding expressions bind the server controls with some data sources. The syntax to bind data is:

```
<%# data-binding-expression %>
```

Examine the following block of code to see the simplest data binding:

```
<asp:Label text='<%# TestData %>' runat=server/>
```

The data-binding expression here indicates that the label's text content is bound to a publicly defined property, TestData, of the Web Form. This means that when data binding occurs for the form, <%# TestData %> will be replaced by the content of the TestData property. Let's define this property for the Web Form:

```
public string TestData = "Hello World";
```

The Web Forms page framework does not perform data binding automatically. The developers must explicitly call the DataBind() method to activate the evaluation of the data-binding expression and perform the substitution. We can call the page's DataBind method upon the page-load event or whenever we change the TestData property and want it reflected on the page. This example calls DataBind() upon page load to bind the Label's text to the TestData variable.

```
<html>
  <head><title>Data Binding Sample</title></head>
  <body>

    <script language="C#" runat=server>
      /* Declare the variable we want to bind to. */
      public string TestData;
      void Page_Load(Object oSender, EventArgs oEvent) {
        TestData = "Hello World!\n";
        Page.DataBind();
      }
    </script>

    <asp:Label text='<%# TestData %>' runat=server/>

  </body>
</html>
```

Let's try something a little more complicated. In the next block of tags, we have three labels bound to three different properties of an object called currStudent:

```
Name: <asp:Label text='<%# currStudent.FirstName %>' runat=server/>
<asp:Label text='<%# currStudent.LastName %>' runat=server/> <br/>
SSN: <asp:Label text='<%# currStudent.SSN %>' runat=server/>
```

The currStudent object is a publicly accessible property of the current page.

```
<script language="C#" runat=server>
  public class CStudent {
    /* Declare the variable we want to bind to. */
    public string FirstName;
    public string LastName;
    public string SSN;
  }
  public CStudent currStudent;
```

```
void Page_Load(Object oSender, EventArgs oEvent) {
  currStudent = new CStudent( );
  currStudent.FirstName = "Jack";
  currStudent.LastName = "Daniel";
  currStudent.SSN = "123-45-6789";
  Page.DataBind( );
}

</script>
```

You can have this currStudent object filled with data coming from any source then perform a DataBind call to update the page with the current student's information. The assumption here, of course, is that the Student class provides the previously mentioned properties.

Server-Side Object Tags

Server-side object tags statically declare and instantiate COM and .NET objects. The syntax to declare server-side objects in *global.asax* is:

```
<object id="id" runat="server" scope="scope" class=".NET class name">
<object id="id" runat="server" scope="scope" progid="COM ProgID">
<object id="id" runat="server" scope="scope" classid="COM classID">
```

Scope can be pipeline, application, or session, which means the object is available on the page, as an application variable, or as a session variable respectively. To dynamically add a server-side object to the page, you would use the Page.LoadControl( ) method.

Other Elements

Server-side includes, server-side comments, and literal text are exactly the same as in ASP. Therefore, we will not go over them here.

ASP.NET Application Development

In conventional ASP programming, developers typically access the Request object to get the parameters needed to render the page and render the content of the page through either the Response object or code rendering blocks. We also use other ASP objects such as the Application, Session, and Server objects to manage application variables, session variables, server settings, and so on.

As mentioned earlier, ASP.NET is intended to change all this spaghetti madness by introducing a much cleaner approach to server-side scripting framework: Web Forms, or programmable pages, and server controls.

In the following sections, we cover the components of a Web Form, its life cycles, the server controls that the Web Form contains, event-handling for these server controls, as well as how to create your own server controls.

Web Form Components

Similar to VB Forms, a Web Form consists of two components: the form with its controls, and the code behind it that handles events associated with the form's controls. A Web Form has the file extension *.aspx* and contains HTML elements, as well as server controls. The code behind the form is usually located in a separate class file. Note that while it is possible to have both the form and the code in one file, it is better to have separate files. This separation of user interface and application code helps improve the spaghetti-code symptom that most ASP-based applications are plagued with.

ASP.NET provides the Page class in the System.Web.UI namespace. This class encapsulates all common properties and methods associated with web pages. The code behind the class derives from this Page class to provide extensions specific to the page we're implementing. The *aspx* file provides the form layout and control declarations. Figure 7-4 illustrates the relationship between the Page base class, the Web Form code behind the class, and the Web Form user interface (UI).

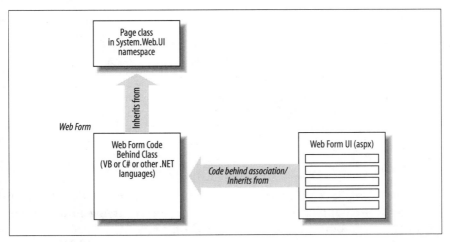

Figure 7-4. Web Form components

As a Web Form developer, you will have to provide the latter two. The Web Form UI is where you declare server controls with appropriate IDs. The code behind the class is where you programmatically access server controls declared in the Web Form UI, as well as handle events from these controls.

The following simple example shows the *aspx* page, the code behind source file, and how they work together. The *aspx* file (*TestEvent.aspx*) contains only HTML tags and a directive that links to the code behind:

```
<%@ Page language="c#" codebehind="TestEvents.cs" inherits="CTestEvents" %>
<html>
  <head><title>Testing Page Events with codebehind</title></head>
  <body>
    <form runat=server>
      Init Time: <asp:Label id=labelInit runat=server/><br/>
      Load Time: <asp:Label id=labelLoad runat=server/><br/>
      <input type=submit />
    </form>
  </body>
</html>
```

The code-behind, *TestEvents.cs*, contains the class CTestEvents to which the *aspx* page is referring:

```
using System;

public class CTestEvents : System.Web.UI.Page {
  protected System.Web.UI.WebControls.Label labelInit;
  protected System.Web.UI.WebControls.Label labelLoad;

  public CTestEvents() {
    labelInit = new System.Web.UI.WebControls.Label();
    labelLoad = new System.Web.UI.WebControls.Label();
  }

  public void Page_Init(Object oSender, EventArgs oEvent) {
    labelInit.Text = DateTime.Now.ToString();
  }

  public void Page_Load(Object oSender, EventArgs oEvent) {
    labelLoad.Text = DateTime.Now.ToString();
    if(IsPostBack) {
      labelLoad.Text += "(PostBack)";
    }
  }
}
```

You must compile *TestEvents.cs* and place the DLL in the */bin* directory under your web application's virtual directory before trying to access the *aspx* page.* The command to compile this C# file is:

```
csc /t:library TestEvents.cs
```

---

* The Web Application directory is the root virtual directory where your web application resides. To set up the virtual directory, use the IIS Administration Tool.

ASP.NET parses the Web Form files to generate a tree of scriptable objects, where the root is the Page-derived object representing the current Web Form. This is similar to how the IE browser parses the HTML file and generates a tree of scriptable objects to be used in DHTML; however, the tree of objects for the Web Form files resides on the server side.

As you are already aware from our survey of the System.Web.UI namespace, the Page class actually derives from the Control class. In a sense, a Web Form is a hierarchy of Control-derived objects. These objects establish the parent-child relationship through the Parent and Controls properties.

Besides the Controls and Parent properties, the Page class also provides other useful properties, which are familiar to ASP developers—such as the Request, Response, Application, Session, and Server properties.

Because the Web Form is nothing but a programmable page object, using this object-oriented model is much more intuitive and cleaner than the conventional ASP development. As opposed to the linear execution of server-side scripts on an ASP page, ASP.NET enables an event-based object-oriented programming model.

Let's take an example of a web page that contains a form with numerous fields. One or more of these fields display list information from a database. Naturally, we have code in the ASP page to populate these fields so that when a user requests this ASP page, the generated page would have the content ready. As soon as the last line of data is written to the browser, the ASP page is done. This means that if there were errors when the user submits the form, we will have to repopulate all the database-driven form fields, as well as programmatically reselect values that the user chose prior to submitting the form. In ASP.NET, we don't have to repopulate the database-driven fields if we know that the page has already been populated. Furthermore, selected values stay selected with no manual handlings. The next couple of sections describe the concept in more detail.

Web Form events

The Page class exposes events such as Init, Load, PreRender, and Unload. Your job as a developer is to handle these events and perform the appropriate task for each of these stages. This is much better than the linear execution model in ASP programming, because you don't have to worry about the location of your initialization scripts.

The first event that happens in the life of a Web Form is the Init event. This is raised so that we can have initialization code for the page. The controls on the page are not yet created at this point. This event is raised once for each user of the page.

The Load event follows the Init event. Subsequently, it is raised each time the page is requested. When this event is raised, all child controls of the Web Form are loaded and accessible. You should be able to retrieve data and populate the controls so that they can render themselves on the page when sent back to the client.

The following example shows the how the Init and Load events can be handled in ASP.NET. In this example, we show both the HTML and its code together in one file to make it simpler:

```
<html>
  <head><title>Testing Page Events</title></head>
  <body>

    <script language="C#" runat="server">
      void Page_Init(Object oSender, EventArgs oEvent) {
        labelInit.Text = DateTime.Now.ToString();
      }

      void Page_Load(Object oSender, EventArgs oEvent) {
        labelLoad.Text = DateTime.Now.ToString();
        if(IsPostBack) {
          labelLoad.Text += "(PostBack)";
        }
      }
    </script>

    <form runat="server">
      Init Time: <asp:Label id="labelInit" runat="server"/><br />
      Load Time: <asp:Label id="labelLoad" runat="server"/><br />
      <input type="submit" />
    </form>
  </body>
</html>
```

The first time you access this page, the Init event happens, followed by the Load event. Because these events happen quickly, both the Init Time and Load Time will probably show the same time. When you click on the submit button to cause the page to reload, you can see that the Init Time stays what it was, but the Load Time changes each time the page is reloaded.

The PreRender event happens just before the page is rendered and sent back to the client. We don't often handle this event; however, it depends on the situation.

The last event in the life of a Web Form is the Unload event. This happens when the page is unloaded from memory. Final cleanup should be done here.

Beside these page-level events, controls on the page can raise events like Server-Click and ServerChange for HtmlControls, as well as Click, Command,

CheckedChanged, SelectedIndexChanged, and TextChanged events for WebControls. It is the handling of these events that makes ASP.NET truly dynamic and interactive.

The Life Cycle of a Web Form

In ASP, the web page starts its life when a client requests a particular page. IIS parses and runs the scripts on the ASP page to render HTML content. As soon as the page rendering is complete, the page's life ceases. If you have forms that pass data back to the ASP page to be processed, the ASP page runs as a new request, not knowing anything about its previous states. Passing data back to the original page for processing is also referred to as postback.

In ASP.NET, things are a little different. The page still starts at the client's request; however, it stays around for as long as the client is still interacting with the page. For simplicity's sake, we say that the page stays around, but in fact, only the view states of the page persist between requests to the page. These view states allow the controls on the server to appear as if they are still present to handle server events. We can detect this postback state of the page via the IsPostBack property of the Page object and forego certain costly reinitialization. The handling of events during these postbacks is what makes ASP.NET so much different than conventional ASP development.

In the following example, we extend the previous example to handle the postback. When the Load event is handled for the first time, we populate the drop-down list box with data. Subsequently, we indicate only the time the event is raised without reloading the data. This example also demonstrates the server event handler handleButtonClick that was bound to the ServerClick event of the button:

```
<html>
  <head><title>Testing Page Events</title></head>
  <body>

    <script language="C#" runat="server">
      void Page_Init(Object oSender, EventArgs oEvent) {
        labelInit.Text = DateTime.Now.ToString();
      }

      void Page_Load(Object oSender, EventArgs oEvent) {
        labelLoad.Text = DateTime.Now.ToString();
        if(!IsPostBack) {
          selectCtrl.Items.Add("Acura");
          selectCtrl.Items.Add("BMW");
          selectCtrl.Items.Add("Cadillac");
          selectCtrl.Items.Add("Mercedes");
          selectCtrl.Items.Add("Porche");
```

```
    } else {
      labelLoad.Text += " (Postback)";
    }
  }

  void handleButtonClick(Object oSender, EventArgs oEvent) {
    labelOutput.Text = "You've selected: " + selectCtrl.Value;
    labelEvent.Text = DateTime.Now.ToString( );
  }
</script>

<form runat="server">
  Init Time: <asp:Label id="labelInit" runat="server"/><br/>
  Load Time: <asp:Label id="labelLoad" runat="server"/><br/>
  Event Time: <asp:Label id="labelEvent" runat="server"/><br/>
  Choice: <select id="selectCtrl" runat="server"></select><br/>
  <asp:Label id="labelOutput" runat="server"/><br/>
  <input type=button value="update"
          OnServerClick="handleButtonClick" runat="server" />
</form>

</body>
</html>
```

The life cycle of a Web Form consists of three main stages: Configuration, Event Handling, and Termination. As mentioned earlier, these stages span across many requests to the same page, as opposed to the serving-one-page-at-a-time policy found in ASP.

Configuration

In the Configuration stage, the page's Load event is raised. It is your job to handle this event to set up your page. Because the Load event is raised when all the controls are already up and ready, your job is now to read and update control properties as part of setting up the page. In the previous code example, we handled the Load event to populate the drop-down list with some data. We also updated the labelLoad control's Text to display the time the Load event happens. In your application, you will probably load the data from a database and initialize form fields with default values.

The page's IsPostBack property indicates whether this is the first time the page is loaded or if it is a postback. For example, if you have a control that contains a list of information, you will only want to load this control the first time the page is loaded by checking the IsPostBack property of the page. When IsPostBack is true, you know that the list control object is already loaded with information. There is no need to repopulate the list. In the previous code example, we skipped over the population of the drop-down and just displayed a string "(Postback)".

You might need to perform data binding and re-evaluate data-binding expressions on the first and subsequent round trips to this page.

Events Handling

In this middle stage, the page's server event-handling functions are being called as the result of some events being triggered from the client side. These events are from the controls you've placed on the Web Form. Figure 7-5 depicts the life cycle of an event.

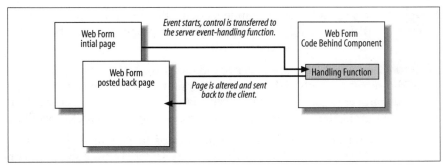

Figure 7-5. The Web Form event life cycle

Termination

At this stage, the page has finished rendering and is ready to be discarded. You are responsible for cleaning up file handles, releasing database connections, and freeing objects. Even though you can rely on the CLR to perform garbage collection for you, we strongly advise you to clean up after yourself because garbage collection only happens periodically. On heavily loaded systems, if the garbage-collection cycle is not optimal, the unfreed resources can exhaust memory and bring your system to a halt.[*]

We can perform the cleanup for the previous example with the Unload event handler as shown here. Because there is nothing to clean up in this simple example, we just show you the function as a template:

```
void Page_Unload(Object oSender, EventArgs oEvent) {
  // cleaning up code here
}
```

---

[*] The garbage collector won't pick up this kind of unintentional memory usage if you have references to objects that are unused, yet remain in scope throughout the life of the application. Therefore, you should not rely solely on this automation.

Server Controls

As we saw from the System.Web.UI.HtmlControls and System.Web.UI.WebControls namespaces, server controls are programmable controls that run on the server before the page is rendered by ASP.NET. They manage their own states between requests to the same page on the server by inserting a hidden field storing the view state of the form. This eliminates the need to repopulate the value of form fields with the posted value before sending the page back the client.

Server controls are also browser-independent. Because they are run on the server side, they can rely on the Request.Browser property to get the client's capability and render appropriate HTML.

Since the server controls are just instantiations of .NET classes, programming the server controls yields easy-to-maintain code. Especially when you have custom server controls that encapsulate other controls, web application programming becomes nothing more than gluing these blocks together.

All HTML controls and web controls mentioned in System.Web.UI.HtmlControls and System.Web.UI.WebControls are server controls shipped with ASP.NET.

Custom Server Controls

As you become more familiar with the ASP.NET framework and the use of server controls on your Web Form, you will eventually need to know how to develop these server controls yourself. In ASP.NET, there are two ways of creating custom server controls: the *pagelet* approach, which is easy to do but rather limited in functionality, and the Control base class (or User-Control) *derivative* approach, which is more complicated but also more powerful and flexible.

Pagelets

Until recently, code reuse in ASP development has been in the form of server-side includes. If you have common UI blocks or scripts, you can factor them into an include file. Use the syntax `<!-- #include file="url" -->` to include the common file into the main page to return to the browser. This approach is fine, but it has serious limitations. The main thing is to make sure the HTML tag IDs and script variable names are unique. This is because IIS does nothing more than merge the include file when it parses server-side includes. The include file ends up being in the same scope with the container file. You cannot include the same file twice because there will be tag ID and script conflicts.

With ASP.NET, you can factor out common HTML and scripts into what is currently called a pagelet and reuse it without worrying about the ID conflicts. A pagelet is a Web Form without a body or a form tag, accompanied by scripts. The HTML portion of the pagelet is responsible for the layout and the user interface, while the scripts provide the pagelet with programmability by exposing properties and methods. Because the pagelet is considered a user control, it provides an independent scope. You can insert more than one instance of the user control without any problem.

The container Web Form must register the pagelet as a user control with the @Register directive and include it on the page with the *<prefix:tagname>* syntax. If more than one copy of the pagelet is used in a container page, each of them should be given different IDs for the container page's script to work correctly. The script on the container Web Form can access and manipulate the pagelet the same way it does any other server controls. The next example shows how an address form is reused as a pagelet. You might display this address form to allow the web user to register with your application or to display the shipping and billing addresses when the web user checks out:

```
<table>
  <tr>
    <td><asp:Label id="labelName" runat="server">Name</asp:Label></td>
    <td><asp:TextBox id="txtUserName" runat="server"
        Width="332" Height="24"></asp:TextBox></td>
  </tr>
  <tr>
    <td><asp:Label id="labelAddr1" runat="server">Address</asp:Label></td>
    <td><asp:TextBox id="txtAddr1" runat="server"
        Width="332" Height="24"></asp:TextBox></td>
  </tr>
  <tr>
    <td><asp:Label id="labelAddr2" runat="server"></asp:Label></td>
    <td><asp:TextBox id="txtAddr2" runat="server"
        Width="332" Height="24"></asp:TextBox></td>
  </tr>
  <tr>
    <td><asp:Label id="labelCity" runat="server">City</asp:Label></td>
    <td>
    <asp:TextBox id="txtCity" runat="server"></asp:TextBox>
    <asp:Label id="labelState" runat="server">State</asp:Label>
    <asp:TextBox id="txtState" runat="server" Width="34" Height="24">
      </asp:TextBox>
    <asp:Label id="labelZIP" runat="server">ZIP</asp:Label>
    <asp:TextBox id="txtZIP" runat="server" Width="60" Height="24">
      </asp:TextBox>
    </td>
  </tr>
  <tr>
    <td><asp:Label id="labelEmail" runat="server">Email</asp:Label></td>
```

```
        <td><asp:TextBox id="txtEmail" runat="server"
            Width="332" Height="24"></asp:TextBox></td>
        </tr>
</table>

<script language="C#" runat="server" ID="Script1">
  public String UserName {
    get { return txtUserName.Text; }
    set { txtUserName.Text = value; }
  }
  public String Address1 {
    get { return txtAddr1.Text; }
    set { txtAddr1.Text = value; }
  }
  public String Address2 {
    get { return txtAddr2.Text; }
    set { txtAddr2.Text = value; }
  }
  public String City {
    get { return txtCity.Text; }
    set { txtCity.Text = value; }
  }
  public String State {
    get { return txtState.Text; }
    set { txtState.Text = value; }
  }
  public String ZIP {
    get { return txtZIP.Text; }
    set { txtZIP.Text = value; }
  }
</script>
```

To use your pagelet, register it as a server control via the @Register directive, as shown in the next block of code. After registering, include the tag for the pagelet as if it was a normal server control. Specify the prefix, the tag name, the server control's ID, and set the runat property to server:

```
<%@ Register TagPrefix="Acme" TagName="Address" Src="Address.ascx" %>
<%@ Page language="c#"%>
<html>
<head>
  <script language="C#" runat="server">
    void Page_Load(Object oSender, EventArgs evt) {
      addr.UserName = "Jack Daniel";
    }
  </script>
</head>
<body>
    Welcome to the E-Shop.
    Registering with E-Shop will allow for monthly updates of bargains...
    <form method="post" runat="server">
      <p><Acme:Address id="addr" runat="server"></Acme:Address></p>
      <p><asp:Button id="cmdClear" runat="server" Text="Clear"></asp:Button>
```

```
          <asp:Button id="cmdSubmit" runat="server" Text="Submit">
          </asp:Button></p>
     </form>
  </body>
</html>
```

You should be able to programmatically access the properties of the pagelet through the server control's ID (addr in this case). In the previous example, we accessed the UserName property of the Address pagelet via its ID:

```
addr.UserName = "Jack Daniel";
```

For an e-commerce checkout page, you could have two instances of <Acme: Address> on the same page: one for the billing and the other for the shipping address. Your script should access these instances of the pagelet via the ID you assign to each address control.

You can also programmatically instantiate instances of the pagelet through the use of the Page's LoadControl method. The first thing is to declare a variable of type Control in your script to host your pagelet. This is because the Control is the root of all objects, including your pagelet. Then instantiate the variable with a call to the LoadControl, passing in the filename of the control page. To make the control visible on the page, add the control to the Page's collection of controls. Because you currently have an instance of the Control object, you won't be able to call the pagelet's properties and methods until you *cast* the variable from Control type to your pagelet type. This is similar to having an Object variable in Visual Basic to hold a COM component. To access the COM-component methods and properties, you would cast the Object variable to the component type. Pagelets when loaded are automatically typed as pagename_extension. For example, if your pagelet were named *myControl.ascx*, the type generated for it would be myControl_ascx. The boldface line in the following example shows you how to cast addr1 from Control to type Address_ascx in order to access the UserName property of the pagelet:

```
<%@ Register TagPrefix="Acme" TagName="Address" Src="Address.ascx" %>
<%@ Page language="C#" %>
<html>
<head>
  <script language="C#" runat="server">
    void Page_Load(Object oSender, EventArgs evt) {
      addr.UserName = "Jack Daniel";
      Control addr1;
      addr1 = LoadControl("Address.ascx");
      ((Address_ascx)addr1).UserName = addr.UserName;
      this.frm.Controls.AddAt(3, addr1);
    }
  </script>
</head>
<body>
  <form id="frm" method="post" runat="server">
```

```
    Billing Address:<br/>
    <Acme:Address id="addr" runat="server"></Acme:Address>
    Shipping Address:<br/>
    <p><asp:Button id="cmdClear" runat="server" Text="Clear">
      </asp:Button>
      <asp:Button id="cmdSubmit" runat="server" Text="Submit">
      </asp:Button>
    </p>
  </form>
</body>
</html>
```

This example, the checkout page, shows you how to declare a pagelet statically in your page with the <Acme:Address> tag, as well as how to dynamically create an instance of the custom control Address with the Page's
LoadControl() method. Once you've created the control dynamically, you
must cast the object to the control type before manipulating it.

The AddAt() method is used to insert the Address pagelet at a particular
location in the checkout page. Instead of declaring the dynamic pagelet as a
Control, you can also declare it as its type, which is Address_ascx. This way,
you just have to cast it once when loading the dynamic control:

```
Address_ascx addr2 = (Address_ascx)LoadControl("Address.ascx");
addr2.UserName = "ABC";
```

Control derivatives

While it is easy to create custom controls using the pagelet approach, this
technique is not flexible enough to create more powerful custom controls,
such as ones that expose events or hierarchy of controls. With ASP.NET,
you can also create custom controls by inheriting from the Control base
class and overriding a couple of methods.

The following example shows you how to create the simplest custom control as a Control derivative.

```
namespace MyWebControls
{
  using System;
  using System.Web.UI;
  using System.Web.UI.WebControls;
  using System.ComponentModel;

  public class MyWebControl : System.Web.UI.WebControls.WebControl
  {
    //protected override void Render(HtmlTextWriter output)
    //{
    //    output.Write("custom control testing via Render()");
    //}
```

```
protected override void CreateChildControls( )
{
    Table tbl = new Table( );
    TableRow row = new TableRow( );
    TableCell cell = new TableCell( );
    HyperLink a = new HyperLink( );
    a.NavigateUrl = "http://msdn.microsoft.com";
    a.ImageUrl = "image url";
    cell.Controls.Add (a);
    row.Cells.Add(cell);
    tbl.Rows.Add(row);

    row = new TableRow( );
    cell = new TableCell( );
    cell.Controls.Add (new LiteralControl("custom control testing"));
    row.Cells.Add(cell);
    tbl.Rows.Add(row);

    tbl.BorderWidth = 1;
    tbl.BorderStyle = BorderStyle.Ridge;

    Controls.Add(tbl);
    }
  }
}
```

As you can see, the MyWebControl object derives from the WebControl class. We have seen that WebControl ultimately derives from the base Control class. All we really do here is override either the Render or the CreateChildControls methods to construct the custom web control. If you choose to override the Render method, you will have to generate the HTML for your custom control through the HtmlTextWriter object, output. You can use methods such as Write, WriteBeginTag, WriteAttribute, and WriteEndTag.

In our example, we override the CreateChildControls method. Instead of worrying about the actual HTML tag and attribute names, we then create ASP.NET objects directly by their class names, such as Table, TableRow, TableCell, HyperLink, and LiteralControl, to construct a hierarchy of objects under a *table*. We can also manipulate attributes for the objects via their properties. At the end of the method, we add the *table* to the custom control's collection of controls.

You will have to compile the previous control code to generate a DLL assembly (i.e., csc /t:library MyWebControls.cs). To use the control, deploy the assembly by copying it to the */bin* directory of your web application. Then you should be able to register the control with the @Register directive and use the control as if it was a server control provided by ASP.NET. If you are using Visual Studio .NET, you can add a reference to the control assembly file or the control project for the test web project that uses the control.

Your custom-control test page should now look like the following:

```
<%@ Page language="c#"%>
<%@ Register TagPrefix="WC" Namespace="MyWebControls"
              Assembly="MyWebControls"%>
<html>
<head>
  <script language="C#" runat=server>
    void Page_Load(object sender, EventArgs e) {
      MyWebControls.MyWebControl myCtrl;
      myCtrl = new MyWebControls.MyWebControl();
      this.Controls.Add(myCtrl);
    }
  </script>
</head>
<body>
  <form method="post" runat="server">
    This is the main page
    <WC:MyWebControl id="myControl1" runat="server" />
  </form>
</body>
</html>
```

As you can see, we register the custom control with the @Register directive and alias the namespace MyWebControls with the WC prefix. In the body of the Web Form, we can add the custom-control tag as <WC:MyWebControl>.

In addition to inserting the custom control onto the page declaratively as shown earlier, we can also programmatically create the custom control at runtime. The Page_Load code demonstrates this point:

```
MyWebControls.MyWebControl myCtrl;
myCtrl = new MyWebControls.MyWebControl();
this.Controls.Add(myCtrl);
```

The output page is shown in Figure 7-6.

Figure 7-6. Custom control test output, statically and dynamically

Event-Driven Programming

There are two ways to associate event handlers—functions that handle the event—to the UI controls.

Refer to the section earlier in this chapter on "Web Form Syntax," particularly where we describe the syntax for server controls. All we do to bind an event from a control to an event handler is to use the *eventname=eventhandlername* attribute/value pair for the control. For example, if we want to handle the onclick event for the HTML control input, all we do is the following. Note that for the HTML controls, the server-side click event is named onserverclick, as opposed to the client-side click event onclick, which can still be used in DHTML scripting:

```
<input id="cmd1" runat="server"
  onserverclick="OnClickHandler"
  type="button" value="click me">
```

For an ASP.NET web control, the syntax is the same:

```
<asp:Button id="cmd2" runat="server"
  onclick="OnclickHandler2"
  Text="click me too"></asp:Button>
```

After binding the event to the event-handling function name, we have to provide the actual event handler:

```
void OnClickHandler(object sender, EventArgs e)
{
  // code to retrieve and process the posted data
}
```

The second way of binding events is delegation. You don't have to have any notion of code in the *aspx* file, not even the event-handling function name. All you have to do is to register the event handler with the control's event-handler property. For web controls, the event-handler property for button click is Click. For HTML controls, it's ServerClick:

```
ControlID.Click += new System.EventHandler (this.EventHandlerName);

ControlID.ServerClick += new System.EventHandler (this.EventHandlerName);
```

ASP.NET and Web Services

The ASP.NET framework simplifies development of web services. All the low-level work, such as packaging and unpackaging data in XML format and utilizing HTTP protocol to transport the web messages between distributed components, are done by the framework. This allows the developers to focus on the application logic.

The .NET Framework uses *asmx* as the default file extension for web services, as opposed to *aspx* for Web Forms and *ascx* for web controls.

The WebService Directive

All *asmx* files start with the @WebService directive that instructs ASP.NET on how to compile the code, as well as the main class name. The WebService directive has the following attributes:

Language
Specifies the language in which the code was written. This instructs the ASP.NET framework to use the appropriate compiler to build your web service. Use VB for Visual Basic, C# for C# and JS for JScript .NET. As other languages emerge, obviously you can specify other languages.

Class
Specifies the main class, which exposes web methods. The ASP.NET framework instantiates this class in order to serve the web methods to the clients.

Codebehind
Specifies the source file for your code, which allows for complete code/ASP separation.

You can easily create a simple web service similar to the following *asmx* file:

```
<%@ WebService Language="VB" class="MathClass" %>
imports System.Web.Services
Public Class MathClass
  <WebMethod> _
  public function Add(a as integer, b as integer) as integer
    return(a + b)
  end function
end class
```

Note the line continuation symbol right after <WebMethod>. If you prefer to separate your code completely from any ASP.NET elements, you could have the code for your web service saved in a separate file and specify the Codebehind attribute of the @WebService directive to point to the code file:

```
<%@ WebService Language="VB" Codebehind="MathClass.vb" Class="MathClass" %>
```

The source for *MathClass.vb* looks exactly like the *asmx* shown earlier minus the first line. You can use the following command line to compile *MathClass.dll*:

```
vbc /t:library /r:System.Web.Services.dll MathClass.vb
```

As with all code-behind, the binary has to be deployed in the */bin* directory under the application.

The WebMethod Attribute

Public methods of any classes can be tagged with the WebMethod attribute to be made accessible from the Web. The syntax for tagging attributes to methods is different for each .NET language. For example, in C# the tag takes the following form:

```
[WebMethod(attribute="value" attribute="value" ...)]
    public returnType FunctionName(paramsList)
```

In VB, angle brackets are used instead of square brackets and the assignment symbol is ":=" instead of just "=". Also note that the whole web method declaration is on a single line. If you want separate them for readability, use the line continuation symbol "_":

```
<WebMethod(attribute:="value" attribute="value" ...)> Public Function
    FunctionName(paramsList) as returnType

<WebMethod(attribute:="value" attribute="value" ...)> Public Sub
    SubName(paramsList)
```

Using Web Services

If you are using Visual Studio.NET, you can choose Project/Add Web Reference and then type in the URL where the web service resides. For our purpose, we'll point to the web service we created in the last chapter, PubsWS. The URL to this web service on our server is *http://localhost/PubsWS/PubsWS.asmx*. After adding the web reference, you can access the proxy object to the web service you are calling via the type servername.proxyObjectName. For your case, it is localhost.PubsWS.[*]

The following code excerpt demonstrates how to use the web service through the proxy. We create an instance of the proxy object and then ask it to relay the message to the real web service to get the list of authors. The result will be streamed back in XML format, which is reconstructed into a DataSet object. We then bind DataGrid1, which is just a DataGrid object that we have on the Web Form, to the default view of the first table of the DataSet. Finally, we ask for the actual binding to take place. The resulting page is the grid populated with rows from the Authors table of the Pubs sample database.

```
localhost.PubsWS ws = new localhost.PubsWS();
DataSet ds = ws.GetAuthors();
DataGrid1.DataSource = ds.Tables[0].DefaultView;
DataGrid1.DataBind();
```

---

[*] You can rename the web reference when adding it to your project. This way the web service will be *<yourwebservicename>*.proxyObjectName instead of *servername*.proxyObjectName.

Instead of using Visual Studio.NET to locate and automatically generate the proxy class, you can also use the information from the previous chapter to generate the source for the proxy class yourself. You can then include this source or compile the source into a DLL and add the DLL to the project as a reference. In any case, the end result is the same. Here is an example that links against the proxy we created in the previous chapter and fills a grid with data:

```
<%@ Page Language="C#" %>
<%@ Import Namespace="System.Data" %>

<!-- Link to the proxy generated by wsdl.exe -->
<%@ Assembly Src="PubsWS.cs" %>

<html>
  <head>
    <title>SOAP Client</title>
  </head>
  <body>

    <!-- Make the SOAP call and fill the data grid. -->
    <%
      PubsWS ws = new PubsWS( );
      DataSet ds = ws.GetAuthors( );
      dg.DataSource = ds.Tables[0].DefaultView;
      dg.DataBind( );
    %>

    <!-- Create a data grid. -->
    <asp:DataGrid id="dg" runat="server"/>

  </body>
</html>
```

Data Binding and the Use of Templates

While all web controls can be data bound, only DataGrid, DataList, and Repeater use a template to control the display of data items. In this section, we show you how to perform simple data binding with some common web controls and how to use an HTML template to provide fully customized data-bound controls.

In its simplest form, data binding is the act of binding a control to a data source. Previously, data binding required that an ADO recordset be a data source, which is not too flexible. There was no way to bind, for example, an array or a collection of objects to a control. With ASP.NET, the whole data-binding business is revamped. The only requirement to make your data source bindable to web controls is that your data source implement the

System.Collections.ICollection interface. In other words, a bindable data source is a collection of homogeneous objects that the web controls can obtain data items from.

While it is possible to write your own data classes that implement the ICollection interface and bind them to web controls, numerous classes exist that do this for you, such as Array, ArrayList, DataView, HashTable, Queue, SortedList, and Stack. All you have to do is put your data in these forms, and you can bind your data to web controls.

Here is the simplest form of data binding. In the form file, all we have are two list boxes with ids list0 and list1:

```
<asp:listbox id="list0" runat="server"></asp:listbox>
<asp:listbox id="list1" runat="server"></asp:listbox>
```

In the Page_Load event handler in the code-behind source file, we construct the data sources of type Array, which implement the ICollection interface we mentioned earlier, and then bind the list controls with the data sources:

```
int[] myArray0 = new int[7] { 1, 2, 3, 5, 7, 11, 13 };
string[] myArray1 = new string[7] {
                        "Monday",
                        "Tuesday",
                        "Wednesday",
                        "Thursday",
                        "Friday",
                        "Saturday",
                        "Sunday"
                            };
list0.DataSource = myArray0;
list0.DataBind( );
list1.DataSource = myArray1;
list1.DataBind( );
```

Figure 7-7 shows the output of this page.

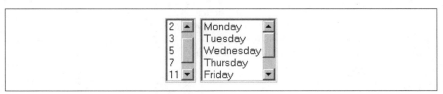

Figure 7-7. Data binding with data from arrays

Most of the time, we tend to bind data from data sources that come from a database. The next example pulls data from the Categories table of the familiar NorthWind database. We can still use the asp:listbox control, but this time, we specify the item's property we want for the text, as well as the value property of the list box. We did not have to do this for the previous example because the items that the list box binds to are of simple types (int and string). If we were to have an array of objects, we would have to specify the property we want to bind to datavaluefield and datatextfield the way we are in the following example:

```
<asp:listbox id=ListBox1 runat="server"
    datavaluefield="CategoryID"
    datatextfield="CategoryName">
</asp:listbox>
```

Again, in the code-behind source file, we have the code to construct the data source and to bind the data source to the list control. Note that because we are using ADO.NET to get the data from the database, we must have references to System.Data and System.Data.OleDb namespaces. The Default-View property of class Table is of type DataView, which implements the ICollection interface.

```
System.Data.DataSet m_ds = new System.Data.DataSet( );
String sConn =
    "provider=SQLOLEDB;server=(local);database=NorthWind;Integrated
Security=SSPI";
String sSQL =
    "select * from Categories";

System.Data.OleDb.OleDbDataAdapter da =
    new System.Data.OleDb.OleDbDataAdapter(sSQL, sConn);
da.Fill(m_ds, "Categories");

ListBox1.DataSource = m_ds.Tables["Categories"].DefaultView;
ListBox1.DataBind( );
```

Figure 7-8 shows the output for this example.

Figure 7-8. Data binding with data from a database

DataGrid

The DataGrid control takes data binding a step further by allowing more than one property of the bound item to be displayed. This section's example shows you how to control the binding of data columns to the grid, as well as how to customize the look and feel of the DataGrid using style.

By default, the DataGrid automatically binds all columns of the data source in the order that they come from the database. Sometimes this is not the behavior you would want. To fully control what columns bind and in which order you want the binding to happen, switch off the `autogeneratecolumns` attribute of the DataGrid, and provide the columns property as shown the following sample:

```
<asp:DataGrid id=DataGrid1 runat="server"
        ForeColor="Black"
        autogeneratecolumns=false>

    <columns>
        <asp:boundcolumn datafield=CategoryID
                            headertext="ID" readonly=True/>
        <asp:boundcolumn datafield=CategoryName
                            headertext="Category" />
        <asp:boundcolumn datafield=Description
                            headertext="Description" />
    </columns>

    <SelectedItemStyle backcolor="#ffcc99" font-bold=True/>

    <AlternatingItemStyle BackColor="Gainsboro"/>

    <FooterStyle BackColor="Silver" ForeColor="White"/>

    <ItemStyle BackColor="White"/>

    <HeaderStyle BackColor="Navy" Font-Bold="True" ForeColor="White"/>

</asp:DataGrid>
```

Figure 7-9 shows the result of this example.

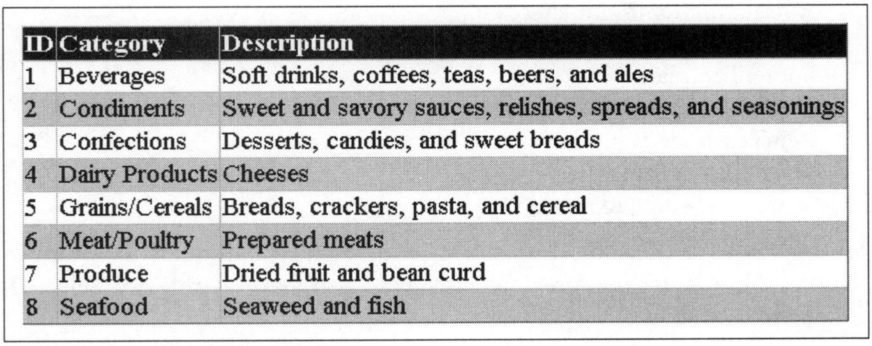

ID	Category	Description
1	Beverages	Soft drinks, coffees, teas, beers, and ales
2	Condiments	Sweet and savory sauces, relishes, spreads, and seasonings
3	Confections	Desserts, candies, and sweet breads
4	Dairy Products	Cheeses
5	Grains/Cereals	Breads, crackers, pasta, and cereal
6	Meat/Poultry	Prepared meats
7	Produce	Dried fruit and bean curd
8	Seafood	Seaweed and fish

Figure 7-9. DataGrid data binding

In addition to using `asp:boundcolumn` to bind a column of the DataGrid to a column of the data source, you can also use `asp:buttoncolumn` to insert a column with buttons that generate notifications. You can handle these notifications to perform predefined tasks such as selecting the item, removing it, and adding it to the shopping basket. You can also have `asp:hyperlinkcolumn` insert links to other pages in a column, `asp:editcommandcolumn` control editing of the selected row of data, or `asp:templatecolumn` customize the display of your column of data.

There are a number of styles that you use to control the visual formatting of your DataGrid control. The HeaderStyle and FooterStyle, as the names imply, control the style for the header and the footer of the DataGrid. The ItemStyle, AlternatingItemStyle, SelectedItemStyle, and EditItemStyle are used for each type of items in the list. The PagerStyle controls the visual appearance and layout of the paging interface.

The code-behind source file for binding of data to the DataGrid is similar to that of the previous example. Basically, we bind the set of the DataSource property of the DataGrid to the DefaultView of the Categories table and perform the binding with the DataBind method:

```
DataGrid1.DataSource = m_ds.Tables["Categories"].DefaultView;
DataGrid1.DataBind( );
```

DataList

Unlike the DataGrid control, where the data binding is still in a tabular form, the DataList control allows to you lay out the list in any way through the use of HTML templates.

Within a DataList tag, you can customize a number of templates. The templates that can be customized include:

AlternatingItemTemplate
EditItemTemplate
FooterTemplate
HeaderTemplate
ItemTemplate
SelectedItemTemplate
SeparatorTemplate

Specific tags are used to set up the style for each type of items you want to display. Similar to the previous list, you also have ItemStyle, SelectedItemStyle, and so on.

In the following example, we only show you one template (the ItemTemplate), which is applied to all items in the list. In this template, we use Web Form data-binding syntax to bind two properties of the data item, the

CategoryID and CategoryName fields. In this simple template, the CategoryID will always be shown with Verdana font in size 10.

You can also control the flow of the DataList by setting attributes such as repeatcolumns, repeatdirection (vertical, horizontal), or repeatlayout (flow, table):

```
<asp:DataList id=DataList1 runat="server"
    repeatcolumns=3
    repeatdirection=Horizontal>

  <AlternatingItemStyle BackColor="Gainsboro"/>
  <ItemTemplate>
    <font face=Verdana size=10>
      <%# DataBinder.Eval(Container.DataItem, "CategoryID") %>
    </font>
    <%# DataBinder.Eval(Container.DataItem, "CategoryName") %>
  </ItemTemplate>

</asp:DataList>
```

The code behind the data binding is shown here:

```
DataList1.DataSource = m_ds.Tables["Categories"].DefaultView;
DataList1.DataBind( );
```

Figure 7-10 shows the output of this DataList data-binding example.

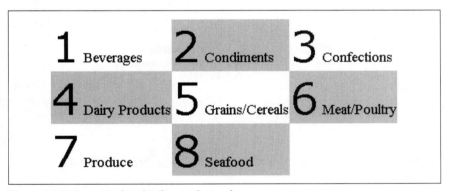

Figure 7-10. DataList data binding with template

Repeater

The ASP.NET Repeater control is completely driven by an HTML template to repeatedly display each of the data items bound to it. When the page renders, the Repeater control loops through all the records in the data source and generates HTML to display the record according to the HTML template. This is as free-form as you can get for data binding. You can have templates to generate bulleted lists, numbered lists, comma-separated lists, and tabs.

There are only five templates in the Repeater control:

> AlternatingItemTemplate
> FooterTemplate
> HeaderTemplate
> ItemTemplate
> SeparatorTemplate

We will use two of these templates to control the display of the item and its separator.

Again, we bind two fields of each item to the template. The end result is a comma-separated list of URLs that link another Web Form to display more detailed information about the clicked category. As you can see, we also use Web Form data-binding tags, <%# and %>, to perform the binding. The CategoryID fills the cat parameter of the query string to the fictitious *Display-Category.aspx* Web Form, and the CategoryName is the display text for the anchor tag.

You could also replace the anchor tag and comma with graphical images to make your page more visually appealing:

```
<asp:Repeater id=Repeater1 runat="server">

  <ItemTemplate>
    <A HREF="http://YourURL/DisplayCategory.aspx?cat=
      <%# DataBinder.Eval(Container.DataItem, "CategoryID") %>"
      ><%# DataBinder.Eval(Container.DataItem, "CategoryName") %>
    </A>
  </ItemTemplate>
  <SeparatorTemplate>, </SeparatorTemplate>

</asp:Repeater>
```

Figure 7-11 shows the result of using the data repeater to bind data.

Beverages , Condiments , Confections , Dairy Products , Grains/Cereals , Meat/Poultry , Produce , Seafood

---

Figure 7-11. Data binding using repeater and template

As with the other controls, the Repeater needs to be bound to a data source:

```
Repeater1.DataSource = m_ds.Tables["Categories"].DefaultView;
Repeater1.DataBind( );
```

As you can see, using a template to bind data to these list-bound controls can be very simple, yet powerful. However, you should be aware of how the generated HTML will look. You should not have complicated, bloated templates that will result in unappealing, large files. In web application development, the page size is directly proportional to the response time the customer experiences.

State Management and Scalability

ASP.NET overcomes all major limitations of ASP when it comes to managing session states. As you are aware from ASP development, a session state is nothing but a named variable that is cached at the server for the duration of the web user's session. As the user navigates through the web application, the session state retains its value as long as the session is not expired.

ASP Session state management can be summarized as follows:

- The session starts, and the web application assigns a unique key to the user.
- This key is stored in an HTTP cookie. Along each subsequent request, the client browser sends the unique key back to the server.
- The server looks up the states stored for this particular key and processes the request accordingly.

While this has worked fine for all these years, we've found out that there were a number of limitations to live with or work around. The biggest limitation is that the session state is process-dependent, which is impossible to implement in a web farm environment without custom session management.

ASP.NET Session-State Management

ASP.NET improves upon ASP session-state management by moving to an out-of-process model. By having all web servers in the farm pointing to a common server that hosts the out-of-process state manager, the web client can be redirected around the farm without losing the session states.

By using an out-of-process model, we no longer have the problem of losing session states when the IIS process is cycled. This means that if the web server application crashed for whatever reason and restarted within the session timeout duration, the web clients could still have all their session states intact. Of course, if the out-of-process state manager crashed, that is a whole different issue. This leads to the next improvement of ASP.NET—the ability to persist session state to a database.

The idea of persisting session state to a database is not new. Many of us have implemented this as the workaround for dealing with web farm configuration. However, ASP.NET makes it easier.

Similar to all other configurations in ASP.NET, session management is done through the use of the *web.config* files. There are two levels of configuration: machine and application. Machine-level configuration associates with the *machine.config* file stored in *WinNT\Microsoft.NET\ Framework\<version>\CONFIG\machine.config*, while the application-level configuration uses the *web.config* file in the application root directory. The application-level configuration overrides the machine-level configuration.

The following code is a portion of the *web.config* file dealing with session-state management:*

```
<configuration>
  <system.web>
    <sessionState
      mode="InProc"
      cookieless="false"
      timeout="20" />
  </system.web>
</configuration>
```

Table 7-2 lists the properties of the SessionState class.

Table 7-2. Properties of the SessionState class

Property	Description
mode	Off indicates that session state is disabled; InProc stores session data locally; StateServer stores session state on a remote server; and SQLServer stores it on a SQL Server.
Cookieless	Specifies whether to rely on the client acceptance of cookie. If this property is set to true, ASP.NET inserts the unique key to the URL for navigation between pages within the application instead of setting it in the client's cookie.
Timeout	Specifies session timeout in minutes. This is a sliding window of time: it starts counting down for each request. The default is 20 minutes.
stateConnectionString	Specifies the server and port of the remote session-state server (not a SQL Server). The format is tcpip=HOST:PORT, as in tcpip=192.168.254.1:42424. Use this only when mode=StateServer.
sqlConnectionString	Represents a SQL Server connection string, such as user id=sa;password=;database=ASPState;server=(local). This is required when mode=SQLServer.

---

* The content of this file is case-sensitive.

Out-of-process session-state management

When you set the session-state mode to run on a remote server (mode=StateServer), you must prepare the remote server to run the state management service automatically.

ASP.NET SDK includes an NT service call *ASP.NET State Service* to be used for out-of-process session-state management. Before setting your *web.config* files to use the out-of-process mode, you will have to start the ASP State service by going to the NT Services Management Console and start the service. You might want to change the *startup type* to automatic so that this service will start automatically at subsequent reboots.

SQL Server session-state management

To use this mode, the SQL Server machine has to be prepared. ASP.NET SDK includes a SQL script to create the ASP State database, which is where all session states are stored. Find this SQL script (*InstallSqlState.sql*) at *%SystemRoot%\Microsoft.NET\Framework\BUILDNUMBER*. To apply the script to your SQL Server, use the SQL Server command-line tool *osql.exe* or SQL Query Analyzer. We use the latter because it allows us to inspect the script to get a better understanding of how this mode of session management is implemented. You will have to stop and restart SQL Server because the script alters the master to run the ASPState_Startup helper procedure at SQL startup time.

Cookieless session-state management

In ASP development, it is a usual practice to impose the requirement that the clients' web browsers be set up to accept cookies so that we can use session state the way it is meant to be used. However, when this requirement is not in place, especially for business-to-consumer (B2C) kinds of applications, the developers have to package the session ID along with the URL as a variable in the query string or as a form field and manage the session states manually.

With ASP.NET, as you can see from the sessionstate section of the configuration file, all you do is flip the setting of cookieless to true, and everything is automatically done for you. Session state can be used as if nothing has changed.

To setup and experiment with these session state configuration, we've created two fictitious *asp.net* pages: login.aspx and main.aspx. The main page redirects the user to the login page if the user has not logged in. The login page redirects the user to the main page when the user is authenticated. When the user logs in, session variable UserName will be populated.

The following is the source for the simplified login page:

```html
<HTML>

<script language="VB" runat="server">
Sub cmdLogin_Click(ByVal sender As System.Object, _
                   ByVal e As System.EventArgs)
  ' more processing here
  Session("UserName") = txtUID.Text
  Response.Redirect("Main.aspx")
End Sub
</script>

<body>
<form id="Form1" method="post" runat="server">
<table>
  <tr>
    <td>User ID</td>
    <td><asp:TextBox id="txtUID"
                     runat="server"></asp:TextBox></td>
  </tr>
  <tr>
    <td>Password</td>
    <td><asp:TextBox id="txtPWD"
                     textmode="password"
                     runat="server">
                     </asp:TextBox></td>
  </tr>
  <tr>
    <td></td>
    <td><asp:Button id="cmdLogin"
                     runat="server"
                     Text="Login"
                     onclick="cmdLogin_Click">
                     </asp:Button></td>
  </tr>
</table>
</form>
</body>
</HTML>
```

The skeleton for the main page is as follows:

```html
<HTML>

<script language="VB" runat="server">
Sub Page_Load(ByVal sender As System.Object, ByVal e As System.EventArgs)
  If (Session("UserName") <> "") Then
    labelData.Text = "Welcome back, " + Session("UserName")
  Else
    Response.Redirect("Login.aspx")
  End If
End Sub
</script>
```

```
<body>
<form id="Form1" method="post" runat="server">
  <asp:Label id="labelData" runat="server"></asp:Label>
</form>
</body>
</HTML>
```

In the first scenario, we will use session state mode InProc. Because the IIS process handles the session state, if we simulate a web server restart by issuing the command iisreset and trying to refresh the main page, it will redirect us to the login page.

In the second scenario, we change the session state mode to StateServer and start the ASP.NET Session State Service (i.e., the command line net start aspnet_state). Note that here we are running the Session State Service on the same machine as the web server even though we can have this service running on a separate server for more reliability. This time around, the session state persists through the resetting the web server. Of course, if we restart the ASP.NET Session State Service itself, the main page will still redirect us to the login page.

Now that we've seen in-process and out-of-process session state management, the last scenario we try will be to have session state persisted to a database. This is as simple as setting the mode and the sqlConnectionString attributes of the sessionState node in the *web.config* file. Of course, we ran *InstallSqlState.sql* on the SQL server to generate the schema and supporting stored procedures needed by ASP.NET to persist state into the database. The result is similar to the previous trials, however. Because the session data are stored in *tempdb*, they are cleared when the SQL server is restarted. As a side note, remember to have SQL Server Agent start automatically so that the cleanup session state job can be run correctly.

Performance Versus Scalability and Reliability

As we've said, ASP.NET introduces an out-of-process model of session-state management, which enables more scalable solutions, but not without a cost. Out-of-process communication performs much worse than in-process communication, not to mention persisting the session states to a database. You should weigh the benefits of each of the different mode of state managements to find the one that is most suitable for your application. Table 7-3 summarizes the different modes and their trade-offs.

Table 7-3. Session-state management communication modes

Mode	Description
In-process	This mode gives you the best performance. It is not reliable, because it is memory-based. It is not scalable, because it is process-based. If you are setting up a web farm, you will have to make sure that subsequent requests are going to the same server.
Out-of-process	The reliable factor is still in question because this mode still is memory based. However, because a separate process manages the session state, it is more reliable than the in-process mode. Because of the out-of-process communication overhead, it is much slower than in-process mode. It is scalable for uses in web farms.
SQL Server	This mode gives you the highest level of reliability at the cost of performance. It is scalable for uses in web farms.

Summary

Throughout this chapter, we've introduced you to ASP.NET and the benefits that it brings to web application development. These benefits include a new and extended web page life cycle that involves events driven from the client browsers, server controls that manage their own states, the separation of user interface and the code behind, the replacement of late-bound scripting languages with strong-typed compiled languages, and the new and improved session-state management that improves scalability.

If you are trying to embrace the web paradigm by using ASP.NET for your web application, along with Web Services for integration between sites, you are right on target. However, not all applications are suitable for the Web. There is a huge market of standard applications where the development is done in traditional VB, C, C++, Java, and so on, and there is no need for it to be web-based. In the next chapter, we cover Windows Forms, which are supposed to map to traditional Windows applications.

CHAPTER 8

Windows Forms

If the goal of Microsoft .NET is to embrace the Web, what will happen to conventional Windows applications? It turns out the .NET Framework not only benefits the development of web applications, but improves the way standard Windows applications are built. In this chapter, we provide you with an understanding of what Windows Forms are, how to use Windows Forms .NET classes to create Windows Forms–based applications, and how you can still "embrace the Web" while creating Windows applications.

Introducing Windows Forms

If you have developed Windows applications since the early 1990s, chances are you have used raw Windows APIs such as RegisterClass, CreateWindow, ShowWindow, GetMessage, TranslateMessage, and DispatchMessage. You certainly had a WinMain entry point in your application. Inside this function, you registered your application with Windows, created and showed the window, and handled messages from the system. Every Windows application has to have a message loop that collects Windows messages and dispatches them to the message-handler function that you've registered through RegisterClass function. As a developer, much of your job is handling Windows messages, such as WM_CREATE, WM_SIZE, or WM_CLOSE, that you create and pump into the system with PostMessage or SendMessage.

Classic Windows development is tedious and error-prone. The result is that application frameworks were built as an abstraction on top of all these Windows APIs. Frameworks such as the Microsoft Foundation Class Library (MFC) and Active Template Library (ATL) were created to help Windows application developers focus more on the task of solving business problems than on how to handle certain Windows messages. These frameworks provide the plumbing, or the template, of a Windows application. The developer's responsibility is to deal with business logic.

While it is much easier to develop Windows applications using these frameworks, it is again sometimes necessary to go down to the Windows API level when the Framework does not give you the controls you need. This situation causes inconsistency in the code. Moreover, there exist numerous frameworks similar to MFC and ATL, such as the Object Windows Library (OWL) from Borland, zApp from Rogue Wave, Windows add-on scripts for Python such as the Win32 Extensions or PythonWin GUI Extensions, Visual Basic, and other homegrown frameworks, causing developers much grief when switching from one to another.

Windows Forms provides a unified programming model for standard Windows application development. It is similar to the native Windows API with regard to level of abstraction; however, it is much richer and more powerful. Instead of depending on functions like the native Windows API, Windows Forms provides a hierarchy of classes. Instead of calling CreateWindow for any type of user-interface widgets, you create the particular type of user-interface control using the appropriate class. You might think that MFC and other frameworks already provide hierarchy of classes. What other benefits can Windows Forms bring that make it stand out from the crowd? The answer is the language-independent aspect of this new framework. Any .NET language can use this collection of classes that make up the Windows Forms object model.

If you've developed Windows applications in C++ and Visual Basic, you might think that it would be nice to have the power of C++ to work in an integrated development environment like that of VB. It is now possible with Visual Studio.NET and Windows Forms. Windows Forms brings a VB-like integrated development environment to C#, Managed C++, and other languages.

In current Windows application development, if you use COM, DCOM, or ActiveX components, deployment of your application requires extensive configuration. You would probably at least use the *regsvr32* utility to register and unregister components from the Windows Registry on the client machine. All these setup-related deployment tasks are eliminated by Microsoft .NET—by Windows Forms in particular. Now, all you have to do to install an application is copy the executable onto the client machine.

Because Windows Forms is part of the Microsoft .NET grand scheme, it fully supports and integrates with Web Services, ADO.NET, and the .NET classes. You can have Windows Forms as the frontend to your web application by using .NET classes such as HttpWebRequest and HttpWebResponse. These classes allow your Windows Forms application to communicate with web servers. Remember that Windows Forms applications are not always stand-alone applications.

The System.Windows.Forms Namespace

In this section, we describe the architecture of Windows Forms and introduce the classes that make up the Windows Forms namespace.

Windows Forms architecture is rather simple. It takes the form of *controls* and *containers*. This is similar to Java JFC model, where container types of classes are Panel, Window, JComponent, and so on, and control types of classes are Button, Checkbox, Label, and so on. Most user-interface classes in the Windows.Forms namespace derive from the Control class. In a sense, everything that you see in a Windows Forms application is a control. If a control can contain other controls, it is a container. The application user interface consists of a form object acting as the main container, as well as the controls and other containers that reside on the form.

Similar to the native Windows API common functions, the System.Windows.Forms namespace provides a common set of classes you can use and derive from to build Windows Forms applications. The classes and interfaces in this namespace allow you to construct and render the user-interface elements on a Windows Form.

As we have seen from the last chapter, the System.Web.UI namespace provides the classes for building web applications. Similarly, the System.Windows.Forms namespace provides the classes for building standard applications. The System.Windows.Forms namespace is analogous to the System.Web.UI namespace, as described in the previous chapter.

Similar to the Control and Page classes in the System.Web.UI namespace, Control and Form are the two most important classes in the System.Windows.Forms namespace.

Control Class

Control is the base class of all UI controls in Windows Forms applications. It provides common properties for all controls, as well as common user-interface control behaviors, such as accepting user input through the keyboard or mouse and raising appropriate events.

Table 8-1 is a list of some representative properties, methods, and events that you will most likely encounter. For the complete list, check out the Microsoft .NET SDK.

Table 8-1. Common Control properties, methods, and events

Properties	Description
Controls	These properties allow for constructing hierarchy of controls. The Controls property lists all child controls, while the Parent property points to the parent of the current control.
Parent	
Enabled	These properties control the visual states of the control.
Focused	
Visible	
Left	These properties control the location and size of the control.
Top	
Right	
Bottom	
Width	
Height	
Size	

Methods	Description
Show	These methods manipulate the control's visual state.
Hide	
Focus	
Select	
Refresh	These methods control when and what portion of the screen needs repainting. The Refresh method immediately forces the control to redraw itself and all of its children. The Invalidate and Update methods selectively control the portion of the screen that needs to be redrawn.
Invalidate	
Update	
ProcessCmdKey	If you develop your own controls, override these methods to intercept the Windows messages. This is similar to how Windows developers handled Windows messages when they developed Win32 applications using the native Win32 API.
WndProc	

Events	Description
Click	To handle default events from the controls, you will most likely override the protected virtual methods provided by the Control class. These mouse-event virtual methods can be overriden to provide custom handling.
MouseDown	
MouseUp	
MouseMove	
MouseWheel	
KeyDown	Similar to the mouse events, these keyboard-event virtual methods can also be overriden.
KeyUp	
KeyPress	

The Control class also provides behaviors, such as data binding, context menu, drag and drop, anchoring and docking, and properties, such as font, color, background, cursor, and so on.

Form Class

A *form* in Windows Forms is similar in concept to a *page* in Web Forms. It is a container type of control that hosts other UI controls. You manipulate the properties of the Form object to control the appearance, size, and color of the displayed form. A Windows Form is basically a representation of any window displayed in your application.

A standard form contains a titlebar, which contains an icon, title text, and control box for the Minimize, Maximize, and Close buttons (see Figure 8-1). Most of the time, a form also contains a menu right under the titlebar. The working area of the form is where child controls are rendered. A border around the whole form shows you the boundary of the form and allows for resizing of the form. Sometimes, the form also contains scrollbars so that it can display more controls or larger controls than the size of the working area of the form.

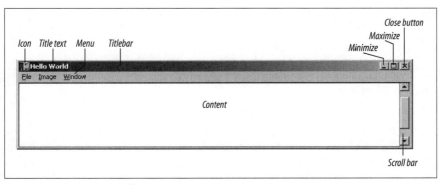

Figure 8-1. An empty application

You can manipulate the form's standard visual elements with properties such as Icon, Text, ControlBox, MinimizeBox, MaximizeBox, and Form-BorderStyle. For example, if you want the title text of the form to read Hello World, you include the assignment formName.Text = "Hello World";. To have a form without the control box in the top right corner, set the ControlBox property to false. If you want to selectively hide the Maximize or the Minimize button in the control box, set the MaximizeBox or MinimizeBox property to false.

You can assign a menu to your form by setting the Menu property of the form with an instance of the MainMenu class. We will show you how to do this in the "Windows Forms Development" section later in this chapter.

Similar to Submit and Reset buttons in a web page's form, a form will frequently include OK and Cancel buttons to submit or to reset the form. In Windows Forms, you can assign any button to the AcceptButton property of the form to make it the default button when the user hits the Enter key. Similarly, you can set up the CancelButton property to handle the Escape key.

The Form class supports a number of methods itself, along with the methods it inherits from the base class. Activate, Show, Hide, ShowDialog, and Close are a few of the imperative methods used in any form to control the window-management functionality of a form. As we get into the "Windows Forms Development" section later in this chapter, you will see these methods in action.

Extending existing controls

Because Windows Forms API is object oriented, extending controls is as easy as deriving from the control you want to extend and adding methods, properties, and events, or overriding the default behavior of the control:

```
class MyCustomTextBox : TextBox
{
  // customization goes here
}
```

Creating composite controls

Composite controls are controls that contain other controls. By definition, it ought to be derived from the ContainerControl class; however, the Windows Forms object model provides the UserControl class, which is a better starting point for your custom composite controls (UserControl actually derives from ContainerControl):

```
class MyCustomComposite : UserControl
{
  // Composite controls go here
}
```

While deriving from UserControl class to create your custom composite controls is not a hard task, Microsoft Visual Studio.NET is an excellent tool for making this task even easier. It truly is an effort to raise the bar on RAD tools. Developers' productivity benefits greatly from support tools like these.

Application Class

The Application class provides static methods to start, stop, or filter Windows messages in an application. All Windows Forms applications contain a reference to this Application class. More specifically, all Windows Forms applications start with something like the following:

```
System.Windows.Forms.Application.Run(new MyForm( ));
```

While this class provides other methods and properties beside the Run method, this method is really the only essential one. The rest of the methods (listed in the rest of this section) are low-level and not frequently used.

The Run method starts the application thread's message loop. This method has two signatures. The first signature involves no parameters, which are normally used for non-GUI applications.

```
System.Windows.Forms.Application.Run( );
```

The second signature takes a form as a parameter, as you can see from the first example. The form MyForm is the entry point to a GUI Windows Forms application.

Table 8-2 summarizes the Application class.

Table 8-2. Common Application properties and methods

Properties	Description
CommonAppDataRegistry	This is the common application registry key under which common data is stored and shared among all users.
StartupPath	This property is the path in which the executable started.
UserAppDataRegistry	This is the registry key where roaming user's data are kept.

Methods	Description
Run	This method starts the application whether it is GUI-based or not.
Exit	This method stops the application by sending the stop message to all message loops in all threads in the application.
ExitThread	Similarly, this method stops the current message loop in the current thread.
AddMessageFilter	You can also add a message filter to the application to intercept and filter Windows messages.[a]
RemoveMessageFilter	You can also remove the message filter.
DoEvents	This method processes all Windows messages currently in the message queue.

[a] The only parameter you need to provide to this method is an object that implements the IMessageFilter interface. Currently, the only method in this interface is PreFilterMessage, which you have to override to intercept and filter any message. If your PreFilterMessage method returns true, the Windows message is consumed and not dispatched to its destination. You can let the message pass through by returning false in this method.

Figure 8-2 illustrates the hierarchy of Windows Controls in the System.Windows.Forms namespace. These controls are placed on the form to create Windows Forms applications and on a UserControl container to create UI Controls (similar to current ActiveX controls). This figure does not include the Application class.

Windows Forms Development

The Form class in the System.Windows.Forms namespace represents a standard window that contains Windows controls. In this section, we walk you through the development of a Windows Forms application and introduce you to the rich set of Windows controls that can be used on a Windows Form.

Windows Forms Application

All Windows Forms applications start out with a derived class from the System.Windows.Forms.Form class. A simple Windows Forms application looks like the following:

```
public class MyForm : System.Windows.Forms.Form
{
  public MyForm( )
  {
    Text = "Hello World";
  }
  public static void Main( )
  {
    System.Windows.Forms.Application.Run(new MyForm( ));
  }
}
```

Basically, you define a class MyForm, which derives from the System.Windows.Forms.Form class. In the constructor of MyForm class, you set the Text property of the Form to Hello World. That's all there is to it. The static Main function is the entry point to all applications. In the entry-point function, you call the static method Application.Run, which starts the message loop for the application. Because you also pass a form-derived object MyForm to the Run method, what we have is a Windows Forms application.

You can also include references to the namespaces to avoid typing the fully qualified name of classes such as System.Windows.Forms.Form or System.Windows.Forms.Application. To do this, include the following line at the beginning of the source file, and omit the System.Windows.Forms prefix to your class names:

```
using System.Windows.Forms;
```

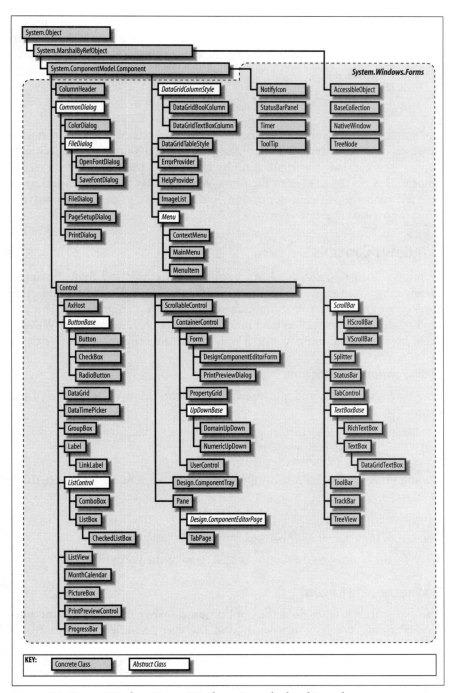

Figure 8-2. System.Windows.Forms Windows Controls class hierarchy

To build the previously listed application, we use the command-line C# compiler. Notice that the target type is an executable, not a DLL, as when we compiled our web service PubsWS (type this command all on one line):[*]

```
csc /t:winexe
    /r:system.dll
    /r:System.Windows.Forms.dll
    MyForm.cs
```

The standard Form object that is shown on the screen doesn't do much; however, it demonstrates the simplicity of creating a Windows Forms application. You can exit the application by clicking on the Close button of the Control Box on the titlebar of the form. When you do this, a quit message is injected into the message loop, and, by default, it is processed and the Application instance will stop.

Windows Controls

Windows Forms applications can be much more involved than the application shown earlier; however, the underlying concepts are the same. In this section, we introduce you to the rich set of Windows controls that you can use on your form, as well as data binding to some of these controls. We also show how event handling works in Windows Forms applications.

Adding controls onto the form

First of all, we create and add the control to the Controls collection of the form:

```
Button btn1 = new Button( );
btn1.Text = "Click Me";
this.Controls.Add(btn1);
```

Adding other types of controls follows the same convention. There are three basic steps:

1. Create the control.

2. Set up the control's properties.

3. Add the control to the Controls collection of the Form object.

Binding the event handler

This is swell, but what does the application do when you click on the button? Nothing. We have not yet bound the event handler to the button's

---

[*] You can also compile the simple file with csc MyForm.cs but it's better to know how to specify the target type and the references that your source relies on.

event. To do that, we first have to create the event handler. An event handler is nothing more than a normal function, but it always has two parameters: object and EventArgs. The object parameter is filled with event originator. For example, if you clicked on a button on a form, causing the onclick event to fire, the object parameter to the event handler will point to the button object that you actually clicked on. The EventArgs object represents the event itself. Using the same example, the EventArgs parameter will be the onclick event with event arguments such as the coordinates of the mouse, which button got clicked and so on. The following code excerpt shows the event handler for the onclick event on a button:

```
void btn1_onclick(Object sender, EventArgs e)
{
    Text = "Sender: " + sender.ToString( ) + " - Event: " + e.ToString( );
}
```

That event handler changes the title of the form each time the button is clicked. Now that we have created the event handler, we assign it to the event click of the button:

```
btn1.Click += new EventHandler(btn1_onclick);
```

That line of code constructs an EventHandler object from the method we passed in and passes the newly created object to the Click event of the button. We basically register a callback function when Click happens. (You may want to review Chapter 2 where we discuss delegates.) Here is the complete example:

```
using System;
using System.Windows.Forms;

public class MyForm : Form
{

    void btn1_onclick(object sender, EventArgs e)
    {
        Text = "Sender: " + sender.ToString( ) +
            " - Event: " + e.ToString( );
    }

    public MyForm( )
    {
        Text = "Hello World";

        Button btn1 = new Button( );
        btn1.Text = "Click Me";
        this.Controls.Add(btn1);

        btn1.Click += new EventHandler(btn1_onclick);
    }
```

```
public static void Main( )
{
  Application.Run(new MyForm( ));
}

}
```

When the user clicks on the button, our event handler is called because we've already registered for the click event. It is possible to add more than one event handler to a single event by repeating the assignment line for other event handlers. All handlers that are registered to handle the event are executed in the order in which they're registered.

You can also easily remove the event handler. Replace += with -=:

```
btn1.Click -= new EventHandler(btn1_onclick);
```

Binding event handlers to events at runtime provides the developer with unlimited flexibility. You can programmatically bind different event handlers to a control based on the state of the application. For example, a button click can be bound to the *update function* when the data row exists or to the *insert function* when it's a new row.

As you can see, the process of binding event handlers to events is the same in Windows Forms as in Web Forms. This consistency of programming model is possibly due their shared substrate, the CLR in both environments.

Data binding

There are two kinds of data binding in Windows Forms. The first involves simple Windows controls such as Label, TextBox, and Button. These simple controls can be bound to a single value only. The second involves Windows controls that can manage lists of data such as ListBox, ComboBox, and DataGrid. These list controls are bound to lists of values.

Let's look at the first type of data binding. In the following example, we bind text boxes to fields in a table from the Pubs database. We extend the simple *Hello, World* Windows Form application to include data access and data binding.

The first thing is to obtain the data from the database. (It's a good time to review ADO.NET in Chapter 5 if you did not read the book in the order presented.) Let's take a look at Example 8-1.

Example 8-1. The C# source file

```
using System;
using System.Windows.Forms;
using System.Data;
using System.Data.OleDb;
```

Example 8-1. The C# source file (continued)

```csharp
public class MyForm : Form
{
  public static void Main( )
  {
    Application.Run(new MyForm( ));
  }

  private TextBox m_txtFirstName, m_txtLastName, m_txtPhone;
  private Button m_btnPrev, m_btnNext;
  private CurrencyManager m_lm;
  private DataSet m_ds;

  public MyForm( )
  {
    Text = "Simple Controls Data Binding";

    // Create the first name text box
    m_txtFirstName = new TextBox( );
    m_txtFirstName.Dock = DockStyle.Top;

    // Create the last name text box
    m_txtLastName = new TextBox( );
    m_txtLastName.Dock = DockStyle.Top;

    // Create the phone text box
    m_txtPhone = new TextBox( );
    m_txtPhone.Dock = DockStyle.Top;

    // Add both first name and last name to the panel1
    Panel panel1 = new Panel( );
    panel1.Dock = DockStyle.Left;
    panel1.Controls.Add(m_txtFirstName);
    panel1.Controls.Add(m_txtLastName);
    panel1.Controls.Add(m_txtPhone);
    // Add panel1 to the left of the form
    this.Controls.Add(panel1);

    // Create the up button and bind click to event handler
    m_btnPrev = new Button( );
    m_btnPrev.Text = "Up";
    m_btnPrev.Dock = DockStyle.Top;
    m_btnPrev.Click += new EventHandler(btnPrev_onclick);

    // Create the down button and bind click to event handler
    m_btnNext = new Button( );
    m_btnNext.Text = "Down";
    m_btnNext.Dock = DockStyle.Top;
    m_btnNext.Click += new EventHandler(btnNext_onclick);

    // Add both the up and down buttons to panel2
    Panel panel2 = new Panel( );
```

Example 8-1. The C# source file (continued)

```csharp
            panel2.Dock = DockStyle.Right;
            panel2.Width = 50;
            panel2.Controls.Add(m_btnNext);
            panel2.Controls.Add(m_btnPrev);
            // Add panel2 to the right of the form
            this.Controls.Add(panel2);

            // Fill the dataset with the authors table from Pubs database
            m_ds = new DataSet();
            string oSQL = "select au_fname, au_lname, phone from authors";
            string oConnStr =
               "provider=sqloledb;server=(local);database=pubs;Integrated Security=SSPI";
            OleDbDataAdapter oDA = new OleDbDataAdapter(oSQL, oConnStr);
            oDA.Fill(m_ds, "tbl");

            // Bind the Text property of last name text box to field au_lname
            m_txtLastName.DataBindings.Add("Text",
                                           m_ds.Tables["tbl"],
                                           "au_lname");

            // Bind the Text property of first name text box to field au_fname
            m_txtFirstName.DataBindings.Add("Text",
                                            m_ds.Tables["tbl"],
                                            "au_fname");

            // Bind the Text property of phone text box to field phone
            m_txtPhone.DataBindings.Add("Text",
                                        m_ds.Tables["tbl"],
                                        "phone");

            // Obtain the list manager from the binding context

            m_lm = (CurrencyManager)this.BindingContext[m_ds.Tables["tbl"]];

        }

        protected void btnNext_onclick(object sender, EventArgs e)
        {
            // Move the position of the list manager
            m_lm.Position += 1;
        }
        protected void btnPrev_onclick(object sender, EventArgs e)
        {
            // Move the position of the list manager
            m_lm.Position -= 1;
        }
}
```

UI controls derive from the Control class, and inherit the DataBindings property (which is of type ControlsBindingCollection). This DataBindings property contains a collection of Binding objects that is used to bind any property of the control to a field in the list data source.

To bind a simple control to a record in the data source, we can add a Binding object to the DataBindings collection for the control using the following syntax:

```
controlName.DataBindings.Add("Property", datasource, "columnname");
```

where controlName is name of the simple control that you want to perform the data binding. The Property item specifies the property of the simple control you want to be bound to the data in column columnname.

Example 8-1 shows how to bind the Text property of the TextBox control m_txtLastName to the au_lname column of Authors table of the DataSet m_ds, as well as m_txtFirstName and m_txtPhone to columns au_fname and phone.

To traverse the list in the data source, we will use the BindingManagerBase object. The following excerpt of code shows you how to get to the binding manager for the data source bound to the controls on the form. In this case, because the data is of list type, the binding manager returned from the BindingContext is a CurrencyManager.*

```
// Obtain the list manager from the binding context

m_lm = (CurrencyManager)this.BindingContext[m_ds.Tables["tbl"]];
```

To demonstrate the use of BindingManagerBase to traverse the data source, we add two buttons onto the form, btnNext and btnPrev. We then bind the two buttons' click events to btnNext_onclick and btnPrev_onclick, respectively:

```
protected void btnNext_onclick(object sender, EventArgs e)
{
  m_lm.Position += 1;
}

protected void btnPrev_onclick(object sender, EventArgs e)
{
  m_lm.Position -= 1;
}
```

As you use BindingManagerBase to manage the position of the list—in this case, the current record in the Authors table—the TextBox controls will be updated with new values. Figure 8-3 illustrates the user interface for the simple controls data-binding example.

---

* If the data source returns only one data value, the BindingManagerBase actually points to an object of type PropertyManager. When the data source returns a list of data value, the type is CurrencyManager.

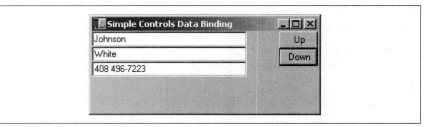

Figure 8-3. Simple controls data binding

Now let's take a look at the other type of data binding. In this example, we will bind the whole authors table to a DataGrid:

```
using System;
using System.Windows.Forms;
using System.Data;
using System.Data.OleDb;

public class MyForm : Form
{
  public static void Main( )
  {
    Application.Run(new MyForm( ));
  }

  private Button m_btn1;
  private TextBox m_txt1;
  private DataGrid m_dataGrid1;

  public MyForm( )
  {
    Text = "Hello World";

    m_txt1 = new TextBox( );
    m_txt1.Text = "select * from authors";
    m_txt1.Dock = DockStyle.Top;
    this.Controls.Add(m_txt1);

    m_btn1 = new Button( );
    m_btn1.Text = "Retrieve Data";
    m_btn1.Dock = DockStyle.Top;
    m_btn1.Click += new EventHandler(btn1_onclick);
    this.Controls.Add(m_btn1);

    m_dataGrid1 = new DataGrid( );
    m_dataGrid1.Dock = DockStyle.Fill;
    this.Controls.Add(m_dataGrid1);

    this.AcceptButton = m_btn1;
  }
```

```
protected void btn1_onclick(object sender, EventArgs e)
{
  try {
    DataSet ds = new DataSet();
    string oConnStr =
      "provider=sqloledb;server=(local);database=pubs;Integrated
Security=SSPI";
    OleDbDataAdapter oDA =
      new OleDbDataAdapter(m_txt1.Text, oConnStr);
    oDA.Fill(ds, "tbl");

    /* You can specify the table directly like this
     *
     *     m_dataGrid1.DataSource = ds.Tables["tbl"];
     *
     * or specify the datasource and the table separately
     * like this:
     */
    m_dataGrid1.DataSource = ds;
    m_dataGrid1.DataMember = "tbl";

  } catch(Exception ex) {
    MessageBox.Show("An error has occured. " + ex.ToString());
  }
 }
}
```

Data binding for controls of type List in Windows Forms is similar to that of Web Forms. However, you don't have to call the DataBind method of the control. All you have to do is set the DataSource property of the UI control to the data source. The data source then has to implement the IEnumerable (or IList, which implements IEnumerable) interfaces. As it turns out, there are hundreds of classes that can be used as data source, including Data-Table, DataView, DataSet, and all array or collection type of classes.

The process for DataGrid data binding is also simple: just set the Data-Source property of the DataGrid object to the data source, and you're all set. We name the table tbl when we add it to DataSet with the data adapter's Fill() method; therefore, the following line of code just indexes into the collection of tables in the DataSet using the table name:

```
m_dataGrid1.DataSource = ds.Tables["tbl"];
```

If the data source contains more than one table, you will also have to set the DataMember property of the control to the name of the table you want the control to bind to:

```
m_dataGrid1.DataSource = ds;
m_dataGrid1.DataMember = "tbl";
```

The results of binding the two tables to the DataGrid are shown in Figure 8-4 and Figure 8-5.

Figure 8-4. Binding the authors table to the DataGrid

au_id	au_lname	au_fname	phone	address	city	state	zip	contract
172-32-1176	White	Johnson	408 496-7223	10932 Bigge	Menlo Park	CA	94025	☑
213-46-8915	Green	Marjorie	415 986-7020	309 63rd St. #	Oakland	CA	94618	☑
238-95-7766	Carson	Cheryl	415 548-7723	589 Darwin L	Berkeley	CA	94705	☑
267-41-2394	O'Leary	Michael	408 286-2428	22 Cleveland	San Jose	CA	95128	☑
274-80-9391	Straight	Dean	415 834-2919	5420 College	Oakland	CA	94609	☑
341-22-1782	Smith	Meander	913 843-0462	10 Mississippi	Lawrence	KS	66044	☐
409-56-7008	Bennet	Abraham	415 658-9932	6223 Batema	Berkeley	CA	94705	☑
427-17-2319	Dull	Ann	415 836-7128	3410 Blonde	Palo Alto	CA	94301	☑
472-27-2349	Gringlesby	Burt	707 938-6445	PO Box 792	Covelo	CA	95428	☑
486-29-1786	Locksley	Charlene	415 585-4620	18 Broadway	San Francisco	CA	94130	☑
527-72-3246	Greene	Morningstar	615 297-2723	22 Graybar H	Nashville	TN	37215	☐
648-92-1872	Blotchet-Halls	Reginald	503 745-6402	55 Hillsdale Bl	Corvallis	OR	97330	☑
672-71-3249	Yokomoto	Akiko	415 935-4228	3 Silver Ct.	Walnut Creek	CA	94595	☑
712-45-1867	del Castillo	Innes	615 996-8275	2286 Cram Pl.	Ann Arbor	MI	48105	☑
722-51-5454	DeFrance	Michel	219 547-9982	3 Balding Pl.	Gary	IN	46403	☑

Figure 8-5. Binding the titles table to the DataGrid

title_id	title	type	pub_id	price	advance	royalty	ytd_sales	notes	pubdate
BU1032	The Busy Exe	business	1389	19.99	5000	10	4095	An overview i	6/12/1991
BU1111	Cooking with	business	1389	11.95	5000	10	3876	Helpful hints o	6/9/1991
BU2075	You Can Com	business	0736	2.99	10125	24	18722	The latest me	6/30/1991
BU7832	Straight Talk	business	1389	19.99	5000	10	4095	Annotated an	6/22/1991
MC2222	Silicon Valley	mod_cook	0877	19.99	0	12	2032	Favorite recip	6/9/1991
MC3021	The Gourmet	mod_cook	0877	2.99	15000	24	22246	Traditional Fr	6/18/1991
MC3026	The Psycholo	UNDECIDED	0877	(null)	(null)	(null)	(null)	(null)	2/8/2001
PC1035	But Is It User	popular_comp	1389	22.95	7000	16	8780	A survey of so	6/30/1991
PC8888	Secrets of Sili	popular_comp	1389	20	8000	10	4095	Muckraking re	6/12/1994
PC9999	Net Etiquette	popular_comp	1389	(null)	(null)	(null)	(null)	A must-read f	2/8/2001
PS1372	Computer Ph	psychology	0877	21.59	7000	10	375	A must for the	10/21/1991
PS2091	Is Anger the E	psychology	0736	10.95	2275	12	2045	Carefully rese	6/15/1991
PS2106	Life Without F	psychology	0736	7	6000	10	111	New exercise,	10/5/1991
PS3333	Prolonged Dat	psychology	0736	19.99	2000	10	4072	What happen	6/12/1991
PS7777	Emotional Se	psychology	0736	7.99	4000	10	3336	Protecting you	6/12/1991

Arranging controls

After adding controls onto the form and setting the event handlings and data bindings, you are fully functional. However, for the visual aspect of your application, you might want to change the layout of the controls on the form. You can do this by setting up physical locations of controls with respect to the container to which the controls belong,* or you can dock or anchor the controls inside the container.

---

* This is similar to VB programming. Controls initially have absolute positions on the form, but they can be programmatically moved and resized while the application is running.

Docking of a control is very simple. You can dock your control to the top, left, right, or bottom of the container. If you dock your control to the top or the bottom, the width of your control will span the whole container. On the same token, if you dock the control to the left or the right, its height will span the height of the container. You can also set the Dock property to DockStyle.Fill, which will adjust the control to fill the container.

The anchoring concept is a bit different. You can anchor your control inside your container by tying it to one or more sides of the container. The distance between the container and the control remains constant at the anchoring side.

You can also use a combination of these techniques by grouping controls into multiple panels and then organizing these panels on the form. With docking and anchoring, there is no need to programmatically calculate and reposition or resize controls on the form.

If you've ever done Java Swing development, you might notice that the current Microsoft .NET Windows Forms framework is similar to JFC with respect to laying out controls; however, it is missing the Layout Manager classes such as GridLayout and FlowLayout to help lay out controls in the containers. We hope that in future releases of the .NET SDK, some sort of layout manager will be included. Currently, if you are writing your Windows Forms application using Visual Studio.NET, you will have more than enough control over the layout of controls on your form.

Visual Inheritance

Visual inheritance was never before possible on the Windows platform using Microsoft technologies. Prior to the release of Microsoft .NET (and we are only talking about VB development here), developers used VB templates to reuse a form. This is basically a fancy name for copy-and-paste programming. Each copy of a VB template can be modified to fit the current use. When the template itself is modified, copies or derivatives of the template are not updated. You either have to redo each one using copy-and-paste or just leave them alone.

With the advent of Microsoft .NET, where everything is now object-oriented, you can create derived classes by inheriting any base class. Since a form in Windows Forms application is nothing more than a derived class of the base Form class, you can actually derive from your Form class to create other Form classes.

This is extremely good for something like a wizard-based application, where each of the forms looks similar to the others. You can create the common

Believe it or not, this is basically all you have to do for the main form of the MDI application! For each of the child forms that we will be spawning from this main form, we will set its MdiParent property to point to this main form.

In the following code excerpt, we load a child form of the main form:

```
...
    Form a = new Form( );
    a.MdiParent = this;
    a.Show( );

    Form b = new Form( );
    b.MdiParent = this;
    b.Show( );
...
```

Again, all it takes to spawn a child form of the MDI application is a single property, MdiParent. In your application, you will replace the type for forms a and b with your own form classes. (As shown later in this chapter, we have ImageForm and TextForm.)

One other point that makes MDI applications interesting is the fact that there is one set of main menus and it is possible for child forms to merge their menus with the MDI frame. We also show you how to incorporate menus into our main MDI form, and later in this section, how the child form's menus are merged to this main menu.

The whole menu architecture in Windows Forms application revolves around two classes:* MainMenu and MenuItem. MainMenu represents the complete menu for the whole form. A MenuItem represents one menu item; however, each menu item contains child menu items in the MenuItems property. Again, you start to see the pattern of *controls* and *containers* here too. For example, if we are to have two top-level menus (e.g., File and Window), then basically, we have to set up the MainMenu object so that it contains two menu items in its MenuItems property. We can do so using the Add method of the MenuItems property to insert menu items dynamically into the collection. If we know ahead of time the number of menu items, we can declaratively assign an array of menu items to this property. Recursively, we can have the File or the Window menu items contain a number of sub-menu items in their MenuItems property the same way we set up the main menu.

---

* The third class is ContextMenu, but we won't discuss it in the scope of this book.

Let's take a look at the source code:

```csharp
using System;
using System.Windows.Forms;

public class MdiMainForm : Form
{
  // Menu Items under File Menu
  private MenuItem mnuOpen, mnuClose, mnuExit;
  // Menu Items under the Window Menu
  private MenuItem mnuCascade, mnuTileHorz, mnuTileVert,
                   mnuSeparator, mnuCloseAll, mnuListMDI;
  // The File and Window Menus
  private MenuItem mnuFile, mnuWindow;
  // The Main Menu
  private MainMenu mnuMain;

  public MdiMainForm( )
  {
    this.Text = "MDI App for Text and Images";

    // File Menu Item
    mnuFile = new MenuItem( );
    mnuFile.Text = "&File";
    mnuFile.MergeOrder = 0;
    // Window Menu Item
    mnuWindow = new MenuItem( );
    mnuWindow.MergeOrder = 2;
    mnuWindow.Text = "&Window";

    // Main Menu contains File and Window
    mnuMain = new MainMenu( );
    mnuMain.MenuItems.AddRange(
        new MenuItem[2] {mnuFile, mnuWindow});

    // Assign the main menu of the form
    this.Menu = mnuMain;

    // Menu Items under File menu
    mnuOpen = new MenuItem( );
    mnuOpen.Text = "Open";
    mnuOpen.Click += new EventHandler(this.OpenHandler);
    mnuClose = new MenuItem( );
    mnuClose.Text = "Close";
    mnuClose.Click += new EventHandler(this.CloseHandler);
    mnuExit = new MenuItem( );
    mnuExit.Text = "Exit";
    mnuExit.Click += new EventHandler(this.ExitHandler);
    mnuFile.MenuItems.AddRange(
        new MenuItem[3] {mnuOpen, mnuClose, mnuExit});

    // Menu Items under Window menu
    mnuCascade = new MenuItem( );
```

```
mnuCascade.Text = "Cascade";
mnuCascade.Click += new EventHandler(this.CascadeHandler);
mnuTileHorz = new MenuItem( );
mnuTileHorz.Text = "Tile Horizontal";
mnuTileHorz.Click += new EventHandler(this.TileHorzHandler);
mnuTileVert = new MenuItem( );
mnuTileVert.Text = "Tile Vertical";
mnuTileVert.Click += new EventHandler(this.TileVertHandler);
mnuSeparator = new MenuItem( );
mnuSeparator.Text = "-";
mnuCloseAll = new MenuItem( );
mnuCloseAll.Text = "Close All";
mnuCloseAll.Click += new EventHandler(this.CloseAllHandler);
mnuListMDI = new MenuItem( );
mnuListMDI.Text = "Windows...";
mnuListMDI.MdiList = true;

mnuWindow.MenuItems.AddRange(
    new MenuItem[6] {mnuCascade, mnuTileHorz, mnuTileVert,
                     mnuSeparator, mnuCloseAll, mnuListMDI});

// This is the MDI container
this.IsMdiContainer = true;
}
public static void Main(string[] args)
{
    Application.Run(new MdiMainForm( ));
}
...
}
```

(Note that this source-code listing is completed in the event handlers listing that follows.)

We first declare all the menu items that we would like to have, along with one MainMenu instance in the class scope. In the main-application constructor, we then instantiate the menu items and set their Text properties. For the two top-level menu items, we also set the MergeOrder property so that we can control where the child forms will merge their menu to the main form menu. In this case, we've set up the File menu to be of order 0 and the Window menu to be of order 2. As you will see later, we will have the child menu's MergeOrder set to 1 so that it is between the File and Window menus.

We then add both the File and the Window menus to the main menu's MenuItems collection by using the AddRange( ) method:

```
mnuMain.MenuItems.AddRange(
    new MenuItem[2] {mnuFile, mnuWindow});
```

Note that at this time, the File and Window menus are still empty. We then assign mnuMain to the MainMenu property of the Form object. At this point, we should be able to see the File and Window menus on the main form; however, there is no drop-down yet.

Similar to how we create menu items and add them to the main menu's MenuItems collection, we add menu items into both the File and Window menu. However, one thing is different. We also bind event handlers to the Click events of the menu items. Let's take one example, the Open menu item:

```
mnuOpen = new MenuItem( );
mnuOpen.Text = "Open";
mnuOpen.Click += new EventHandler(this.OpenHandler);
```

Note that the syntax for binding the event handler OpenHandler to the event Click of the MenuItem class is similar to any other event binding that we've seen so far. Of course, we will have to provide the function body in the MDI main class.

While we are talking about menus, another interesting piece of information is the mnuListMDI MenuItem at the end of the Window menu. We set the MdiList property of this MenuItem to true, as shown in the following code fragment, so that it will automatically show all the opened documents inside the MDI application.

```
mnuListMDI.Text = "Windows...";
mnuListMDI.MdiList = true;
```

See Figure 8-6 for an example of how this feature shows up at runtime.

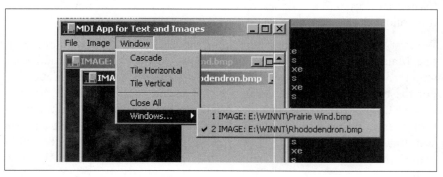

Figure 8-6. MdiList autogenerated menu entries

The following code is for the event handlers that we've set up for various menu items in this main form (this completes the MdiMainForm class listing):

```
protected void OpenHandler(object sender, EventArgs e)
{
  //MessageBox.Show("Open clicked");
```

```csharp
    OpenFileDialog openFileDlg = new OpenFileDialog( );
    if(openFileDlg.ShowDialog( ) == DialogResult.OK)
    {
      try
      {
        String sFN = openFileDlg.FileName;
        String sExt = sFN.Substring(sFN.LastIndexOf("."));
        sExt = sExt.ToUpper( );
        //MessageBox.Show(sFN + " " + sExt);
        if(sExt == ".BMP" || sExt == ".JPG" || sExt == ".GIF")
        {
          ImageForm imgForm = new ImageForm( );
          imgForm.SetFileName(sFN);
          imgForm.MdiParent = this;
          imgForm.Show( );
        }
        else if(sExt == ".TXT" || sExt == ".VB" || sExt == ".CS")
        {
          TextForm txtForm = new TextForm( );
          txtForm.SetFileName(sFN);
          txtForm.MdiParent = this;
          txtForm.Show( );
        }
        else
        {
          MessageBox.Show("File not supported.");
        }
      }
      catch(Exception ex)
      {
        MessageBox.Show ("Error: " + ex.ToString( ));
      }
    }
}

protected void CloseHandler(object sender, EventArgs e)
{
    if(this.ActiveMdiChild != null)
    {
      this.ActiveMdiChild.Close( );
    }
}

protected void ExitHandler(object sender, EventArgs e)
{
    this.Close( );
}

protected void CascadeHandler(object sender, EventArgs e)
{
    this.LayoutMdi(MdiLayout.Cascade);
}
```

```
protected void TileHorzHandler(object sender, EventArgs e)
{
  this.LayoutMdi(MdiLayout.TileHorizontal);
}

protected void TileVertHandler(object sender, EventArgs e)
{
  this.LayoutMdi(MdiLayout.TileVertical);
}

protected void CloseAllHandler(object sender, EventArgs e)
{
  int iLength = MdiChildren.Length;
  for(int i=0; i<iLength; i++)
  {
    MdiChildren[0].Dispose();
  }
}
```

The functionality of the OpenHandler event handler is simple. We basically open a common file dialog box to allow the user to pick a file to open. For simplicity's sake, we will support three image formats (BMP, GIF, and JPG) and three text file extensions (TXT, CS, and VB). If the user picks the image-file format, we open the ImageForm as the child form of the MDI application. If a text-file format is selected instead, we use the TextForm class. We will show you the source for both the ImageForm and TextForm shortly.

To arrange the children forms, we use the LayoutMdi method of the Form class. This method accepts an enumeration of type MdiLayout. Possible values are Cascade, ArrangeIcons, TileHorizontal, and TileVertical.

The form also supports the ActiveMdiChild property to indicate the current active MDI child form. We use this piece of information to handle the File → Close menu item to close the currently selected MDI child form.

To handle the CloseAll menu click event, we loop through the collection of all MDI child forms and dispose them all.

The following is the source for ImageForm class:

```
using System;
using System.Drawing;
using System.Windows.Forms;

public class ImageForm : System.Windows.Forms.Form
{
  private MenuItem mnuImageItem;
  private MenuItem mnuImage;
  private MainMenu mnuMain;

  private Bitmap m_bmp;
```

```
public ImageForm( )
{
    mnuImageItem = new MenuItem( );
    mnuImageItem.Text = "Image Manipulation";
    mnuImageItem.Click += new EventHandler(this.HandleImageItem);

    mnuImage = new MenuItem( );
    mnuImage.Text = "&Image";
    mnuImage.MergeOrder = 1;     // merge after File but before Window
    mnuImage.MenuItems.AddRange(new MenuItem[1] {mnuImageItem});

    mnuMain = new MainMenu( );
    mnuMain.MenuItems.AddRange( new MenuItem[1] {mnuImage});
    this.Menu = mnuMain;
}

public void SetFileName(String sImageName)
{
    try
    {
        m_bmp = new Bitmap(sImageName);
        Invalidate( );
        this.Text = "IMAGE: " + sImageName;
    }
    catch(Exception ex)
    {
        MessageBox.Show ("Error: " + ex.ToString( ));
    }
}

protected override void OnPaint(PaintEventArgs e)
{
    if(m_bmp != null)
    {
        Graphics g = e.Graphics;
        g.DrawImage(m_bmp, 0, 0, m_bmp.Width, m_bmp.Height);
    }
}

protected void HandleImageItem(object sender, EventArgs e)
{
    MessageBox.Show("Handling the image.");
}
}
```

Because this ImageForm class needs to draw the image file on the form, we include a reference to the System.Drawing namespace. To render the image file onto the form, we rely on the Bitmap and Graphics classes. First of all, we get the input filename and construct the Bitmap object with the content of the input file. Next, we invalidate the screen so that it will be redrawn. In the overriden OnPaint method, we obtained a pointer to the Graphics object and asked it to draw the Bitmap object on the screen.

One other point that we want to show you is the fact that the Image menu item has its MergeOrder property set to 1. We did this to demonstrate the menu-merging functionality of MDI applications. When this form is displayed, the main menu of the MDI application changes to File, Image, and Window.

To complete the example, following is the source to the TextForm class:

```
using System;
using System.Windows.Forms;
using System.IO;

public class TextForm : Form
{
  private MenuItem mnuTextItem;
  private MenuItem mnuText;
  private MainMenu mnuMain;

  private TextBox textBox1;

  public TextForm( )
  {
    mnuTextItem = new MenuItem( );
    mnuTextItem.Text = "Text Manipulation";
    mnuTextItem.Click += new EventHandler(this.HandleTextItem);

    mnuText = new MenuItem( );
    mnuText.Text = "&Text";
    mnuText.MergeOrder = 1;     // merge after File but before Window
    mnuText.MenuItems.AddRange(new MenuItem[1] {mnuTextItem});

    mnuMain = new MainMenu( );
    mnuMain.MenuItems.AddRange(new MenuItem[1] {mnuText});
    this.Menu = mnuMain;

    textBox1 = new TextBox( );
    textBox1.Multiline = true;
    textBox1.Dock = System.Windows.Forms.DockStyle.Fill;
    this.Controls.Add (this.textBox1);
  }

  public void SetFileName(String sFileName)
  {
    StreamReader reader = File.OpenText(sFileName);
    textBox1.Text = reader.ReadToEnd( );
    reader.Close( );
    textBox1.SelectionLength = 0;
    this.Text = "TEXT: " + sFileName;
  }
```

```
protected void HandleTextItem(object sender, EventArgs e)
{
  MessageBox.Show("Handling the text file.");
}

}
```

Similar to the ImageForm class, the TextForm class also has its menu inserted in the middle of File and Window. When a TextForm becomes the active MDI child form, the menu of the MDI application becomes File, Text, and Window. This menu-merging is done automatically. All we have to do is set up the MergeOrder properties of the menu items.

For the functionality of the TextForm, we have a simple TextBox object. We set its Multiline property to true to simulate a simple text editor and have its docking property set to fill the whole form. When the main form passes the text filename to this form, we read the input file and put the content into the text box.

Figure 8-7 illustrates the screen shot for this MDI application at runtime. In this instance, we have three TextForms and three ImageForms open concurrently.

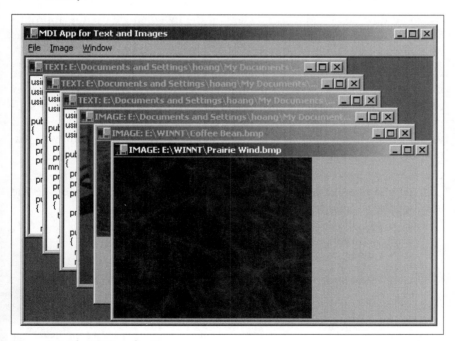

Figure 8-7. The MDI application

The following script is used to build this MDI application. As you can see, the target parameter is set to winexe to indicate that the result of the compilation will be an executable instead of library, which would result in a DLL. Because we make use of the graphics package for our image rendering, we also have to add the reference to the System.drawing.dll assembly. We have three forms in this application: the main form, which is named MDIApp, and the two MDI child forms, ImageForm and TextForm (make sure you type these commands all on one line).*

```
csc /t:winexe
    /r:System.Windows.Forms.dll
    /r:system.drawing.dll
    MDIApp.cs
    ImageForm.cs
    TextForm.cs
```

Stage Deployment

Imagine the MDI application from the previous example with hundreds of different types of files supported. For each of the file types, we'd probably have a class similar to the ImageForm and TextForm classes. Instead of compiling and linking all of these classes into your application, wouldn't it be nice if we could download and install a class on the fly when we use the appropriate file type? In this section, we show how you can convert the previous MDI application to allow just that.

Conceptually, we will have the main executable act as a controller. It will be the first assembly downloaded onto the client machine. Once the user chooses to open a particular file type, this controller determines which supporting DLLs should be downloaded to handle the file type, download and install the DLL and then asks the class in the downloaded assembly to display the selected file.

In order for the controller to communicate with all supporting classes, we abstract the commonality out of ImageForm and TextForm to create the abstract class BaseForm.†

```
using System;
using System.Windows.Forms;
using System.Security;
[assembly:AllowPartiallyTrustedCallers]
namespace BaseForm
{
```

---

* Again, you can compile the executable without specifying the target type or the references.

† Because we will demonstrate running *MDIApp.exe* from a browser later, *BaseForm.dll* has to be explicitly flagged to grant *MDIApp.exe* usage via the AllowPartiallyTrustedCallers attribute. This is to accomodate the Version 1 security changes for Microsoft .NET Framework from RCs.

```
abstract public class BaseForm : Form
{
    abstract public void SetFileName(String sFileName);
}
}
```

We will rewrite both ImageForm and TextForm to make them inherit from BaseForm. Any other form that you will need to write for other file types will have to also inherit from BaseForm. This way, all the controller module has to do is to know how to talk to BaseForm and everything should be fine.

The followings are the changes to *ImageForm.cs* source file. All we did was to wrap the class inside a namespace call ImageForm, make ImageForm class inherit from BaseForm, and providing the implementation for the abstract method SetFileName( ). The rest of the code is the same with the original *ImageForm.cs*.

```
//...

namespace ImageForm
{
  public class ImageForm : BaseForm.BaseForm
  {

    //...

    override public void SetFileName(String sImageName)
    {
      //...
    }

    //...

  }
}
```

We apply the same thing to *TextForm.cs* as we do for *ImageForm.cs*. The following summarizes the changes.

```
//...

namespace TextForm
{
  public class TextForm : BaseForm.BaseForm
  {

    //...

    override public void SetFileName(String sFileName)
    {
      //...
    }
```

```
//...

    }
}
```

Now, instead of having the MDIApp compiled and linked with *ImageForm. cs* and *TextForm.cs* and directly using ImageForm and TextForm class in OpenHandler( ) function, we utilize the reflection namespace to load each assembly from a predetermined URL on the fly. Replace the old code for handling images in OpenHandler( ):

```
ImageForm imgForm = new ImageForm( );
imgForm.SetFileName(sFN);
```

with:

```
Assembly ass = Assembly.LoadFrom("http://localhost/MDIDLLS/ImageForm.dll");
BaseForm.BaseForm imgForm =
        (BaseForm.BaseForm) ass.CreateInstance("ImageForm.ImageForm");
imgForm.SetFileName(sFN);
```

The three lines of code essentially do the following:

1. Download the assembly from the specified URL.
2. Create an instance of ImageForm class in ImageForm namespace and cast it to BaseForm.
3. Instruct the BaseForm derived class to deal with the image file.

For the TextForm, replace the following old code for handling text files in OpenHandler( ):

```
TextForm txtForm = new TextForm( );
txtForm.SetFileFile(sFN);
```

with:

```
Assembly ass = Assembly.LoadFrom("http://localhost/MDIDLLS/TextForm.dll");
BaseForm.BaseForm txtForm =
        (BaseForm.BaseForm) ass.CreateInstance("TextForm.TextForm");
txtForm.SetFileName(sFN);
```

The last thing to do is to make MDIApp use the Reflection namespace by inserting the following line of code:

```
using System.Reflection;
```

You will have to compile *BaseForm.cs*, *ImageForm.cs*, and *TextForm.cs* into *BaseForm.dll*, *ImageForm.dll*, and *TextForm.dll* in that order because Image-Form and TextForm derive from BaseForm.

The following command lines will do the job:

```
csc /t:library /r:System.Windows.Forms.dll baseform.cs
csc /t:library /r:System.Windows.Forms.dll;baseform.dll imageform.cs
csc /t:library /r:System.Windows.Forms.dll;baseform.dll textform.cs
```

You will also have to compile the main module *MDIApp.cs*. Notice that the only thing the MDIApp.cs needs to know is BaseForm.

```
csc /t:winexe
     /r:System.Windows.Forms.dll;system.drawing.dll;baseform.dll MDIApp.cs
```

Once you have all the components compiled, copy them all into a virtual directory call MDIDLLs because this is the predefined location where these components are to be downloaded.*

One last step you will have to do is to use the .NET Framework Configuration tool to give file I/O permission to adjust zone security and give Local Intranet full trust level.† It is not recommended that you use this setting without knowing all consequences; however, this is the simplest thing to do to quickly demonstrate the experiment. For your enterprise application, consult the .NET security documentation for further recommendation.

And now everything is setup. All you have to do is to point your browser to *http://localhost/MDIDLLs/MDIApp.exe* and see how the components are automatically downloaded and run.

Another utility you might want to use to inspect the global assembly cache (where the downloaded components reside) is gacutil. Use gacutil /ldl to list all downloaded assemblies and gacutil /cdl to clear the downloaded assemblies. When you first see the MDIApp main form, the only assembly downloaded is MDIApp. But as soon as you try to open an image file or a text file, ImageForm or TextForm along with BaseForm will be downloaded.

As you can see, with this setup, you won't have to have hundreds of DLLs when you only use a couple of file types. Another cool thing is that when the DLLs on the server are updated, you will automatically have the latest components.

Of course, you can make this MDIApp more production-like by having the main module accessing a web service that lists the *file types* this application supports and the *class names* as well as the *assembly filenames* needed to be downloaded. Once this is setup, you can have conditioning code based on the file type; you can pass the *assembly filename URL* to Assembly. LoadFrom() method; you can use the class name to create the class instance; all of these make the main module more generic. Suppose the web service that lists the supporting file types for this MDIApp reads information from a

---

* Make sure this virtual directory execute permission does not have executable enabled. In other words, just create the virtual directory with the default settings.

† The tool can be found at Adminstrative Tools/Microsoft .NET Framework Configuration. Choose to Configure Code Access Security and then Adjust Zone Security. Give Local Intranet full trust level for the duration of this experiment.

database or an XML file. When you need to introduce new file type and supporting assembly to deal with the new file type, all you have to do is to add an entry to your database or your XML file and add the assembly file into the virtual directory. We think this is an exercise you should definitely try out.

Windows Forms and Web Services

Previously, Windows DNA tended not to use fat clients, rich Windows applications on PCs, because of the need for an intrusive installation program. With .NET "copy" deployment, there is no such problem. Now fat Windows clients can interface easily with business logic in the middle tier through XML/HTTP. The rich client application will, in fact, perform better than a web-based frontend. However, everything depends on the requirements of the application.

You can still add web references to Web Services that auto-generate proxy classes for use in your Windows Forms applications just as for Web Forms applications. This is further evidence that .NET as a whole is intended to embrace the Web. In Windows Forms, data binding is automatic once you've set the control's DataSource to the appropriate data source, as seen in the next block of code. Note that there is no explicit call to the DataBind method as in Web Forms data binding.

```
localhost.PubsWS ws = new localhost.PubsWS( );
DataSet ds = ws.GetAuthors( );
DataGrid1.DataSource = ds.tables[0].DefaultView;
```

Again, you can also generate the source for the proxy class yourself using the *wsdl.exe* tool, along with the WSDL obtained from the web service. You can then include this source to your Windows Forms project or compile the source into a DLL and add the DLL to the project as a reference.

Conclusion

Windows Forms provides a unified programming model for standard Windows application development. It does not matter what language you are using—you can always be productive because the common substrate has been developed to benefit all.

Windows Forms brings a true object-oriented programming model to Windows GUI development, allowing for an extensible framework that is much cleaner and easier to use compared to previous attempts.

In this chapter, we've shown you the architecture of the Windows Forms application. The Controls and Containers architecture, while very simple, is powerful and flexible for developing Windows-based applications. We have also shown you how to build a Windows Forms application, starting with a simple do-nothing application, then data binding, and finally a multiple-document interface application.

.NET Languages

This appendix contains two lists of languages (Microsoft-supported and third-party) with compilers that generate IL to target the CLR.

Microsoft-Supported Languages for .NET

Table A-1 lists commercial languages that Microsoft supports. You can find more information about each of these languages by browsing the provided URLs.

Table A-1. Microsoft-supported languages for .NET

Language	Link
C#	*http://msdn.microsoft.com/vstudio/nextgen/technology/csharpintro.asp*
JScript	*http://msdn.microsoft.com/workshop/languages/clinic/scripting07142000.asp*
Managed C++	*http://msdn.microsoft.com/vstudio/nextgen/Technology/managedext.asp*
VB.NET	*http://msdn.microsoft.com/vstudio/nextgen/technology/language.asp*

Third-Party Languages for .NET

Table A-2 shows a list of third-party languages with compilers that target the CLR. Some of these are research languages, while others are commercial languages that target .NET. Browse the provided web sites to read more about the languages that interest you. As noted earlier, this list of languages could grow by the time this book hits the market, so be sure to check the following sites for the most up-to-date listings: *http://www.gotdotnet.com* and *http://msdn.microsoft.com/net/languages/default.asp*.

Table A-2. Third-party languages

Language	Link
APL	*http://www.dyadic.com*
COBOL	*http://www.adtools.com/info/whitepaper/net.html*
Component Pascal	*http://www2.fit.qut.edu.au/CompSci/PLAS//ComponentPascal*
Delta Forth	*http://www.dataman.ro/dforth/*
Eiffel#	*http://www.eiffel.com/doc/manuals/technology/dotnet/eiffelsharp/white_paper.html*
Fortran	*http://www.lahey.com/dotnet.htm,*
	http://www.salfordsoftware.co.uk/compilers/ftn95/dotnet.shtml
Haskell	*http://haskell.cs.yale.edu/ghc*
Mercury	*http://www.cs.mu.oz.au/research/mercury/dotnet.html*
Mondrian	*http://www.mondrian-script.org*
Oberon	*http://www.oberon.ethz.ch/lightning*
Perl	*http://www.activestate.com/ASPN/NET*
Python	*http://www.activestate.com/ASPN/NET*
RPG	*http://www.asna.com/pr2%5F20%5F01.asp*
Scheme	*http://rover.cs.nwu.edu/~scheme*
Smalltalk	*http://www.qks.com*
Standard ML	*http://www.research.microsoft.com/Projects/SML.NET*
TMT Pascal	*http://www.tmt.com/net.htm*

For more information, visit the O'Reilly .NET Center at *http://dotnet.oreilly. com* and the .NET DevCenter at *http://www.oreillynet.comdotnet.*

Common Acronyms

Table B-1 provides a listing of common acronyms or terms that you will come across in .NET-related reading materials and conversations. Some of these acronyms or terms have little relevance to .NET, but appear occasionally in this book, so we've provided them in this table for your convenience.

Table B-1. List of common acronyms

Acronym	Description
.ASMX	File extension for Web Services source-code files.
.ASPX	File extension for ASP.NET source-code files.
.config	File extension of .NET application configuration files.
ADO	ActiveX Data Objects.
ADO.NET	With goals similar to ADO, ADO.NET is the way to access data sources in .NET.
API	Application Programming Interface.
AppDomain	Short term to mean an application domain.
ASP	Active Server Pages.
ASP.NET	With goals similar to ASP, ASP.NET is the technology that supports the rapid development of Web Forms.
ATL	Active Template Library.
BLOB	Binary Large Object.
CAB Files	Cabinet files.
CCW	COM Callable Wrapper.
CLI	Common Language Infrastructure. This is the specification of the infrastructure and base class libraries that Microsoft has submitted to ECMA so that a third-party vendor can build a .NET runtime on another platform. The CLR is Microsoft's implementation of the CLI.
CLR	Common Language Runtime.
CLS	Common Language Specification.
CLSID	Class identifier used in COM.

Acronym	Description
COFF	Common Object File Format.
COM	Component Object Model.
COM Interop	Short for COM interoperation.
COM+ 2.0	This term is no longer used as of Beta 1 of the .NET SDK. The new accepted term is .NET Framework.
COM+ Runtime	This term is no longer used as of Beta 1 of the .NET SDK. The new and accepted term is Common Language Runtime.
CTS	Common Type System.
DB	Database.
DCOM	Distributed Component Object Model.
DHTML	Dynamic HyperText Markup Language.
DISCO	Discovery of Web Services. A Web Service has one or more .DISCO files that contain information on how to access its WSDL.
DISPID	Dispatch identifier. Used in COM to identify a method or a property for dynamic invocation.
DLL	Dynamically Linked Library.
DNA	Distributed interNet Applications Architecture.
DOM	Document Object Model.
DTD	Datatype Document. This has been superceded by XSD schemas.
EXE	Executable.
GC	Garbage Collector.
GDI	Graphical Device Interface.
GDI+	A .NET library that supports advanced graphics management.
Global.asax	The global configuration file for an ASP.NET application.
GUID	Globally Unique Identifier.
HTML	HyperText Markup Language.
HTTP	HyperText Transfer Protocol.
IDE	Integrated Development Environment.
IDL	Interface Definition Language.
IE	Internet Explorer.
IID	Interface Identifier.
IIS	Internet Information Server.
IJW	It Just Works.
IL	Intermediate Language.
ILDASM	Intermediate Language Disassembler.
Inproc	In-Process.
ISAPI	Information Server Application Programming Interface.

Table B-1. List of common acronyms (continued)

Acronym	Description
Machine.config	Configuration file for administrative policy for an entire machine.
MBR	Marshal-By-Reference.
MBV	Marshal-By-Value.
MFC	Microsoft Foundation Classes.
MSI	Microsoft Windows Installer Package.
MSIL	Microsoft Intermediate Language.
MSVCRT	Microsoft Visual C++ Runtime.
MSXML	Microsoft eXtensible Markup Language.
MTS	Microsoft Transaction Server.
NGWS	This term is no longer used as of Beta 1 of the .NET SDK. The new and accepted term is .NET.
NTFS	NT Filesystem.
N-Tier	Multi-tier.
NTLM	NT Lan Manager.
OBJREF	Object Reference.
Out of proc	Out-of-process.
P/Invoke	Platform Invoke.
PE	Portable Executable.
perm	Permissions.
RAD	Rapid Application Development.
RCW	Runtime Callable Wrapper.
REGASM	Register Assembly tool.
RPC	Remote Procedure Call.
SCL	SOAP Contract Language.
SDK	Software Development Kit.
SEH	Structured Exception Handling.
SMTP	Simple Mail Transfer Protocol.
SOAP	Simple Object Access Protocol.
SQL	Structured Query Language.
Standard JIT	Optimized native code that includes verification of IL (generaged by the standard JIT compiler).
STL	Standard Template Library.
TCP	Transport Control Protocol.
TLB	Type Library.
TLBEXP	Type Library Exporter Tool.
TLBIMP	Type Library Importer Tool.

Acronym	Description
UDDI	Universal Description, Discovery, and Integration Service. UDDI is a platform-independent framework for describing and discovering Web Services.
UDF	Uniform Data Format.
UI	User Interface.
URI	Uniform Resource Identifier.
URL	Uniform Resource Locator.
URT	Universal Runtime. This term is no longer used as of Beta 1 of the .NET SDK. The new and accepted term is the .NET Framework.
VB	Visual Basic.
VBRUN	Visual Basic Runtime.
VES	Virtual Execution System. The VES is a subset of the CLR. The VES doesn't include features such as debugging, profile, and COM interoperation.
Visual Studio 7	This term is no longer used as of Beta 1 of the .NET SDK. The new and accepted term is Visual Studio.NET.
VOS	Virtual Object System. This is now called the CTS.
VS.NET	Visual Studio .NET.
WAP	Wireless Application Protocol.
web.config	Configuration file for ASP.NET. You define HTTP modules, handlers, session state management, and other ASP.NET configurable parameters in this file.
WebForms	This term is no longer used as of Beta 1 of the .NET SDK. The new and accepted term is Web Forms (with a space).
WebServices	This term is no longer used as of Beta 1 of the .NET SDK. The new and accepted term is Web Services (with a space).
Win32	Windows 32-bit.
WinForms	This term is no longer used as of Beta 1 of the .NET SDK. The new and accepted term is Windows Forms (with a space).
WML	Wireless Markup Language.
WSDL	Web Service Description Language. Think of this as IDL for Web Services. Unlike IDL, WSDL is expressed using only XML schemas. SDL is used in Beta1 of the .NET SDK, but WSDL replaced SDL in Beta 2 and later installments.
XML	Extensible Markup Language.
XPath	XML Path.
XSD	XML Schema Definition.
XSL	Extensible Stylesheet Language.
XSLT	Extensible Stylesheet Language Transformations.

look-and-feel form as your base class and then create each of the wizard forms by deriving from this base class.

MDI Applications

There are two main styles of user interfaces for Windows-based applications: Single Document Interface (SDI) and Multiple Document Interface (MDI).* For SDI applications, each instance of the application can have only one document. If you would like more than one open document, you must have multiple instances of the application running. MDI, on the other hand, allows multiple documents to be open at one time in one instance of the application. Another good thing about MDI application is that, depending of the type of document currently open, the main menu for the application changes to reflect the operations that you can perform on the document.

While it is easy to implement both SDI and MDI applications using the Windows Forms architecture, we only show an example of MDI in this section.

MDI application architecture borrows the same pattern of Windows Forms architecture. Basically, you have one form acting as the container form and other forms acting as child forms.

The Form class provides a number of properties and methods to help in the development of MDI applications, including IsMdiContainer, IsMdiChild, MdiParent, MdiChildren, ActiveMdiChild, and LayoutMdi().

The first thing we want to show you is the bare minimum main form for our MDI application:

```
using System;
using System.Windows.Forms;

public class MdiMainForm : Form
{
  public MdiMainForm( )
  {
    this.Text = "MDI App for Text and Images";
    // This is the MDI container
    this.IsMdiContainer = true;
  }
  public static void Main(string[] args)
  {
    Application.Run(new MdiMainForm( ));
  }
}
```

---

* Other styles are Explorer, Wizard, etc., but we are not going discuss all of them in this book.

APPENDIX C
Common Data Types

Each of the .NET languages might provide its own keywords for the types it supports. For example, a keyword for an integer in VB is Integer, whereas in C# or C++ it is int; a boolean is Boolean in VB, but bool in C# or C++. In any case, the integer is mapped to the the class Int32, and the boolean is mapped to the class Boolean in the System namespace. Table C-1 lists all simple data types common to the .NET Framework. Non-CLS-compliant types are not guaranteed to interoperate with all CLS- compliant languages.

Table C-1. Common data types

Type	Description
Boolean	True or false.
Byte	8-bit unsigned integer: 0 to 255.
Char	Character. Unicode 16-bit character.
DateTime	Represents a date and time value.
Decimal	Can represent positive and negative values with 28 significant digits: −79,228,162,514,264,337,593,543,950,335 through 79,228,162,514,264,337,593,543,950,335 .
Double	Stores 64-bit floating-point values: −1.79769313486231570e308 to 1.79769313486231570e308.
Guid	Represents a globally unique identifier (GUID).
Int16	Stores 16-bit signed integers: −32,768 to 32,767.
Int32	Stores 32-bit signed integers: −2,147,483,648 to 2,147,483,647.
Int64	Stores 64-bit signed integers: −9,223,372,036,854,775,808 to 9,223,372,036,854,775,807.
SByte	Represents an 8-bit signed integer. The SByte type is not CLS-compliant. −128 to 127.
Single	Represents an IEEE 754f, single precision, 32-bit value: −3.40282346638528859e38 to 3.40282346638528859e38.
String	Represents a string of Unicode characters.
UInt16	Represents a 16-bit unsigned integer. The UInt16 type is not CLS- compliant. 0 to 65,535.
UInt32	Represents a 32-bit unsigned integer. The UInt32 type is not CLS- compliant. 0 to 4,294,967,295

Table C-1. Common data types (continued)

Type	Description
UInt64	Represents a 64-bit unsigned integer. The UInt64 type is not CLS- compliant. The UInt64 data type can represent positive integers with 18 significant digits: 0 to 184,467,440,737,095,551,615.
Void	Void.

Table C-2 shows a number of useful container types that the .NET Framework provides.

Table C-2. Container types

Type	Description
ArrayList	This class implements the IList interface. The array can grow dynamically in size.
BitArray	This class represents a compact array of bit values. Each element represents a Boolean value (true/false).
HashTable	This class represents a collection of associated keys and values that are organized based on the hash code of the key.
Queue	This class represents a first-in, first-out collection construct.
SortedList	This class is similar to HashTable except that all elements are sorted by their actual keys (not hashed) and elements are accessible through either key or index.
Stack	This class represents a first-in, last-out stack construct.

Usage

This section demonstrates how you can take advantage of container types. We don't illustrate all methods and properties, but we show the important characteristics of these types. All examples in this chapter are in C#; however, you can use these CLS types from any other CLS-compliant languages.

ArrayList

In the following code listing, we demonstrate some of the critical usages of the ArrayList class, such as adding data to the end of the list, inserting data anywhere in the list, iterating through the list, and sorting the list.

```
using System;
using System.Collections;
public class TestArrayList {

    public static void Main( )  {

        ArrayList arrList = new ArrayList( );
        arrList.Add("Monday");
        arrList.Add("Tuesday");
        arrList.Add("Wednesday");
```

```
arrList.Add("Thursday");

// We'll try to insert Friday afterward
// arrList.Add("Friday");

arrList.Add("Saturday");
arrList.Add("Sunday");

int i = 0;
IEnumerator arrIterator = arrList.GetEnumerator( );
Console.WriteLine("There are: {0} days in a week.", arrList.Count);
while(arrIterator.MoveNext( )) {
    Console.WriteLine("[{0}] {1}", i++, arrIterator.Current);
}

Console.WriteLine("Insert Friday");
arrList.Insert(4, "Friday");

i = 0;
arrIterator = arrList.GetEnumerator( );
Console.WriteLine("There are: {0} days in a week.", arrList.Count);
while(arrIterator.MoveNext( )) {
    Console.WriteLine("[{0}] {1}", i++, arrIterator.Current);
}

arrList.Sort( );

i = 0;
arrIterator = arrList.GetEnumerator( );
Console.WriteLine("Sorted as text");
while(arrIterator.MoveNext( )) {
    Console.WriteLine("[{0}] {1}", i++, arrIterator.Current);
}

Object oDay = "Friday";
Console.WriteLine("Index for Friday using BinarySearch: {0}",
                  arrList.BinarySearch(oDay));
Console.WriteLine("Index for Sunday using BinarySearch: {0}",
                  arrList.BinarySearch("Sunday"));
    }
}
```

BitArray

The sample code for BitArray is self-explanatory, as shown in the following
code listing. We use the bit array to store and retrieve access rights in the
following example. You can use the Set and Get methods as well as the []
operator.

```
using System;
using System.Collections;
```

```
public class TestBitArray {

    enum Permissions {canRead, canWrite, canCreate, canDestroy};

    public static void Main() {

        BitArray bitArr = new BitArray(4);
        bitArr.Set((int)Permissions.canRead, true);
        bitArr[(int)Permissions.canWrite] = false;
        bitArr[(int)Permissions.canCreate] = true;
        bitArr[(int)Permissions.canDestroy] = false;

        Console.WriteLine("bitArr count: {0}\tlength: {1}",
                          bitArr.Count,
                          bitArr.Length);

        Console.WriteLine("Permissions:");
        Console.WriteLine("Read: {0}",
                          bitArr[(int)Permissions.canRead]);
        Console.WriteLine("Write: {0}",
                          bitArr[(int)Permissions.canWrite]);
        Console.WriteLine("Create: {0}",
                          bitArr[(int)Permissions.canCreate]);
        Console.WriteLine("Destroy: {0}",
                          bitArr[(int)Permissions.canDestroy]);
    }
}
```

HashTable

The HashTable data type is similar to the dictionary object, which is basically an associated array. Each element stored in the table is associated with a key. Because HashTable implements the IDictionaryEnumerator, we can obtain the enumerator to help us iterate through the data collection. As you can see from the sample code, we can also loop through the data using the keys or values collection.

```
using System;
using System.Collections;
public class TestHashtable {

    public static void Main() {

        Hashtable hashTbl = new Hashtable();
        hashTbl.Add("Param1", "UserName");
        hashTbl.Add("Param2", "Password");

        IDictionaryEnumerator hashEnumerator = hashTbl.GetEnumerator();
        Console.WriteLine();
        Console.WriteLine("Loop through with enumerator:");
        while (hashEnumerator.MoveNext()) {
```

```
            Console.WriteLine("Key: {0}\tValue: {1}",
                               hashEnumerator.Key,
                               hashEnumerator.Value);
        }

        Console.WriteLine();
        Console.WriteLine("Loop through Keys:");
        foreach(string key in hashTbl.Keys) {
            Console.WriteLine(key);

        }

        Console.WriteLine();
        Console.WriteLine("Loop through Values:");
        foreach(string val in hashTbl.Values) {
            Console.WriteLine(val);

        }

        Console.WriteLine();
        Console.WriteLine("Loop through Keys:");
        foreach(string key in hashTbl.Keys) {
            Console.WriteLine("Key: {0}\tValue: {1}", key, hashTbl[key]);

        }
    }
}
```

Queue

To demonstrate the use of a queue Abstract Data Type (ADT), we create a
fictitious order-processing code listing. Each enqueued item represents a line
item in a typical order. We will then dequeue each line item and perform the
total calculation.

```
using System;
using System.Collections;

public class TestQueue  {

    public static void Main()  {
        string sLineItem1, sLineItem2;
        Queue myQueue = new Queue();

        sLineItem1 = "123\tItem 123\t4\t3.39";
        sLineItem2 = "ABC\tItem ABC\t1\t9.49";
        myQueue.Enqueue(sLineItem1);
        myQueue.Enqueue(sLineItem2);

        Console.WriteLine("\nProcessing Order:\n");
        String sLineItem = "";
```

```
          String [] lineItemArr;
          Decimal total = 0;
          while(myQueue.Count > 0) {
             sLineItem = (String)myQueue.Dequeue( );
             Console.WriteLine( "\t{0}", sLineItem);
             lineItemArr = sLineItem.Split(new Char[] {'\t'});
             total += Convert.ToInt16(lineItemArr[2]) *
                      Convert.ToDecimal(lineItemArr[3]);
          }
          Console.WriteLine("\nOrder Total: {0}\n", total);

       }
    }
```

SortedList

The following code demonstrates the sorted list ADT. A sorted list is similar
to a hash table or a dictionary type. Each item of data is associated with the
key with which the list is sorted. Notice that the strings are added to the list
in no particular order. However, when we iterate through the list, all strings
are sorted by their associated keys.

```
using System;
using System.Collections;
public class TestSortedList  {

    public static void Main( )  {

        SortedList mySortedList = new SortedList( );
        mySortedList.Add("AA", "Hello");
        mySortedList.Add("AC", "!");
        mySortedList.Add("AB", "World");

        Console.WriteLine("\nLoop through manually:\n");
        for(int i=0; i< mySortedList.Count; i++) {
           Console.WriteLine("Key: {0}\tValue: {1}",
                        mySortedList.GetKey(i),
                        mySortedList.GetByIndex(i));
        }

        IDictionaryEnumerator myIterator = mySortedList.GetEnumerator( );
        Console.WriteLine("\nLoop through with enumerator:\n");
        while (myIterator.MoveNext( )) {
           Console.WriteLine("Key: {0}\tValue: {1}",
                        myIterator.Key,
                        myIterator.Value);
        }
    }
}
```

Stack

The following code demonstrates the first-in, last-out characteristics of the stack abstract data type. The output from the pop operation initially shows the fourth item, the third item, and so on.

```
using System;
using System.Collections;
public class TestStack{

    public static void Main()  {

        Stack myStack = new Stack();
        myStack.Push("Item 1");
        myStack.Push("Item 2");
        myStack.Push("Item 3");
        myStack.Push("Item 4");

        while(myStack.Count > 0) {
            Console.WriteLine(myStack.Pop());
        }
    }
}
```

Common Utilities

Microsoft .NET Framework provides many tools to help developers make the best use of the Framework. In the following sections, we document the commonly used subset of .NET tools that we've used throughout this book:

- Assembly Generation Utility (*al.exe*)
- Assembly Registration Utility (*gacutil.exe*)
- MSIL Assembler (*ilasm.exe*)
- MSIL Disassembler (*ildasm.exe*)
- C++ Compiler (*cl.exe*)
- C# Compiler (*csc.exe*)
- VB Compiler (*vbc.exe*)
- PE File viewer (*dumpbin.exe*)
- Type Library Exporter (*tlbexp.exe*)
- Type Library Importer (*tlbimp.exe*)
- XML Schema Definition Tool (*xsd.exe*)
- Shared Name Utility (*sn.exe*)
- Web Service Utility (*wsdl.exe*)

Assembly Generation Utility (al.exe)

al.exe is generally used to generate assemblies with manifests. The following table shows some of the common usages of the Assembly Generation Utility.

Option	Description
/flags:*flags*	Specifies a value for the Flags field in the assembly.
	• 0x0000: side-by-side compatible.
	• 0x0010: cannot execute with other versions in the same application domain.
	• 0x0020: cannot execute with other versions in the same process.
	• 0x0030: cannot execute with other versions on the same computer.
/help or /?	Use to get help for this command.
/keyfile:*keyfilename* or /keyf:*keyfilename*	Use to create shared components. *keyfilename* contains a key pair generated with the Shared Name Utility (*sn.exe*). The compiler inserts the pub lic key into the assembly manifest and then signs the assembly with the private key.
/keyname:*keycontainer* or /keyn:*keycontainer*	Use to create shared components. *keycontainer* contains a key pair generated and installed into a key container with the Shared Name Utility (*sn.exe*). The compiler inserts the public key into the assembly manifest and then signs the assembly with the private key.
/main:*entrymethod*	Specifies the entry-point method name when converting a module to an executable.
/out:*filename*	Specifies the output filename.
/target:lib|exe|win or /t:lib|exe|win	Specifies the file format of the output file (lib for library, exe for console executable, and win for win32 executable). The default setting is lib.
/version:*major. minor.revision.build*	Specifies version information for the assembly. The default value is 0.

Assembly Registration Utility (gacutil.exe)

You can use *gacutil.exe* to install and uninstall an assembly, as well as to list the content of the GAC. The following table shows some of the common usages of the Assembly Registration Utility.

Option	Description
/l	To list the content of the GAC.
/ldl	To list the content of the downloaded files cache.
/cdl	To clear the content of the downloaded file cache.
/i *filename*	To install an assembly with file named *filename* into the GAC.
/u *assemblyname*	To uninstall an assembly from the GAC by specifying the assembly name. If multiple versions of the same assembly exist, all of them will be removed unless a version is specified with the *assemblyname* (i.e., gac –u myAssembly,ver=1.0.0.1).
/h or /help or /?	To display command syntax and options

MSIL Assembler (ilasm.exe)

This tool takes MSIL as input and generates a portable executable (PE) file containing the MSIL and the metadata required to run on the .NET Framework. This is most useful to vendors who would like to create MSIL-compliant compilers. All they have to do is write the compiler to translate the source language to MSIL. *Ilsam.exe* will take the second step to put the MSIL content into the PE format where it can be executed on the .NET Framework. The general syntax for MSIL assembler is:

```
ilasm [options] MSILfilename
```

The following table shows some of the common usages of the assemblers.

Option	Description
/debug	This option ensures that the output PE contains debugging information such as local variables, argument names, and line numbers. This is useful for debug build.
/dll	This option produces a .dll output.
/exe	This option produces an .exe output.
/listing	This option produces a listing of the output on STDOUT.
/output=*filename*	*filename* is the output filename.
/?	This option is used to obtain command-line help.

MSIL Disassembler (ildasm.exe)

This tool extracts the MSIL code from a PE file targeted for .NET Framework. The general syntax for this tool is:

```
Ildasm [options] PEFilename
```

The following table shows some of the common usages of the disassembler.

Option	Description
/linenum	This includes references to original source lines.
/output=*filename*	The output goes to a file instead of in a GUI dialog box.
/source	This shows original source lines as comments.
/text	The output goes in a console window.
/tokens	This shows metadata tokens of classes and members.

C++ Compiler (cl.exe)

The following table shows some of the common usages of the C++ compiler.

Option	Description
/CLR	This option flags the compiler to compile .NET-runtime managed code.
/entry:*methodname*	For C++ managed code, this link setting should point to the main entry-point function.
/link	This option combines the compile and link steps.
/subsystem: |windows|windowsce|console|	This link option specifies the type of output.
/out:*filename*	This option allows for the output filename.

C# Compiler (csc.exe)

The following table shows some of the common usages of the C# compiler.

Option	Description
/debug	With this option, the compiler will emit debugging information in the output file.
/define:*symbol* or /d:*symbol*	This option is similar to C++. Use this option to define preprocessor symbols.
/doc:*docname*	*docname* is the XML output file for the autogenerated XML comment embedded in C# code.
/help	This option shows the command-line help for the C# compiler.
/main:*classname*	If there is more than one Main entry in different classes, you will have to specify the Main entry in which class you want the entry point of the application.
/out:*filename*	This option represents the output filename.
/reference:*libname* or /r:*libname*	This option allows single or multiple libraries be included with this compilation. For multiple libraries to be included, use a semicolon as the delimiter.
/target:exe|library|winexe|module or /t:exe|library|winexe|module	This option allows you to specify the type of the output: exe for console executables, library for DLLs, and winexe for Windows Form applications. When you set the target to module, the compiler outputs binary for the module but not a .NET assembly. Modules can be added to a .NET assembly later.
/unsafe	If you use unsafe keywords in your C# code, you will have to use this option when compiling your source.

Visual Basic Compiler (vbc.exe)

The following table shows some of the common usages of the Visual Basic compiler.

Option	Description
/debug	With this option, the compiler will emit debugging information in the output file.
/define:*symbol* or /d:*symbol*	Use this option to define preprocessor symbols.
/help or /?	This option shows the command-line help for the Visual Basic compiler.
/keycontainer:*keycontainer*	*keycontainer* specifies the key container that contains the key pair for signing the assembly. See *sn.exe* for information on generating the key container.
/keyfile:*keyfile*	*keyfile* specifies the key file that contains the key pair for signing the assembly. See *sn.exe* for information on generating the key file.
/main:*classname*	If there is more than one Main entry in different classes, you will have to specify the Main entry in which class you want the entry point of the application.
/out:*filename*	This option represents the output filename.
optionexplicit[+/-]	Turn on or off optionexplicit to enforce explicit or implicit declaration of variables. The default setting is on.
optionstrict[+/-]	Turn on or off optionstrict to disallow or allow casting with truncation. The default setting is on.
/reference:*libname* or /r:*libname*	This option allows single or multiple libraries be included with this compilation. For multiple libraries to be included, use a semicolon as the delimiter.
/target:exe|library|winexe|module or /t:exe|library|winexe|module	This option allows you to specify the type of the output: exe for console executables, library for DLLs, and winexe for Windows Form applications. When you set the target to module, the compiler outputs binary for the module but not a .NET assembly. Modules can be added to a .NET assembly later.

PE File Format Viewer (dumpbin.exe)

dumpbin is not a new utility. However, since .NET Framework stores the IL inside the extended PE format, this old utility is still very useful for examining the structure of executable or DLLs, as well as listing import and export entries of the binaries. The general syntax for this utility is:

```
Dumpbin [options] PEFilename
```

The following table shows some of the common *dumpbin* usages.

Option	Description
/all	Displays all information from the PE file.
/exports	Displays all exports from the PE file.
/header	Displays the header information from the PE file.
/imports	Displays all imports for the PE file.

Type Library Exporter (tlbexp.exe)

Type library exporter and importer are the two tools necessary for COM interop. The exporter generates a type library for a .NET Framework assembly so that other COM components can interop with .NET components. The general syntax for *tlbexp.exe* is:

```
tlbexp AssemblyName [options]
```

The following table shows some of the common usages of *tlbexp.exe*.

Option	Description
/nologo	This option suppresses the logo of the tlbexp executable.
/out:*filename*	*filename* is the name of the type library file.
/silent	This option suppresses all messages from the tlbexp executable.
/verbose	This option displays extra information while converting the component.
/? or /help	This option displays the help information for the tool.

Type Library Importer (tlbimp.exe)

Because it is the reverse tool of the type library exporter, the importer generates a .NET proxy component for a COM component so that .NET components can use legacy COM components. The general syntax for *tlbimp.exe* is:

```
tlbimp PEFile [options]
```

The following table shows some of the common usages of *tlbimp.exe*.

Option	Description
/keycontainer: *keycontainer*	This option signs the resulting assembly with the private key in the *keycontainer*. The public key in the *keyfile* will be used in the assembly manifest. See *sn.exe* for the *keycontainer* generation.
/keyfile: *keyfile*	This options signs the resulting assembly with the private key in the *keyfile*. The public key in the *keyfile* will be used in the assembly manifest. See *sn.exe* for *keyfile* generation.
/nologo	This option suppresses the logo of the tlbimp executable.
/out:*filename*	*filename* is the name of the type library file.
/silent	This option suppresses all messages from the tlbimp executable.
/unsafe	This option produces interfaces without .NET Framework security checks.
/verbose	This option displays extra information while converting the component.
/? or /help	This option displays the help information for the tool.

XML Schema Definition Tool (xsd.exe)

XML Schema Definition (XSD) is useful when working with XML schemas that follow the XSD language. With XSD, you can perform the following transformations:

- XDR to XSD
- XML to XSD
- Classes to XSD
- XSD to Classes
- XSD to DataSet

XDR to XSD

To convert an XDR-formatted file to XSD, use the following syntax:

```
xsd [options] file.xdr
```

Note that the file extension *.xdr* dictates the conversion from XDR to XSD.

XML to XSD

To convert an XML-formatted file to XSD, use the following syntax:

```
xsd [options] file.xml
```

Note that the file extension *.xml* dictates the conversion from XML to XSD.

Classes to XSD

You can convert classes to XSD by specifying the runtime assembly file (*.exe* or *.dll* extension) as the filename to the utility. You can also specify a particular type within the assembly you want to convert to XSD using the /type flag. The typename can be a wildcard match. If you omit the /type flag, all types in the assembly will be converted. The syntax follows:

```
Xsd [/TYPE:typename] assemblyFile
```

or:

```
Xsd [/T:typename] assemblyFile
```

XSD to Classes

To convert XSD back to classes, use the `/classes` or `/c` flag. You can specify a particular element in the XSD schema to be converted to a class. You can also specify the language for the class source file. The general syntax follows:

```
xsd /CLASSES
    /ELEMENT:element
    /NAMESPACE:namespace
    /LANGUAGE:language /URI:uri file.xsd
```

or:

```
xsd /C E:element /N:namespace /L:language /U:uri file.xsd
```

Note that namespace, language, and uri can be specified only once.

XSD to DataSet

To convert XSD to dataset, use the `/dataset` or `/d` flag. Again, you can narrow down to a particular element in the XSD schema to be converted. The general syntax follows:

```
xsd /D [/DATASET] file.xsd
```

Shared Name Utility (sn.exe)

sn.exe guarantees unique names for shared components because these components will end up in the GAC. Each shared component is signed with a private key and published with the public key. The following table shows some common usages of *sn.exe*.

Option	Description	
`/?`	This option displays more command-line help.	
`-d keycontainer`	This option is used to remove the `keycontainer` from the CSP.	
`-i keyfile keycontainer`	This option reads the key pair in `keyfile` and installs it in the key container `keycontainer` in the Cryptographic Service Provider (CSP).	
`-k keyfile`	This option generates a new key pair and writes it to `keyfile`.	
`-v assembly`	This option is used to verify the shared name in an `assembly`.	

Web Service Utility (wsdl.exe)

wsdl.exe helps create ASP.NET Web Services and proxies for their clients. The most common usage of *wsdl.exe* is to generate proxy classes for web services:

```
wsdl
    /language:language
```

```
/namespace:namespace
/out:output
/protocol:protocol
path
```

The *path* parameter is a local path to a service-description file or URI where the SDL file can be retrieved. The *language* parameter specifies the language for the output-proxy source file. It can be C#, VB, or JS. The generated class will be in the specified namespace. The output source file is controlled by the *output* option. The *protocol* controls which protocol the proxy will use to communicate with the Web Service. The choices of protocols provided by the .NET Framework are SOAP, HttpGet, and HttpPost. You can also have your own protocol here if you've extended the WebClientProtocol or Http-WebClientProtocol class.

For short names options, use the following.

```
wsdl
        /l:language
        /n:namespace
        /o:output
        /protocol:protocol
        path
```

Index

Symbols

<%‰...‰%>, enclosing code rendering blocks, 201

A

ABCs (abstract base classes), 39
abstract attribute for .class IL declaration, 61
Abstract Data Type (ADT), 280
abstract keyword, signaling the C# compiler with, 58
abstraction, engineering concept for software, 32
Acceleration Server 2000, 3
AcceptChanges( ) method, 108
access control lists (ACLs), 93
acronyms, 272–275
Activate( ) method, 91
activation information in COM, 70
Activator class, calling the GetObject method, 83
Active Server Pages (ASP), 186, 272
Active Template Library (see ATL)
ActiveMdiChild property, 254, 260
ActiveX Data Objects (ADO), 102
Add( ) method, 89
AddAt( ) method, 216
AddMessageFilter Application property, 241
AddRange( ) method, 257
Administrators group, 94–98

ADO (ActiveX Data Objects), 102, 272
ADO.NET, 10, 104–144
    architecture, 102
    content components for, 107–121
    interoperability of, 104
    managed providers for, 121–132
    performance of, 107
    productivity of, 106
    scalability of, 105
ADT (Abstract Data Type), 280
Agents role, 94–98
al.exe (Assembly Generation Utility), 283
    using assemblies, 32
AlternatingItemStyle, controlling visual formatting of DataGrid control, 226
AlternatingItemTemplate, 226
anchoring controls inside containers, 252
ansi attribute, 61
AOL Instant Messenger, 146
API (Application Programming Interface), 272
APL language, 271
AppDomain class, 49, 272
AppendChild( ) method, constructing XML document tree, 135
Application Center 2000 server products, 3
Application class, 241
Application Programming Interface (API), 272

We'd like to hear your suggestions for improving our indexes. Send email to *index@oreilly.com*.

J

K

L

M

W

WAP (Wireless Access Protocol), 275
Web
  forms (see Web Forms)
  GUIs, 11
  Microsoft Services, 3
  paradigm shifts, 2
  services (see Web Services)
Web Forms, 186–234
  application development, 204–219
  ASP.NET and, 187
  components, 205–209
  configuring, 210
  custom server controls, 212–218
  events, 207
  life cycle of, 209–211
  server controls for, 212
  syntax, 197–204
  System.Web.UI namespace
    and, 188–197
web methods, 159
Web Service Discovery (DISCO), 133,
  273
Web Service Utility (wsdl.exe), 283
Web Services, 145–185, 275
  for ASP.NET, 219–222
  consumers, 163–182
  discovery, 155–157
  framework, 147–158
  namespaces, 157
  providers, 158–163
  security and, 182–185
  using, 221
  Web Forms and, 268
  wire formats, 148
  WSDL and, 150–155
Web Services Description Language (see
  WSDL)
web.config files, 162, 163
  managing sessions, 230
  setting, 192
WebControls object, 196
WebMethod attribute, 221
WebMethodAttribute class in
  System.Web.Services
  namespace, 158
WebService class in
  System.Web.Services
  namespace, 157

@WebService directive, 220
WebServiceAttribute class in
  System.Web Services
  namespace, 157
widgets, 189
Width control property, 238
Win32, 275
  Extensions (Python), 236
%windir% setting, 76
Windows 2000, 3
  class loaders and, 41
  DLL Hell, avoiding, 7
  PE file formats and, 18
  role-based security, 97
  security features for, 9
Windows 98
  class loaders and, 41
  PE file formats and, 18
Windows authentication, 163
Windows CE, 3
Windows Forms, 235–269
  application, 242
  control class, 237
  controls, 244–253
  developing, 242–264
  form class, 239–240
  stage deployment, 264–268
  System.Windows.Forms namespace
    and, 237
  Web Services and, 268
Windows Me, 3
  class loaders and, 41
  PE file formats and, 18
Windows NT security features, 9
Windows XP, 3
WinForms, 275
wire formats (Web Services), 148
Wireless Access Protocol (WAP), 275
Wireless Markup Language
  (WML), 275
WM_CLOSE, 235
WM_CREATE, 235
WML (Wireless Markup
  Language), 275
WM_SIZE, 235
WndProc control property, 238
WriteLine( ) method, 13, 35
WriteXml( ) method, 111
WriteXmlSchema( ) method, 111

About the Authors

Thuan Thai is also the author of *Learning DCOM*, published by O'Reilly & Associates. He has been giving technical presentations on the .NET platform to clients since the announcement of the initiative in July 2000.

Hoang Q. Lam is an application architect at CrossTier and an instructor in web development at George Washington University through DevXpert. At CrossTier, he specializes in developing B2B and B2C applications using Microsoft tools.

Colophon

Our look is the result of reader comments, our own experimentation, and feedback from distribution channels. Distinctive covers complement our distinctive approach to technical topics, breathing personality and life into potentially dry subjects.

The animals on the cover of *.NET Framework Essentials*, Second Edition, are shrimp. Different species of shrimp are found in marine and fresh water—shallow and deep—all over the world. Swimming backward by rapidly flexing its abdomen and tail, and with the assistance of specialized legs for swimming, the shrimp feeds on smaller plants and animals, as well as carrion. In fact, several species engage in symbiotic (mutually benefical or dependent) relationships with other organisms. The coral shrimp (*Stenopus hispidus*) cleans the scales of the coral fish, while the fish in turn swims backward through the shrimp's pincers (presumably to clean them).

Colleen Gorman was the production editor and the proofreader for *.NET Framework Essentials*. Sarah Sherman and Mary Anne Weeks Mayo provided quality control. Joe Wizda wrote the index.

Ellie Volckhausen designed the cover of this book, based on a series design by Edie Freedman. The cover image is a 19th-century engraving from the Dover Pictorial Archive. Emma Colby produced the cover layout with QuarkXPress 4.1 using Adobe's ITC Garamond font.

David Futato designed the interior layout. Mike Sierra converted the files from Microsoft Word to FrameMaker 5.5.6. The text font is Linotype Birka; the heading font is Adobe Myriad Condensed; and the code font is Lucas-Font's TheSans Mono Condensed. The illustrations that appear in the book were produced by Robert Romano and Jessamyn Read using Macromedia FreeHand 9 and Adobe Photoshop 6. The tip and warning icons were drawn by Christopher Bing. This colophon was written by Jeff Holcomb.